France

A Study of the Educational System of France and a Guide to the Academic Placement of Students in Educational Institutions of the United States

A. Mariam Assefa
Executive Director
World Education Services, Inc.
New York, New York

1988

Ministry of Education, Ontario
Information Centre, 13th Floor,
Mowat Block, Queen's Park,
Toronto, Ont.   M7A 1L2

A Service of the International Education Activities Group of the
American Association of Collegiate Registrars and Admissions Officers

Washington, D.C.

Placement Recommendations and Grade Equivalencies Approved by the
National Council on the Evaluation of Foreign Educational Credentials

Library of Congress Cataloging-in-Publication Data

Assefa, A. Mariam.
France: a study of the educational system of France and a guide to the academic placement of students in educational institutions of the United States.

(World education series)
Bibliography: p.
Includes index.
1. Education—France. 2. School credits—France.
3. Students, Foreign—United States. 4. School credits—United States. 5. School grade placement—United States. I. American Association of Collegiate Registrars and Admissions Officers. International Education Activities Group. II. Title. III. Series.
LA692.A77 1988   370'.944   88-3505
ISBN 0-910054-90-8

Publication of the World Education Series is funded by grants from the Bureau of Educational and Cultural Affairs of the United States Information Agency.

Contents

Preface	ix
Map	x
Facts About France	xi
Historical Highlights	xi
Educational Overview	xii

Section I. Elementary and Secondary Education ... 1
Chapter I. Elementary and Secondary Education ... 1
  Preschool Education ... 1
  Primary Education ... 1
  Secondary Education ... 2
    Lower Secondary Education ... 2
      Observation Cycle (6° and 5°) ... 2
      Orientation Cycle (4° and 3°) ... 3
    Upper Secondary Education: The *Lycée* ... 3
      Seconde (2°) (First Year of *Lycée*) ... 4
      The *Première* (1°) (Second Year of *Lycée*) ... 5
      The *Terminale* (Final Class) ... 9
      The *Baccalauréat* ... 14
        The International Option *(Option Internationale)* of the *Baccalauréat* ... 18
        The Examination by Section ... 18
        Grades on the *Baccalauréat* ... 26
        Credit for the *Baccalauréat* ... 27
  Vocational Education ... 28
    Lower Secondary Programs ... 28
    Upper Secondary Programs ... 29

Section II. Higher Education in France ... 31

  Legal Basis of the Educational System ... 32
  Organization of Higher Education ... 32
    Central Administration ... 32
    Regional Administration ... 33
    Institutions of Higher Education ... 33
  Enrollment ... 33
  Student Life ... 34

Chapter II. University Education ... 35
  History ... 35
    The Reform of 1968 ... 35
    The Reform of 1984 ... 36
  Current University Structure and Administration ... 37

Academic Organization 38
  The Units of Teaching and Research 38
  University-Affiliated Institutes and Schools 38
  Libraries 39
  University Admission 39
  Academic Calendar 39
  National Diplomas of Higher Education 39
  University Diplomas 40
  Teaching 40
  Examinations 42
  Grading 42
  Documentation 43
Program Structure 43
  First Cycle *(Premier Cycle)* 43
    Orientation Programs 46
    DEUG Program Descriptions 47
  Second Cycle *(Second Cycle)* 60
    Traditional *Licence* and *Maîtrise* Programs 60
    Professional *Maîtrise* Programs 62
    The *Magistère* 67
    The *Diplôme d'Etudes Politiques* 69
  Third Cycle *(Troisième Cycle)* 71
    The *Diplôme d'Etudes Supérieures Spécialisées*/DESS 71
    The *Diplôme d'Etudes Approfondies*/DEA 72
    The *Doctorat* 73
    The *Habilitation à Diriger des Recherches* 74
    Doctoral Degrees Prior to the Reform of 1984 75
International Education 78
  Admission 78
  Language Proficiency Assessment 78
  French Language and Civilization Programs for Foreigners 79
  Diplomas in Teaching French as a Foreign Language 79

Chapter III. Short Higher Technical Education 81
  The *Diplôme Universitaire de Technologie*/DUT 81
  The *Brevet de Technician Supérieur*/BTS 83

Chapter IV. Engineering Education 86
  Introduction 86
  The Commission des Titres d'Ingénieur/CTI 86
  Special Features 87
  Traditional *Grandes Ecoles* 87
  Pre-Engineering Education *(Classes Préparatoires)* 88
  Admission to *Grandes Ecoles* 89
  Program Structure 91
  Five-Year Integrated Programs 92

Four-Year Programs 101
Continuing Education Programs 101
Post-*Diplôme d'Ingénieur* Programs 101
   DEA and Doctoral Studies 103
   Studies at Specialized Institutes 103
   The *Mastère* 104

Chapter V. Agricultural Education 109
Short Programs 109
Long Programs 110
   Traditional *Grandes Ecoles* 110
      Program Structure 110
   Integrated Five-Year Programs 112
   Four-Year Programs 112
   Specialized and Post-*Diplôme d'Ingénieur* Programs ... 116
Veterinary Medicine 116

Chapter VI. Business Education 118
Short (Two-Year) Programs 118
Long Programs 118
   Recognition of Institutions 118
   Credentials 120
   Grandes Ecoles 121
      Classes Préparatoires 121
      Admission to Business *Grandes Ecoles* 123
   Other Business Schools 125
Post-*Diplôme* Programs 125
   The *Mastère* 125
   The Master of Business Administration 126
   University Business Education 127
   Professional Accounting Programs 127

Chapter VII. Teacher Training 131
Elementary School Teacher Training 131
Special Education Teachers 132
   Teaching of the Handicapped 132
   School Psychologists 133
   Vocational Education Teachers 133
Secondary School Teachers 133
   Lower Secondary School *(Collège)* Teachers 133
   Upper Secondary School *(Lycée)* Teachers 134
   Physical Education Teachers 135
   Ecoles Normales Supérieures 135
      Classes Préparatoires 136
      Study at *Ecoles Normales Supérieures* 137
      The *Agrégation* 137

Chapter VIII. Health and Social Education 139
  Medical Studies 139
    Medicine 139
    Dentistry 141
    Pharmacy 141
  Paramedical Education 142
    University Paramedical Education 142
      Audioprosthesis 142
      Midwifery 142
      Speech Therapy 143
    Nonuniversity Paramedical Education 143
      Medical Laboratory Technology 144
      Nursing 144
        Specialization 145
        Psychiatric Nursing 145
      Occupational Therapy 146
      Physical Therapy 146
      Chiropody 147
      Radiology 147
      Rehabilitation Counselors 147
  Social Professions 149
    Social Work 149
    Social and Cultural Organizers 149
    Child Care Workers 150

Chapter IX. Architecture, Art, Music, Drama 151
  Architecture 151
    Schools of Architecture 151
    Other Institutions 153
    Further Education 154
  Art Education 154
    Studio Arts 154
      Higher National Institutions 154
      National, Regional and Municipal Institutions 155
      Other Institutions 156
    Graphic Art 156
    Cinema and Photography 157
    Art History, Restoration and Conservation 157
  Music 158
    General Music Education 158
    Professional Music Education 160
      The National Conservatories of Music 160
      Private Institutions 160
    Music Therapy 160
    Music Education 161
  Dance 161
  Drama 161

Chapter X. Suggestions for U.S. Admissions Officers 162
  Credentials and Documentation 162
  Examinations and Grades 162
  Concours Grades 163
  Additional Resources 163
  The Role of the National Council on the Evaluation
    of Foreign Educational Credentials 164
  Placement Recommendations 165

Appendix A. French Universities and Institutions Deemed to be
    Universities 187
Appendix B. Institutions Which Award the *Diplôme d'Ingénieur* 198
Appendix C. Postsecondary Schools of Business and Commerce 213
Appendix D. Special Institutions 223
Acronyms 225
Useful Addresses 228
Glossary 230
Useful References 234
Index 236

Tables and Charts

1.	Structure of the French Education System	xiv
2.1.	Sample DEUG Program in Social Sciences	59
2.2.	Sample DEUG A Program in Analytical and Physical Sciences	59
2.3.	Sample DEUST Program in Music Professions	60
2.4.	Sample *Licence* and *Maîtrise* Programs in Sociology	62
2.5.	Sample *Licence* and *Maîtrise* Programs in Mathematics	63
2.6.	Sample MST Program in Applied Biological and Medical Science ..	64
2.7.	Sample MSG Program	65
2.8.	Sample *Diplôme d'Etudes Politiques* Program	69
2.9.	Sample DEA Program in Social Psychology and Etiology	73
3.1.	Sample Curriculum in Civil Engineering	82
3.2.	Sample BTS Curriculum for Assistant Engineering Technician	84
3.3.	Sample BTS Marketing and Distribution Program	85
4.1.	Types of *Classes Préparatoires* Classified by *Baccalauréat*	89
4.2.	Sample *Classe Préparatoire* Program, Mathematics and Physics	90
4.3.	1983 Results of the *'Concours Mines-Ponts'*	91
4.4	1985 Admissions on the *'Concours Mines-Ponts'*	91
4.5.	Sample Traditional *Grande Ecole* Program	93
4.6.	Sample Integrated Five-Year Program in Engineering	96
4.7.	Sample Four-Year Engineering Curriculum	102
4.8.	Sample Specialized Program in Engineering	104
4.9	Sample *Mastère* Program in Electronics	104
5.1.	Sample Curriculum for a *Classe Préparatoire Biologique*	111
5.2.	Sample Program, ENSAIA	111
5.3.	Sample Five-Year Integrated Program in Agriculture	114

5.4.	Sample Four-Year Program in Agriculture	115
6.1.	Classes *Préparatoires* Programs	123
6.2.	Sample Program, HEC	124
7.1.	Sample *Classe Préparatoire* Program in Literature	136
8.1.	Sample Program in Nursing	144
8.2.	Sample Physical Therapy Program	146
9.1.	Second Cycle Curriculum, *Ecoles d'Architecture*	152

Sample Documents

1.1.	*Brevet des Collèges*	15
1.2a.	Academic *Baccalauréat* Diploma	15
1.2b.	*Baccalauréat* "B" Transcript	16
1.2c.	Technical *Baccalauréat* Diploma	17
2.1.	*Diplôme d'Université*	41
2.2a.	Transcript of *Diplôme d'Etudes Universitaires Générales*/DEUG and *Licence* Courses	44
2.2b.	Provisional *Maîtrise* Diploma	45
2.3.	*Diplôme d'Etudes Universitaires Générales*/DEUG Diploma	61
2.4.	*Licence*	61
2.5.	Traditional *Maîtrise* Diploma	66
2.6.	Professional *Maîtrise*	67
2.7.	Diploma Awarded by the Institute of Political Studies of Grenoble	72
2.8.	*Diplôme d'Etudes Supérieures Specialisées*/DESS	75
2.9.	*Diplôme d'Etudes Approfondies*/DEA	76
2.10.	Provisional Certificate of New *Doctorat*	76
3.1.	University Diploma of Technology	84
3.2.	Higher Technician's Certificate	85
4.1.	*Diplôme d'Ingénieur* from a Traditional *Grande Ecole*	92
4.2.	Diploma of Engineer from INSA	95
5.1.	Certificate of Diploma of General Agriculture	113
5.2.	Certificate of Diploma of Agricultural Engineer	113
6.1a.	Diploma Awarded by the Ecole Supérieure de Commerce de Paris	119
6.1b.	*Diplôme d'Etudes Supérieures Commerciales, Administratives et Financières*/DESCAF	120
6.2.	*Certificat de Fin d'Etudes* from a Recognized Institution	122
6.3	Degree from MBA Institute	122
6.4.	*Mastère*	126
6.5.	*Certificat d'Aptitude à l'Administration des Entreprises*/CAAE	127
6.6	*Diplôme d'Etudes Comptables Supérieures*	130
8.1.	Certificate of Qualification of Speech Therapist	143
8.2.	State Diploma of Nurse	145
8.3.	State Diploma of Masseur-Kinesitherapist	148
9.1.	Provisional Certificate of Diploma of Architect	153
9.2.	First Cycle Diploma of the Ecole du Louvre	158
9.3.	*Médaille d'Or*	159

Preface

The purpose of this book is to explain French educational credentials to U.S. college and university admissions officers and credentials evaluators. France has a highly complex educational system, influenced by a rich culture, centuries of tradition, and major economic, philosophical, political and social conditions. Given its specific purpose, this book does not attempt to provide an in-depth study of the foundations, history and development of French education except briefly as they apply to specific institutions or credentials.

The preparation of this book was a major challenge which took the help of many people to whom I am forever grateful. I would like to express special thanks to Erika Popovych and all my colleagues at World Education Services, Inc. whose competence, dedication and hard work gave me the freedom to devote much time to writing; to the Board of Directors of World Education Services, Inc. and its former Chairman, Ivan Putman, for their encouragement and support and for giving me a leave of absence in the Fall of 1986; to my excellent monitor Ann Fletcher of Stanford University who gave me invaluable advice and guidance; to Norbert Blanc, formerly with the Cultural Services of the French Embassy in Washington, D.C., for helping me on short notice establish contacts with French educational authorities; to the staff of the United States Information Service in Paris and in Lyon, namely Carol Madison, who gave me a home away from home and offered every assistance I sought; to Gerard Communeti of the Académie de Lyon and the administrators of the various institutions in Lyon and Saint-Etienne who extended a warm welcome to me and devoted many hours of their time to discussing and explaining their institutions and the educational system as a whole; to Mrs. Jeannine Feneuille, Director of the Centre International d'Etudes Pédagogiques and her staff for granting me access to their library and for opening the doors of the Ministry of Education for me. My appreciation also goes to members of the AACRAO World Education Series Committee. The members of the National Council on the Evaluation of Foreign Educational Credentials who have the very difficult task of establishing placement recommendations are owed recognition by the users of this and other WES volumes. Henny Wakefield and Miranda Knowles, AACRAO editors, I thank for their excellent suggestions and patience and for their good humour through it all. Montroe Headd was responsible for typing the lists of engineering and business schools.

Writing this book has brought back fond memories of my student days in the French system and has made me appreciate the benefits of a rich educational experience. I hope that this book contributes in some small way to making French education better understood in the United States and to the expansion of educational exchange between the two countries.

A. Mariam Assefa
New York, New York
January 1988

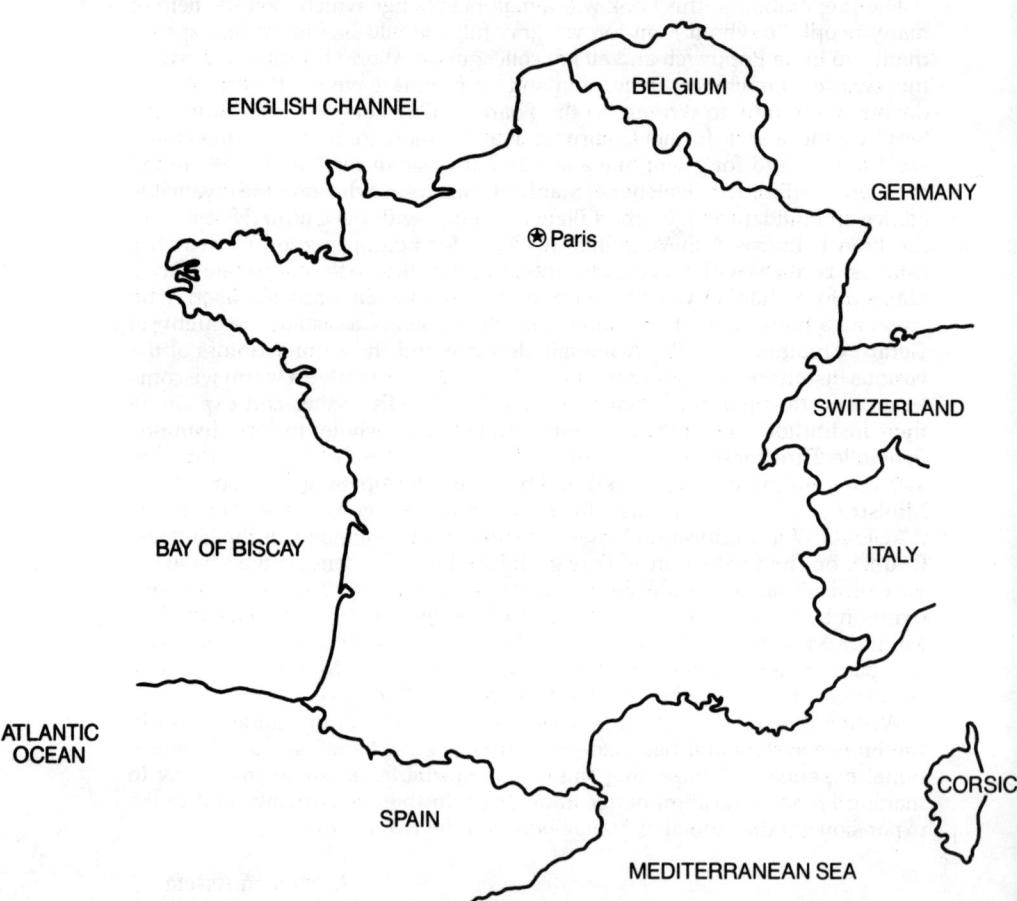

Facts About France

Name: French Republic (République Française)

Location: Western Europe, bounded on the north by the English Channel, on the northeast by Belgium and Luxembourg, on the east by West Germany and Switzerland, on the southeast by Italy, on the south by the Mediterranean Sea, on the southwest by Spain and on the west by the Atlantic Ocean. France has overseas departments and territories in the Caribbean (French Guyana, Guadeloupe and Martinique); in the Indian Ocean (Mayotte and Réunion); and in the Pacific Ocean (French Polynesia, New Caledonia and St. Pierre et Miquelon).

Size: 212,973 square miles

Population: Circa 55 million in 1986

Capital City: Paris. Major Cities: Marseille, Lyon, Toulouse, Nice, Nantes, Strasbourg, Bordeaux

Government: A President, elected for a seven-year term, is the head of state and a Prime Minister, appointed by the President, heads the government and the cabinet. The legislative branch consists of a lower house, the National Assembly, elected for five years, and an upper-house, the Senate, elected for nine years. France is a founding member of the European Community.

Language: French

Economy: *Industries*—aircrafts, automobiles, chemicals, electronics, instruments, perfume, plastics, ships, steel, textiles, wine. *Minerals*—asphalt, bauxite, coal, cobalt, iron, nickel, potash, rock salt, silver, uranium. *Agriculture*—barley, corn, dairy products, grapes, meat, vegetables, wheat (France is the largest exporter of agricultural products in the European Community.)

Currency: The franc (December 1987: 5.40 = $1 U.S.). *Gross Domestic Product* (1986): approximately $640 billion. *Per Capita Income* (1986): approximately $9,750.00

Literacy: 99%

Historical Highlights

In 58–51 B.C., Celtic Gaul is conquered by Julius Caesar and the Romans rule for 500 years. Under Charlemagne, Frankish rule is extended over much of Europe and after his death France emerges as one of the successor kingdoms. The monarchy is overthrown by the French Revolution (1789–1793) and is succeeded by the First Republic which is followed by the First Empire (1804–1815), a monarchy (1815–1848), the Second Republic (1848–1852), the Second

Empire (1852–1848), the Third Republic (1871–1946), the Fourth Republic (1946–1958), and the Fifth Republic (1958 to the present). A major colonial power in former times, France withdraws from Indochina in 1954, from Morocco and Tunisia in 1956, from Algeria in 1962 and from its remaining African colonies in 1958–1962 while retaining strong economic, political and cultural ties.

Educational Overview

During the Middle Ages education in France was organized and controlled by the Church. The Renaissance saw the development of education. The reigns of Louis XIII and Louis XIV in the seventeenth century were marked by the growing influence of the Jesuits over education and by the writings of Descartes and Pascal, among others. Education was limited to the aristocracy and at the onset of the French Revolution in 1789, three-quarters of the population was illiterate.

In 1791, the Constitutional Assembly proclaimed the right of all citizens to an education, an idea which was not immediately put into practice. The First Empire saw the creation of the *lycées* as elite secondary schools while an Imperial University exercised total authority over secondary and higher education. In 1850, the Falloux Law ended the state monopoly over secondary education and led to the establishment of private schools primarily by religious orders. By the end of 1870, the rules governing education were even more relaxed and secondary education was extended to young women.

In 1882, elementary education became secular, free of charge and compulsory for children between the ages of 6 and 13 years. Secondary education became free of charge in 1933 and the number of years of compulsory education was raised to 14. In 1959 compulsory education was extended to the current 16 years.

Although based on the principles of liberty and equality, French education had been very selective and children were streamed out of academic programs at an early age to be placed into vocational education. This inequity was addressed by the 1975 reform of elementary and secondary education whose principal objective was to grant all children access to the *collège* (lower secondary school), thus opening the way for a greater number to attend the *lycée* (upper secondary school). The current goal of French educational authorities is to raise the proportion of students graduating from the *lycée* from the present 30% to 80% of the 18-year-old population by the year 2000. There were 12,786,800 students enrolled in elementary and secondary schools in 1982.

School Administration

All education is administered by the Ministry of Education, which is the largest state agency. In 1984, 18% of the national budget was allocated to education. Also in that year the Ministry employed more than 890,000 people, of whom some 75% were teachers.

France is divided in 27 educational administrative districts known as *académies* (academies) headed by a *recteur* (rector), a senior official appointed by the State as the local representative of the Minister of Education. The rector is responsible for all educational, administrative and financial matters for the elementary and secondary schools in the district, including the training and appointment of elementary school teachers, and oversees the administration of national examinations and the award of diplomas. The *recteur* is assisted by several inspectors *(inspecteurs)* who are directly responsible for the supervision of schools and teachers.

Private Schools

Relations between the State and private schools are ruled by a 1959 law. Schools contract with the government for financial assistance in exchange for their adherence to certain rules. Under the terms of the "simple contract" which applies mainly to elementary schools, the government pays the salaries of teachers provided they hold the requisite teaching qualifications. Secondary schools enter into a "contract of association" under which the State pays the salaries of teachers (who are public employees) and provides operating expenses while the schools agree to follow the same curriculum as public schools and to submit to the supervision of public inspectors. Students sit for the same national examinations as public school students. In 1982–1983, some 2 million children were enrolled in private schools.

For an overview of tertiary education, see "Section II. Higher Education in France."

Chart 1 presents the educational system of France.

FACTS ABOUT FRANCE

Chart 1. STRUCTURE OF THE FRENCH EDUCATION SYSTEM

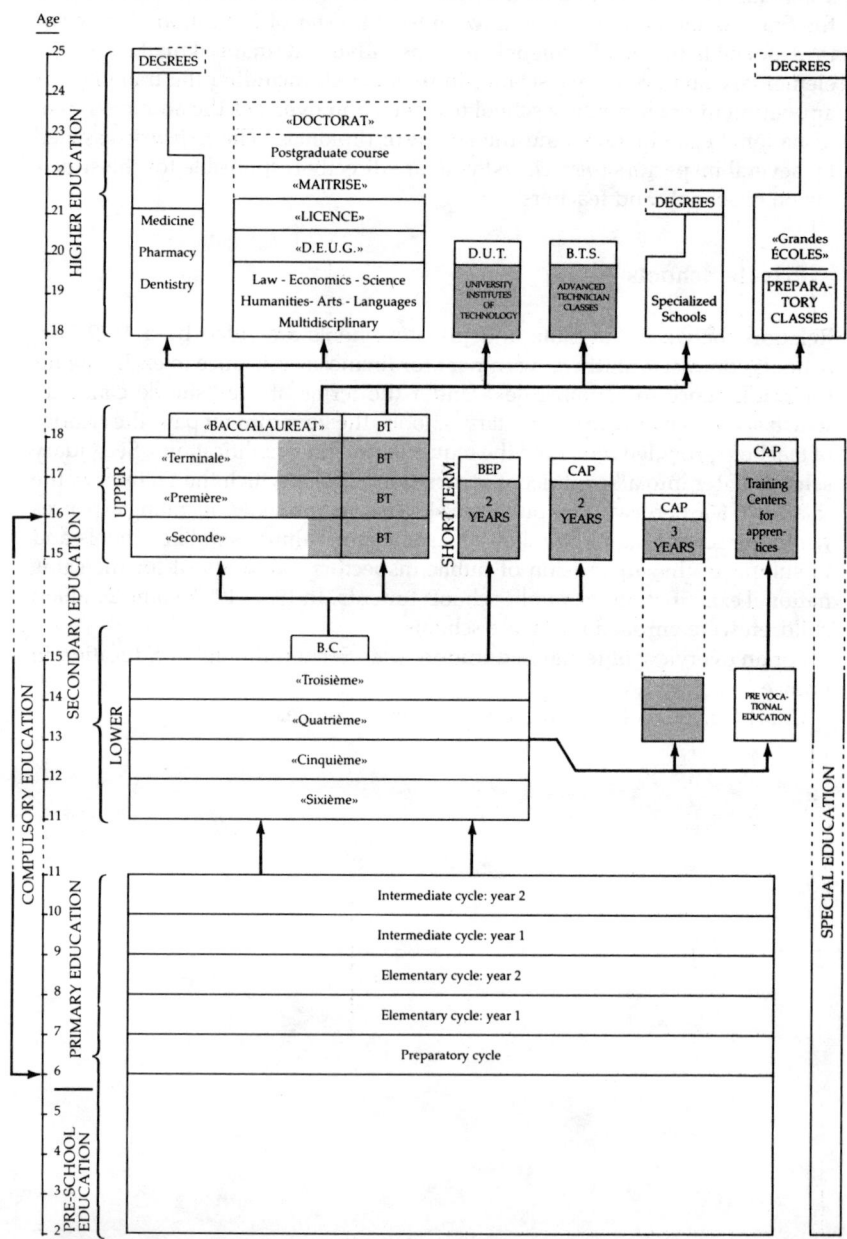

Courtesy of the Ministry of Education
Note: Shaded areas indicate vocational education.

Section I. Elementary and Secondary Education

Chapter I

Elementary and Secondary Education

Preschool Education

Preschool education is optional and caters to children between 2 and 6 years of age. Children are generally distributed into three sections according to their age: 2- to 4-year-olds—lower section, 4- to 5-year-olds—middle section, and 5- to 6-year-olds—upper section. There is total voluntary attendance from the age of 4, though compulsory attendance remains fixed at 6 years.

Primary Education

Attendance at primary school, which is five years long, is compulsory and begins when the child reaches 6 years of age. Special provisions allow 5-year-olds to attend primary school.

Municipal authorities are responsible for the construction and maintenance of primary schools while the State controls the curriculum, trains and employs teachers.

Primary education is organized in three cycles as follows:

> *Cycle Préparatoire*/CP (Preparatory Cycle)
> 6 to 7 years of age.

> *Cycle Elémentaire*/CE (Elementary Cycle)
> First year (CE1) 7 to 8 years of age
> Second year (CE2) 8 to 9 years of age

> *Cycle Moyen*/CM (Intermediate Cycle)
> First year (CM1) 9 to 10 years of age
> Second year (CM2) 10 to 11 years of age

Primary school stresses the acquisition of basic skills in reading, writing and arithmetic. Close to half of the time is devoted to activities which promote the development of observation, reasoning, imagination and physical abilities in children.

The academic year lasts 35 to 36 weeks. The week, which is divided into nine half days, contains 27 hours of instruction. The school day begins at 8:30 a.m. and runs until 4:30 p.m. Schools are usually closed on Wednesday and open on Saturday morning.

The weekly schedule is as follows:

1. Basic Education (15 hours) including French (9 hours) and mathematics (6 hours).
2. Developmental Activities *(Activités d'Eveil)* (7 hours) including arts and crafts, initiation to natural and social sciences (history and geography), moral and civic education, music.
3. Physical Education (5 hours).

Secondary Education

Secondary education, which is seven years long, is divided into two levels. Lower secondary school *(collège)* lasts four years and upper secondary school *(lycée)* is three years long. French grades are numbered in descending order beginning with the 6° (first year) of *collège* and through the *lycée*. The four years of *collège* are known as *sixième* - 6°, *cinquième* - 5°, *quatrième* - 4° and *troisième* - 3°.

Lower Secondary Education

Promotion from primary school to *collège* is automatic. The four-year lower secondary program is divided into two cycles of two years each. The lower cycle is the *cycle d'observation* (observation cycle) and consists of 6° and 5°. It is followed by a two-year upper cycle, *cycle d'orientation* (orientation and guidance cycle) which consists of 4° and 3°. The *collège* was the subject of a major reform in 1975 intended to stop the early definition and streaming of students by aptitude as had been the tradition in France. Students are now enrolled in classes of mixed aptitude and provisions have been made for additional hours of remedial work for students who could not otherwise keep pace with their peers.

OBSERVATION CYCLE (6° and 5°)

The two-year common cycle enrolls 96% of the children who have completed primary school. The remaining 4% are enrolled in special classes for the handicapped *(sections d'études spécialisées)*. The program consists of 24 hours of instruction per week to which may be added one hour of remedial or enrichment class in each of the three principal subjects: French, mathematics and foreign language. The weekly schedule is as follows: art and music (2 hours); foreign language I (3 hours); French (5 hours); history, geography, economics, civics (3 hours); manual and technical subjects (2 hours); mathematics (3 hours); physical and natural sciences (3 hours); and physical education (3 hours).

Promotion from 6° to 5° is automatic. Even though teachers can recommend that a student repeat the class, they may not impose that decision against student or parental wishes. At the end of the 5°, which is also the end of the observation cycle, only teachers may determine whether a student proceeds to the next grade, 4°. Students may appeal the decision but reversals are not common. Of the students who began secondary school in 6°, 65% are admitted to the next level, approximately 15% repeat the 5°, and the remaining 20% are streamed into vocational programs.

ORIENTATION CYCLE (4° and 3°)

The orientation cycle offers a minimum of 27½ hours of instruction per week and is made up of the same core subjects studied in the observation cycle, supplemented by one optional subject. Students may also take an elective, for a total weekly load of approximately 30 hours. The weekly schedule is as follows: *Common Subjects*—art and music (2 hours), foreign language I (3 hours), French (5 hours), history and geography (3 hours), manual and technical education (1.5-3 hours), mathematics (4 hours), physical and natural sciences (3 hours), physical education (3 hours). *Optional Subjects* (one of the following)—ancient Greek (3 hours), economics and business (3 hours), foreign language II (3 hours), enrichment of foreign language I (2 hours), industrial technology (3 hours), Latin (3 hours).

Promotion from 4° to 3° is automatic but only teachers determine whether a student passes from 3° to upper secondary education at a *lycée*. At the end of *collège* (3°), students sit for a national examination known as *brevet des collèges* which was introduced in 1985-86. (See sample document 1.1.) The *brevet des collèges* is not required for promotion into upper secondary school. It is an achievement examination designed to gauge the standard of education offered in lower secondary school.

Upper Secondary Education: The *Lycée*

The *lycée* enrolls students who have completed lower secondary education and prepares them in three years for a *baccalauréat*. Created under Napoleon, the *lycée* has undergone several reforms but its symbolic value remains largely intact. Still today, fewer than 30% of 18-year-olds graduate from a *lycée* even though the enrollment has tripled in the past twenty-five years from 421,900 in 1960-61 to 1,141,700 in 1983-84. In 1985, the government declared that, by the year 2000, 80% of the 18-year-olds must complete a *lycée*.

There are two types of *lycée*: *Lycée d'Enseignement Général et Technique*/LEGT (Comprehensive *Lycée*) and *Lycée Professionnel* (Vocational *Lycée*). *Lycée* classes are known as *seconde* (2°), *première* (1°) and *terminale*.

The distribution of students in the various streams of a *lycée* mirrors social distinctions in France. *Lycée* programs and the *baccalauréat* have been expanded to include technical streams and options in order to open up upper secondary education to segments of the population that had previously been excluded. The result of these measures has been an increase in the total number of students reaching the *lycée* and earning the *baccalauréat* even though middle class and urban children attend in greater proportion than those from modest backgrounds and rural areas. Between 1947 and 1980, the proportion of working class children enrolled in the *terminale* of academic *lycées* increased from 7.5% to 18.3% while it reached 30% for middle class children. In the desirable and highly selective mathematics and science section *(série* C), the gap is even wider: 8.8% are drawn from the working class whereas 40% are from the middle class.

SECONDE (2°) (FIRST YEAR OF *LYCÉE*)

In 1980, the structure and content of education in 2° was completely revised and implementation of the new plan began in the 1981-82 academic year. The new *seconde de détermination* is common for all students except for those majoring in music. As its name implies, this class serves to determine the subsequent streaming of students in the final two years of study. The objective of the reform was to postpone the decision students must make regarding their future academic and professional orientations, thus allowing them to sample various disciplines before making a choice. The revised curriculum consists of a common core of disciplines, stressing equally literature and science, complemented by compulsory optional subjects.

The weekly schedule is as follows: *Core Disciplines* (common for all students): foreign language I (3 hours), French (5 hours), history and geography (4 hours), mathematics (4 hours), natural sciences (1-2 hours), physics (3-5 hours), and sports (2 hours). *Compulsory Options* (one option to be chosen from one of the following groups): Group 1 (11 hours each)—applied arts, industrial technology, laboratory sciences and technology, and medical and social sciences. Group 2 (2-3 hours each)—art, business and computer science, foreign language, Greek, Latin, sports, technology, and typing. Students who choose an option from the Group 2 subjects must also take introduction to economics and social studies (2 hours). *Electives* (one or two additional subjects chosen either from the compulsory options of Group 2 or from the following): art or music (2 hours), manual and technical education (2 hours), modern language III (3 hours), preparation for social and family life (2 hours), and typing (2 hours).

Promotion from 2° to 1° is not automatic but depends on the results achieved and the type of optional subjects taken. The *seconde de détermination* is the subject of controversy because the course load is considered to be heavy and demanding. Students are expected to master both scientific and literary disciplines as specialists since they could end up in either type of 1°. Furthermore, the choice of options can increase the weekly load of 23 hours of class by up to 11 hours. Students repeating the class in 1984-85 totalled 17.8%.

ELEMENTARY AND SECONDARY EDUCATION

THE *PREMIÈRE* (1°) (SECOND YEAR OF *LYCÉE*)

After a 2°, 57% of students proceed to *première* (1°), which constitutes the first year of a two-year sequence leading to the *baccalauréat*. Students are streamed into different sections according to results achieved in 2° and the type of *baccalauréat* sought. The A-B-E-S sections lead to a *baccalauréat de l'enseignement du second degré (baccalauréat* of secondary education) and the F-G-H sections to a *baccalauréat de technicien* (technician's *baccalauréat*). D' is a special academic program in agricultural sciences.

The following sections are offered in 1°.

Academic

A Literature and Art
  (A1—Literature and Mathematics, A2—Literature and Languages, A3—Literature and Art)
B Economics and Social Sciences
D' Agriculture
E Mathematics and Technology
S Mathematics and Science

Technical

F Technical
  (F1—Mechanical Construction, F2—Electronics, F3—Electrotechnics, F4—Civil Engineering, F5—Applied Physics, F6—Applied Chemistry, F7—Biological Sciences [Biochemistry Option], F7'—Biological Sciences [Biology Option], F8—Medical-Social Sciences, F9—Energy and Equipment, F10—Microtechnics [Instruments or Optics], F11—Music and Dance, F12—Visual Art)
G Business
H Data Processing

Weekly schedules are as follows. The hours listed in parentheses indicate laboratory or studio work.

A—LITERATURE AND ART

Core Subjects	A1	A2	A3
Foreign Language I	3	3	3
French	5	5	5
History/Geography/Civics	4	4	4
Mathematics	5	2	2
Natural Sciences	2	2	2
Physical Education	2	2	2
Physics	1.5	1.5	1.5

continued

ELEMENTARY AND SECONDARY EDUCATION

Optional Subjects

1. Either Latin or Ancient Greek or Foreign Language II   3   –   3
2. Either Latin + Ancient Greek or Latin + Foreign
   Language II or Foreign Language II + III   –   3+3 –
3. Either Studio Arts and Architecture or Music Education –   –   4

Electives

Ancient Greek; Computer Science/Data Processing; Economics and Business; Economics and Social Sciences; Foreign Language II; and III; Latin; Manual and Technical Education; Music Education; Studio Arts; Technology

B—ECONOMICS AND SOCIAL SCIENCES

Core Subjects		Electives
Economics and Social Sciences	4	Ancient Greek; Computer Science/ Data Processing; Economics and Business; Foreign Language II; and III; Latin; Manual and Technical Education; Music Education; Studio Arts; Technology
Foreign Language I	3	
French	4	
History/Geography/Civics	4	
Mathematics	5	
Natural Sciences	2	
Physical Education	2	
Physics	1.5	

Optional Subjects

1. Either Latin or Ancient Greek or
   Foreign Language II   3

S—MATHEMATICS AND SCIENCE/E—MATHEMATICS AND TECHNOLOGY

Core Subjects	S	E
Foreign Language I	3	3
French	4	4
History/Geography/Civics	4	2
Mathematics	6	6
Natural Sciences	2.5	–
Physical Education	2	–
Physics	5	5
Technology	–	12

Electives

Ancient Greek; Computer Science/Data Processing; Economics and Business; Economics and Social Sciences; Foreign Language II; and III; Latin; Manual and Technical Education; Music Education; Studio Arts

ELEMENTARY AND SECONDARY EDUCATION

F—TECHNICAL

General Education	F1	F2	F3	F4	F9	F10A	F10B
Foreign Language I	2	2	2	2	2	2	2
French	3	3	3	3	3	3	3
History/Geography/Civics	2	2	2	2	2	2	2
Mathematics	4	4	4	4	4	4	4
Measurements	–	–	(3)	–	–	–	–
Physical Education	2	2	2	2	2	2	2
Physics	3	5+(3)	5	2+(1)	2+(1)	2+(1)	5+(3)
Technology							
A. Study of Constructions	4+(4)	4+(2)	4+(2)	4+(4)	8+(4)	4+(4)	3+(2)
B. Applications							
1. Preparation and Organization Methods	3+(1)	–	–	4+(2)	–	1+(3)	1+(1)
Electronic Systems	–	(4)	–	–	–	–	–
Electrical Systems	–	–	3	–	–	–	–
Equipment Systems	–	–	–	–	4	–	–
2. Operation and Control Systems	2+(6)	–	–	2+(4)	–	2+(6)	1+(7)
Electronic Systems	–	(5)	–	–	–	–	–
Electrical Systems	–	–	(6)	–	–	–	–
Equipment Systems	–	–	–	–	(4)	–	–

Electives

Art Education; Preparation for Family and Social Life

F—TECHNICAL

General Education	F5	F6	F7	F7'	F8
Foreign Language I	2	2	2	2	2
French	3	3	3	3	3
Biochemistry	–	–	2+(5)	2+(5)	–
Biology	–	–	–	–	3+(1)
Chemistry	–	4	–	–	–
History/Geography/Civics	2	2	2	2	2
Mathematics	5	4	3	3	3
Microbiology	–	–	(5)	–	–
Microbiology/Immunology and Parasitology	–	–	–	(5)	–
Physics	8	3	5+(6)	5+(6)	2+(1)
Physiology	–	–	1	1	–
Social Sciences for Health Care					
Psycho-Socio-Legal Aspects	–	–	–	–	3+(3)
Professional Techniques	–	–	–	–	3+(2)
Physical Education	2	2	2	2	2

continued

Laboratory Work, Industrial Laboratory and Research

Chemistry	(1)	(8)	–	–	–
Design and Technology	(4)	(3)	–	–	–
Instruments	–	(1)	–	–	–
Physics	(9)	(3)	–	–	–
Workshop	(2)	–	–	–	–

Electives

Art Education; Initiation to Family and Social Life; Speed Writing (F8 section)

F-11—MUSIC AND DANCE/F-12—VISUAL ART

General Education	F11	*General Education*	F12
Additional Mathematics	1	Foreign Language	2
Foreign Language I	3	French	3
French	4	History/Geography/Civics	2
History of Arts and Cultures	1	Mathematics	3
Introduction to		Physical Education	2
Contemporary Society	1	Physics	3
Mathematics	4	*Professional Subjects*	
Physics	2	Foundations in Arts:	
Professional Education		Three-Dimensional Design	(3)
Instrumental Track:		Color, Study of Documents	
		and Research	(3)
Analysis	1.5	Arts, Techniques and	
Dictation	1	Cultures	2
Ensemble Music	1.5	Graphic Arts:	
History of Music	1.5	Composition	(5)
Performance	2	Practical Studio Work	(3)
Reading Scores	0.5	Technology	2
Sound Techniques	1	Traditional Representation	
Dance Track:		(Technical Drawing/	
Anatomy	1	Descriptive Geometry/	
Choreographic		Perspective)	3
Performance	5	*Electives*	
Dictation	1	Initiation to Family and Social Life; Modern Language II; Music Education	
History of Music and Dance	1.5		
Musical Analysis	1		
Physical Education	5		

Electives

Ancient Language; Foreign Language II; Harmony, Solfeggio, Choreography; Introduction to Social and Family Life; Studio Arts

G—BUSINESS

General Education		Optional Subjects	
Administrative and Commercial Techniques	2	Communication	2
Communication Techniques and Tools	3	Mathematics	2
Data Processing Applications	(3)		
Economics, Business Economics, Law	6		
Foreign Language I	3		
French	3		
Introduction to Contemporary Society	2		
Mathematics	1.5		
Physical Education	2		
Quantitative Techniques for Business	3		

H—DATA PROCESSING

General Education		Technology	
Applied Physics	2	Business Economics and Techniques	5
English	2	Data Processing Application	(4)
French	3	Data Processing Methods	5
Introduction to Contemporary Society	2	Data Processing Technology	2
Mathematics	5	*Electives*	
Physical Education	2	Foreign Language II; Initiation to Family and Social Life	

THE *TERMINALE* (FINAL CLASS)

The *terminale* is reached by roughly 30% of 18-year-olds. Of those enrolled in 1984-85, 64.7% were in the general academic streams (A-B-C-D-E) and 35.3% in the technical streams (F-G-H). Among the classes of the academic track, the *terminale* D (mathematics and natural sciences) had the largest enrollment—18.2%, followed by *terminale* A (literature and philosophy)—17%, *terminale* B (economics)—15.2%, *terminale* C (mathematics and physical sciences)—11.8% and *terminale* E (mathematics and technology)—2.4%. In the technical sections, *terminale* G (business) accounted for 19.4%, followed by *terminale* F (applied sciences)—13% and *terminale* H (data processing science)—0.4%.

The *terminale* is dedicated to the *baccalauréat* examination which is administered nationwide in June. There are as many sections of *terminale* as there are options on the *baccalauréat*: 31 in all, including the newly instituted vocational *baccalauréat professionnel* which has five options. Students pass into the *terminale* which corresponds to the 1° they have just completed. Those who have successfully completed 1°S proceed to either *terminale* C (mathematics and physical sciences) or to *terminale* D (mathematics and natural sciences). Those who have completed 1°E proceed to *terminale* E (mathematics and technology). The single 1°G leads to one of three *terminales:* G1 (administrative/secretarial techniques); G2 (quantitative techniques/accounting and bookkeeping); G3 (commercial/sales techniques). A few students from 1°A will enter *terminale* G and a few from 1°B, *terminale* A or G.

The hours of instruction remain largely identical to those of 1°, but the distribution of hours among different subjects varies; French is no longer offered except as an elective and philosophy is added to the curriculum of all sections.

Weekly schedules are as follows. The hours listed in parentheses indicate laboratory or studio work.

Academic
- A Literature and Art
  (A1—Literature and Mathematics, A2—Literature and Languages, A3—Literature and Art)
- B Economics and Social Sciences
- C Mathematics and Physical Sciences
- D Mathematics and Natural Sciences
- D' Agricultural Science
- E Mathematics and Technology

Technical

- F Technical
  (F1—Mechanical Construction, F2—Electronics, F3—Electrotechnics, F4—Civil Engineering, F5—Applied Physics, F6—Applied Chemistry, F7—Biological Sciences [Biochemistry Option], F7'—Biological Sciences [Biology Option], F8—Medical-Social Sciences, F9—Energy and Equipment, F10—Microtechnics [Instruments or Optics], F11—Music and Dance, F12—Visual Art)
- G Business
  (G1—Secretarial Science, G2—Quantitative Techniques, G3—General Business)
- H Data Processing

A—LITERATURE AND ART

Core Subjects	A1	A2	A3
Foreign Language I	3	3	3
History/Geography/Civics	4	4	4
Mathematics	5	2	2
Philosophy	8	8	8
Physical Education	2	2	2

continued

ELEMENTARY AND SECONDARY EDUCATION

Optional Subjects

1. *Either* Latin *or* Ancient Greek *or* Foreign Language II   3 — 3
2. *Either* Latin + Ancient Greek *or* Latin + Foreign Language II
   or Ancient Greek + Foreign Language II   — 3+3 —
3. *Either* Studio Arts and Architecture *or* Music Education   — — 4

Electives

Ancient Greek; Computer Science/Data Processing; Economics and Business; Economics and Social Sciences; Foreign Language II; and III; French; Latin; Manual and Technical Education; Music Education; Studio Arts; Technology

B—ECONOMICS AND SOCIAL SCIENCES

Core Subjects		*Electives*
Economics and Social Sciences	5	Ancient Greek; Computer Science/ Data Processing; Economics and Business; Foreign Language II; and III; French; Latin; Manual and Technical Education; Music Education; Physics; Studio Arts; Technology
Foreign Language I	3	
History/Geography/Civics	4	
Mathematics	5	
Philosophy	5	
Physical Education	2	

Optional Subjects

1. *Either* Latin *or* Ancient Greek *or* Foreign Language II   3

C, D—MATHEMATICS AND SCIENCE/E—MATHEMATICS AND TECHNOLOGY

Core Subjects	C	D	E
Foreign Language I	3	2	2
History/Geography/Civics	3	3	—
Mathematics	9	6	9
Natural Sciences	2	2.5	—
Philosophy	3	3	3
Physical Education	2	2	2
Physics	5	5	5
Technology	—	—	11

Electives

Ancient Greek; Computer Science/Data Processing; Economics and Business; Economics and Social Sciences; Foreign Language II; and III; French; Latin; Manual and Technical Education; Music Education; Studio Arts; Technology

F—TECHNICAL

General Education	F1	F2	F3	F4	F9	F10A	F10B
Foreign Language I	2	2	2	2	2	2	2
Mathematics	3.5	3.5	3.5	3.5	3.5	3.5	3.5
Measurements	—	—	(4)	—	—	—	—

continued

Philosophy	2	2	2	2	2	2	2
Physical Education	2	2	2	2	2	2	2
Physics	4	6+(4)	5	3+(1)	3+(1)	3+(1)	6+(4)

Technology

A. Study of Constructions	4+(4)	4+(2)	4+(2)	4+(4)	8+(4)	4+(4)	3+(2)
B. Applications							
1. Preparation and Organization:							
Electrical Systems	—	—	4	—	—	—	—
Electronic Systems	—	(5)	—	—	—	—	—
Equipment Systems	—	—	—	—	5	—	—
Methods	1+(4)	—	—	5+(2)	—	1+(4)	1+(1)
2. Operation and Control:							
Electrical Systems	—	—	(8)	—	—	—	—
Electronic Systems	—	(6)	—	—	—	—	—
Equipment Systems	—	—	—	—	(6)	—	—
Systems	2+(8)	—	—	2+(6)	—	2+(8)	1+(9)

Electives

Art; Education; French; Preparation for Family and Social Life

F—TECHNICAL

General Education	F5	F6	F7	F7'	F8
Biochemistry	—	—	2+(7)	2+(4)	—
Biology	—	—	—	—	3+(1)
Chemistry	1	4	—	—	—
Economics	—	—	—	—	2
Foreign Language I	2	2	2	2	2
Hematology/Histology/Cytology	—	—	—	1+(4)	—
Mathematics	5	3.5	2	2	2
Microbiology	—	—	1+(3)	—	—
Microbiology/Immunology and Parasitology	—	—	—	2+(8)	—
Philosophy	2	2	2	2	3
Physical Education	2	2	2	2	2
Physics	7	1	3+(8)	2+(1)	2
Physiology	—	—	2	3	—
Physiopathology and Medical Terminology	—	—	—	—	3
Professional Techniques	—	—	—	—	(6)
Psycho-Socio-Legal Aspects	—	—	—	—	3+(2)
Laboratory Work, Industrial Laboratory and Research					
Chemistry	(1)	(9)	—	—	—
Design and Technology	(2)	(3)	—	—	—
Instruments	—	(1)	—	—	—
Physics	(11)	(3)	—	—	—
Workshop	(2)	—	—	—	—

continued

ELEMENTARY AND SECONDARY EDUCATION

Electives

Art Education; French; Initiation to Family and Social Life; Secretarial Science; Speed Writing (F8 section); Workshop

MUSIC AND DANCE (F11, F11')/VISUAL ART (F12)

General Education	F11	General Education	F12
Additional Mathematics *or* Philosophy	2	Foreign Language	2
Foreign Language I	3	Mathematics	3
History of Arts and Cultures	1	Philosophy	3
Mathematics	3	Physical Education	2
Philosophy	4	Physics	3
Physics	2	*Professional Subjects*	
Professional Education		Foundations in Arts:	
Instrumental Performance Track:		Three-Dimensional Design	(3)
Analysis	1.5	Color, Study of Documents and Research	(3)
Dictation	1	Arts, Techniques and Cultures	2
Ensemble Music	1.5	Applied Arts:	
History of Music	1.5	Composition	2+(5)
Organ	1	Practical Studio Work	(4)
Performance	2	Technology	3
Reading Scores	0.5	Traditional Representation:	
Sound Techniques	1	Technical Drawing/ Descriptive	
Dance Track:		Geometry/Perspective)	3
Anatomy	1	*Electives*	
Choreographic Performance	5	Foreign Language II; French; Initiation to Family and Social Life; Foreign Language II; Music Education	
Dictation	1		
History of Music and Dance	1.5		
Musical Analysis	1		
Physical Education	5		
Stage Design	1		

Electives

Ancient Language; Foreign Language II; Harmony, Solfeggio; Choreography; Introduction to Social and Family Life; Studio Arts

G—BUSINESS

General Education	G1	G2	G3
Administrative (Secretarial) Methods	3	—	—
Application and Synthesis	4	6	6
Commercial (Sales) Techniques	—	—	7
Communication Techniques and Tools	9	—	—

continued

Economics, Business Economics, Law	5	5	5
Foreign Language I	3	3	3
Introduction to Contemporary Society	1.5	1.5	1.5
Mathematics	—	2.5	2.5
Philosophy	2	2	2
Physical Education	2	2	2
Quantitative Techniques for Business	—	7	—

H—DATA PROCESSING

General Education		*Technology*	
Applied Physics	3	Business Economics and Techniques	6
English	2	Data Processing Application	(5)
Mathematics	5	Data Processing Methods	5
Philosophy	2	Data Processing Technology	1+(1)
Physical Education	2	*Electives*	
		Foreign Language II; French; Initiation to Family and Social Life	

THE *BACCALAURÉAT*

Established under Napoleon in 1809, the *baccalauréat* remains an important educational milestone. The diploma is earned by national examination administered by each *académie* under the auspices of the Ministry of Education. (An *académie* is an educational administrative district.) It is classified as a national diploma of higher education *(diplôme national de l'enseignement supérieur)*. Initially offered solely in philosophy and science, the *baccalauréat* has been extended, since 1967, to technical disciplines. A vocational *baccalauréat* was created in 1985 and first administered in 1987. There are 31 options on the *baccalauréat* today in fields encompassing computer science, literature and humanities, pure and applied sciences, and secretarial science.

There are three types of *baccalauréats:*

> *Baccalauréat de l'Enseignement du Second Degré (Baccalauréat of Secondary Education) (A-B-C-D-E)*
> *Baccalauréat de Technicien (Baccalauréat of Technician) (F-G- H)*
> *Baccalauréat Professionnel (Vocational Baccalauréat)*

Actual diplomas are identified as *Diplôme de Bachelier de l'Enseignement du Second Degré* and *Diplôme de Baccalauréat de Technicien*.

By law, all *baccalauréats* are deemed to be equal and give access to university education even though fields such as science, engineering and medicine are reserved for holders of a scientific *baccalauréat*. See documents 1.2a, 1.2b, and 1.2c for sample *baccalauréats*.

Of the students entering a *lycée*, 80% will eventually earn a *baccalauréat*, albeit not always within three years. In any given year, 65% of the candidates attempting the examination will pass it. The highest rate of success (75%)

ELEMENTARY AND SECONDARY EDUCATION

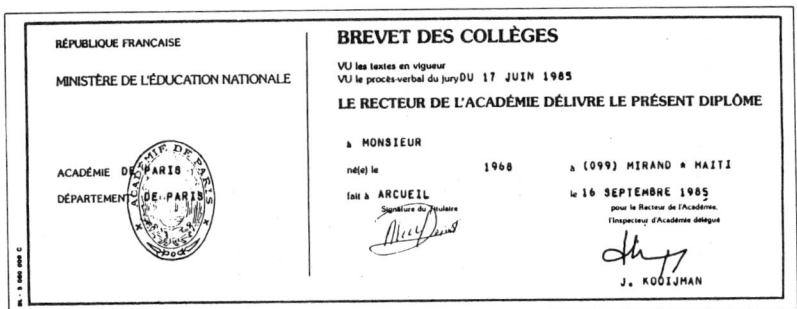

1.1. *Brevet des Collèges*

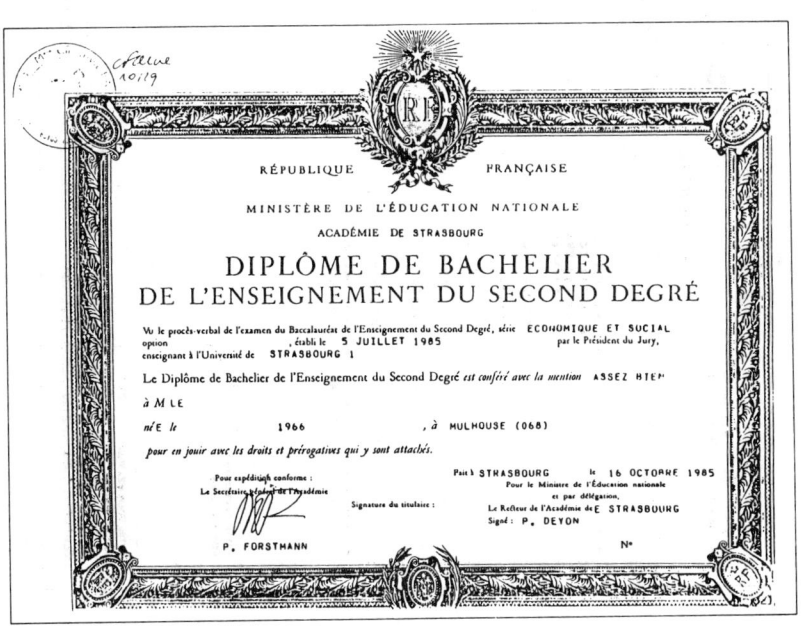

1.2a. Academic *Baccalauréat* Diploma

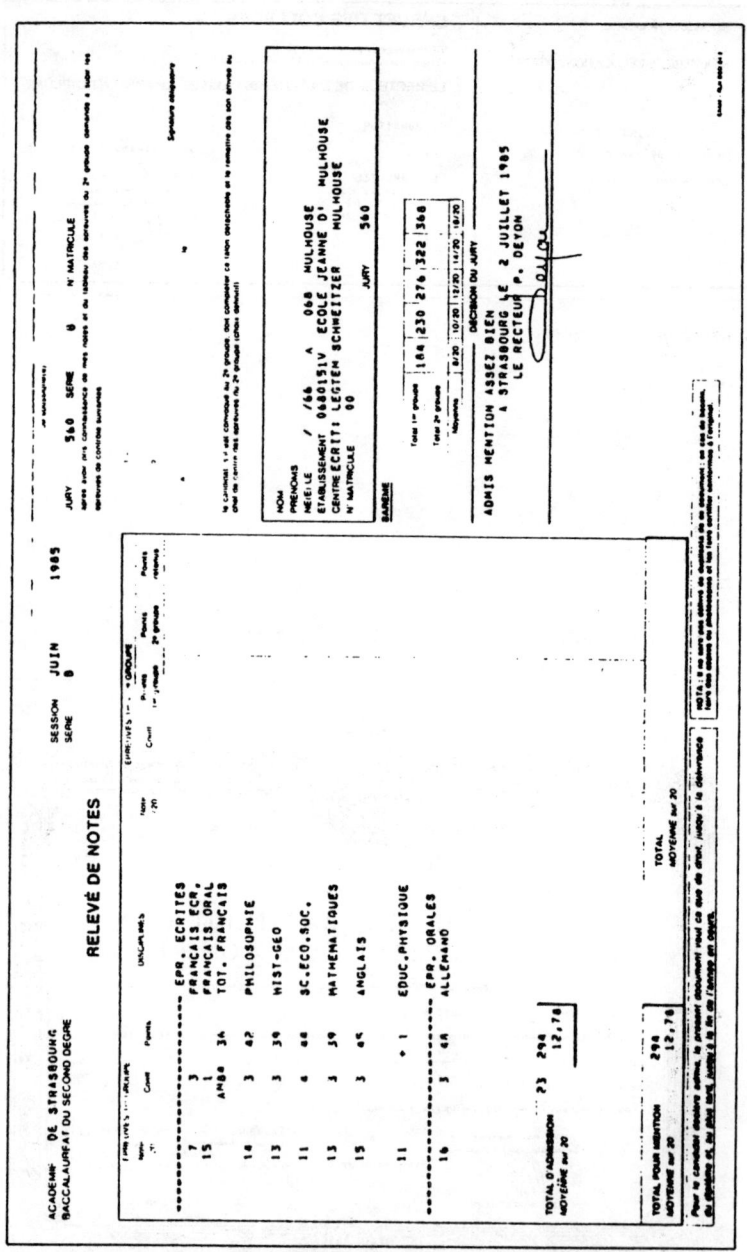

1.2b. *Baccalauréat "B"* Transcript Issued by the Académie de Strasbourg

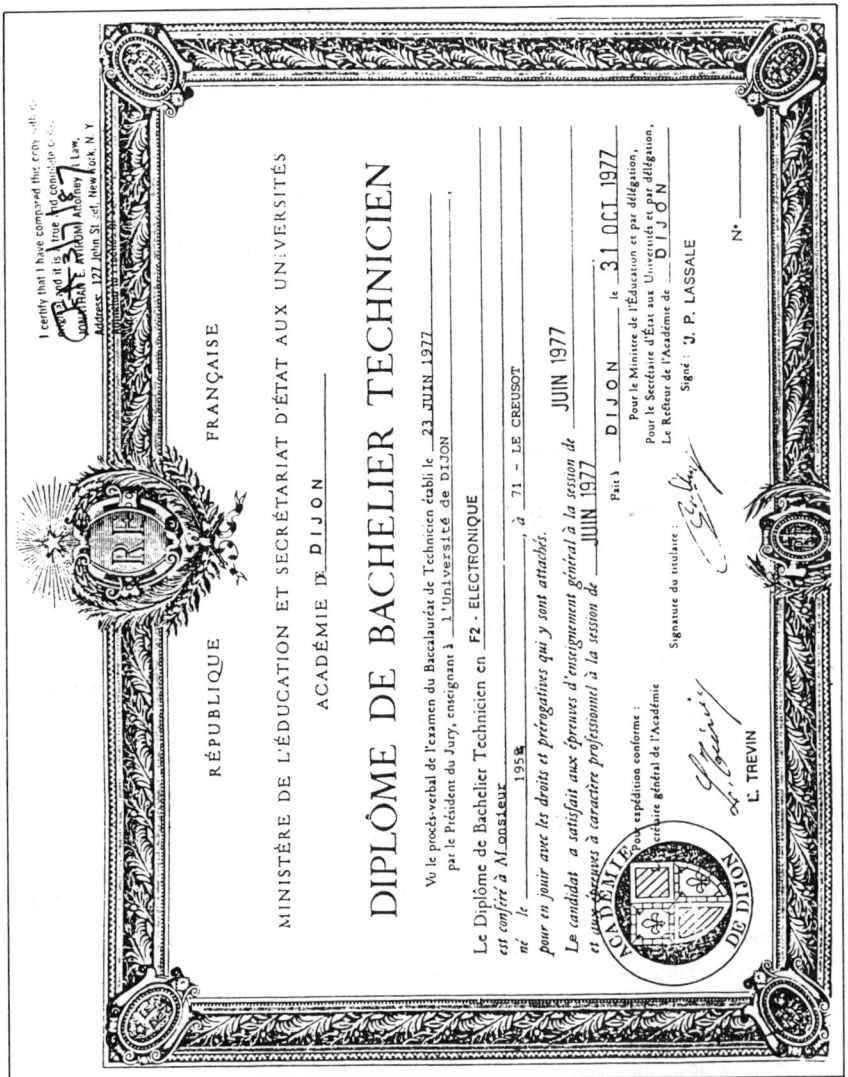

1.2c. Technical *Baccalauréat* Diploma

occurs in the selective mathematics and physical sciences stream (*série* C). The *baccalauréat* examination is administered by an examination panel (jury) composed of *lycée* teachers external to the institution and chaired by a university professor. Each year examination questions are developed by special committees following instructions laid down by the Ministry of Education. French is examined at the end of the 1° one year ahead of the rest of the *baccalauréat* and the results are carried over and included in the final tally. The relative weight of each subject is determined by the value of its coefficient on the examination. The highest coefficient factor is assigned to the field of concentration of each section and is an indication that a large number of hours of instruction are devoted to it both in 1° and in *terminale*. The *baccalauréat* examination consists of a series of written essays in the principal subjects; minor subjects are examined orally.

The International Option *(Option Internationale)* of the *Baccalauréat*

This is not a *baccalauréat* stream but represents additional optional study in 1° and *terminale* for selected students who are enrolled in traditional academic streams. Introduced in the mid-1980's, this unique program provides supplemental education in the language, literature, culture, history, and geography of foreign countries in a curriculum developed with the assistance of the relevant foreign educational authorities. The international option is offered in English and British Literature, Dutch, German, Italian, Spanish, Swedish and American Studies and Literature, at a few *lycées* in France and at French schools abroad. The program, which is taught entirely in the language of the chosen country, preferably by native teachers, consists of five-six weekly hours of additional instruction in literature and civilization, and two-three weekly hours in history, geography, and social studies. These subjects constitute supplemental examinations on the *baccalauréat*.

The Examination by Section

A1 (Literature and Mathematics)	Coeff.	A2 (Literature and Foreign Languages)	Coeff.
First Round		*First Round*	
Written Examination		Written Examination	
Foreign *or* Classical Language	3	Foreign Language I	4
French	5	Foreign Language II, *or* III *or* Classical Language	3
History/Geography	3	French	5
Mathematics	4	History/Geography	3
Philosophy	5	Philosophy	5
Oral Examination		Oral Examination	
Foreign *or* Classical Language	3	Foreign *or* Classical Language	3
Second Round		Mathematics	2
Oral Examination		*Second Round*	
Two subjects previously examined in writing		Oral Examination	
		Two subjects previously examined in writing	

ELEMENTARY AND SECONDARY EDUCATION

A3 (Literature and Fine Arts)

First Round	Coeff.
Written Examination	
Arts	3
Foreign *or* Classical	
Language	3
French	5
History/Geography	3
Philosophy	5
Oral Examination	
Mathematics	2
Practical Examination:	3
Music *or* Art	3
Foreign *or* Classical	
Language	

Second Round

Oral Examination
  Two subjects previously
    examined in writing

B (Economics and Social Sciences)

First Round	Coeff.
Written Examination	
Economics and Social	
Sciences	4
Foreign Language	3
French	4
History/Geography	3
Mathematics	3
Philosophy	3
Oral Examination	
Foreign Language II *or*	
Classical Language	3

Second Round

Oral Examination
  Two subjects previously
    examined in writing

C (Mathematics and Physical Sciences)

First Round	Coeff.
Written Examination	
French	3
History/Geography	2
Mathematics	5
Natural Sciences (Biology)	2
Philosophy	2
Physics	5
Oral Examination	
Foreign Language I	3

Second Round

Oral Examination
  Two subjects previously
    examined in writing

D (Mathematics and Natural Science)

First Round	Coeff.
Written Examination	
French	3
History/Geography	2
Mathematics	4
Natural Sciences (Biology)	4
Philosophy	2
Physics	4
Oral Examination	
Foreign Language I	3

Second Round

Oral Examination
  Two subjects previously
    examined in writing

D' (Agricultural Science)

First Round	Coeff.
Written Examination	
Biology	4
French	3
History/Geography	2
Mathematics	3
Philosophy	2

E (Mathematics and Technology)

First Round	Coeff.
Written Examination	
French	3
Mathematics	5
Mechanical Construction	4
Philosophy	2
Physics	4

continued

Physics	3
Oral Examination	
Agricultural Science	5
Economics	3
Foreign Languages	3

Second Round

Oral Examination
  Two subjects previously examined in writing

Oral Examination	
Foreign Language I	3
Laboratory	3

Second Round

Oral Examination
  Two subjects previously examined in writing

F1 (Mechanical Construction)

First Round	Coeff.
General Education	
Written Examination	
French	4
Mathematics	5
Oral Examination	
Foreign Language	2
Technical Education	
Written Examination	
Mechanics	3
Project *or* Study	6
Oral Examination	
Practical Examination	5
Second Round	
General Education	
Oral Examination	
French	4
Mathematics	5
Physics	4
Professional Education	
Written Examination	
Study of Production	4
Study of Production Tools	4
Technology	4
Oral Examination	
Mechanics	3

F2 (Electronics)

First Round	Coeff.
General Education	
Written Examination	
French	3
Mathematics	5
Philosophy	1
Oral Examination	
Foreign Language	2
Technical Education	
Written Examination	
Physics	5
Study of a Technical System	6
Oral Examination (Presentation of Case Study)	5
Electronic Construction	3
Second Round	
General Education	
Oral Examination	
French *or*	3
Mathematics	5
Professional Education	
Practical Examination	5
Electronic Construction *or* Physics	5
Presentation of a Case Study of a Technical System	6

F3 (Electrical Technology)

First Round	Coeff.
General Education	
Written Examination	
French	3

F4 (Civil Engineering Technology)

First Round	Coeff.
General Education	
Written Examination	
French	3

continued

ELEMENTARY AND SECONDARY EDUCATION

Mathematics	5		Mathematics	5
Philosophy	1		Philosophy	1
Oral Examination			Oral Examination	
Foreign Language	2		Foreign Language	2

Technical Education / *Technical Education*

Written Examination			Written and Practical	
Physics	3		Examination	
Study of Constructions	3		Applied Mechanics and	
Study of Equipment	3		Resistance of Materials	4
Practical Examination			Drafting	4
Operation and Control	5		Project	6
			Oral Examination	

Second Round / *Second Round*

General Education / *General Education*

Oral Examination			Oral Examination	
French	3		French	3
Mathematics	5		Mathematics	5
Mechanics	3		Physics	4

Professional Education / *Professional Education*

Written Examination			Written and Practical	
Blueprints	3		Examination	
Measurements	2		Cost Estimating	3
Technology	3		Legislation	2
Trials	2		Materials and Construction	
Oral Examination			Technology	6
Physics	3		Oral Examination	
			Applied Mechanics and	
			Resistance of Materials	4

F5 (Applied Physics) | F6 (Applied Chemistry)

	Coeff.			Coeff.
First Round			*First Round*	
General Education			*General Education*	
Written Examination			Written Examination	
French	3		French	3
Mathematics	6		Mathematics and Physics	6
Philosophy	1		Philosophy	1
Oral Examination			Oral Examination	
Foreign Examination	2		Foreign Language	2
Technical Education			*Technical Education*	
Written Examination			Written Examination	
Electricity	4		Chemistry	4
Physics	4		Laboratory Techniques	3
Practical Laboratory	4		Technology and Blueprint	4
Second Round			*Second Round*	
General Education			*General Education*	
Oral Examination			Oral Examination	
Chemistry	3		French *or* Mathematics *or*	
French	3		Physics	3
Mathematics	6			

continued

Professional Education

Written Examination
- Electrical Measurements — 5
- Physical Measurements — 5
- Physics Laboratory Techniques — 5

Oral Examination
- Physics *or* Electricity — 4

Technical Education

Written Examination
- Chemical and Physical Analysis — 5
- Preparation and Assembly — 5

Optional
- Chemistry (Oral) — 4
- Scientific Documentation and Typing — 4

F7 (Biological Sciences—Biochemistry Option)

First Round	Coeff.
General Education	
Written Examination	
French	3
Philosophy	1
Physiology and Chemistry	4
Oral Examination	
Foreign Language	2
Technical Education	
Written Examination	
Biochemistry	4
Biochemistry Lab Techniques	3
Microbiology and Lab Techniques	3
Second Round	
General Education	
Written Examination	
Mathematics and Physics	3
Oral Examination	
French	3
Physiology and Chemistry	4
Technical Education	
Practical Examination	
Biochemistry	
Microbiology	6
Preparation and Assembly	4
Oral Examination	5
Biochemistry	4

F7' (Biological Sciences—Biology Option)

First Round	Coeff.
General Education	
Written Examination	
French	3
Philosophy	1
Physiology and Chemistry	4
Oral Examination	
Foreign Language	2
Technical Education	
Written Examination	
Biochemistry and Lab Techniques	3
Biological Lab Techniques	3
General Immunology and Microbiology	4
Second Round	
General Education	
Written Examination	
Mathematics and Physics	3
Oral Examination	
French	3
Physiology and Chemistry	4
Technical Education	
Practical Examination	
Bacteriology	5
Biochemistry	4
Hematology and Immunology; Serology *or* Parasitology *or* Histology; Cytology *or* Physiology	6
Oral Examination	
General Immunology and Microbiology	4

continued

ELEMENTARY AND SECONDARY EDUCATION

F8 (Medico-Social Sciences)

First Round	Coeff.
General Education	
Written Examination	
Biology and Chemistry	4
French	3
Philosophy	1
Oral Examination	
Foreign Language	2
Technical Education	
Written Examination	
Case Study (Typed)	4
Medico-Social Sciences	3
Physiopathology and Medical Terminology	3
Second Round	
General Education	
Oral Examination	
Biology and Chemistry	4
Economics	2
French	3
Mathematics and Physics	3
Medico-Social Sciences	3
Professional Education	
Oral and Practical Examination	
Medico-Social Sciences	3
Presentation and Discussion of Internship Report	3
Study of Document and Typed Report	4

F9 (Energy and Equipment)

First Round	Coeff.
General Education	
Written Examination	
French	3
Mathematics	5
Philosophy	1
Oral Examination	
Foreign Language	2
Technical Education	
Written Examination	
Applied Fluid Dynamics and Thermodynamics	4
Graphic Representation of an Installation	4
Study of an Installation	6
Second Round	
General Education	
Oral Examination	
French	3
Mathematics	5
Physics	4
Professional Education	
Written Examination	
Equipment and Construction Technology	2
Practical Work and Study	2
Resistance and Mechanics of Materials	3
Social and Construction Legislation	4
Oral Examination	
Applied Fluid Dynamics and Thermodynamics	4

F10 (Microtechnology—Instruments or Optics)

First Round	Coeff.
General Education	
Written Examination	
French	3
Mathematics	5
Philosophy	1
Oral Examination	
Foreign Language	2
Technical Education	
Written Examination	
Mechanics *or* Optics	3
Study *or* Project	6

F11 (Music—Instruments Option)

First Round	Coeff.
General Education	
Written Examination	
Either Mathematics and Physics *or* Philosophy	2
French	3
Oral Examination	
Foreign Language	2
Technical Education	
Practical Examination	
History of Music	2

continued

Practical Examination	
Production	5

Second Round

General Education

Oral Examination	
Electricity:	
Instrumentation Option	3
Optics Option	2
French	3
Instrumentation Option:	
Physics and Chemistry	
of Materials	1
Mathematics	5
Optics Option: Mechanics	2
Physics	4

Professional Education

Written Examination	
Instrumentation Option:	
Production Tools Study	4
Optics Option: Optical	
Metrology and Physical	
Measurement	4
Study of Production	4
Technology	3
Oral Examination	
Instrumentation Option:	
Mechanics	3
Optics Option: Optics	3

Instrumental Performance	2
Musical Techniques	3

Second Round

General Education

Oral Examination (one from each group)	
1. History of Arts and	
Culture	2
Mathematics	2
Philosophy	2
2. French	3
Mathematics and	
Physics	2
Philosophy	2

Technical Education

Practical Examination (one of the following)	
Instrumental Reading	2
Music Writing	2
Musical Performance	4
Organs	2
Sound Techniques	2

F11' (Music—Dance Option)

First Round	Coeff.
General Education	
Written Examination	
Either Mathematics and	
Physics *or* Philosophy	2
French	3
Oral Examination	
Foreign Language	2
Technical Education	
Written Examination	
Choreographed Rendition	4
History of Music	2
Musical Techniques	3
Second Round	
General Education	
Oral Examination	
1. History of Arts and	
Culture	2
Mathematics	2
Philosophy	2

F12 (Visual Art)

First Round	Coeff.
General Education	
Written Examination	
French	3
Mathematics	4
Philosophy	1
Oral Examination	
Foreign Language	2
Technical Education	
Written Examination	
Arts/Techniques and	
Cultures	4
Practical Examination	
Graphic Art Composition	6
Oral Presentation	4
Second Round	
General Education	
Oral Examination	
Either French *or*	3
Mathematics	4

continued

ELEMENTARY AND SECONDARY EDUCATION

2. French	3	Physics	3
Mathematics and Physics	2	*Technical Education*	
Philosophy	2	Written Examination	
Technical Education		Artistic Expression	4
Practical Examination (one of the following)		Technology	3
		Traditional Representation Techniques	3
Anatomy	2	Oral Examination	
Choreographed Rendition	4	Arts/Techniques and Cultures	4
Choreographic Improvisation (Dance)	2		
Command Performance (Choreographed)	2		
Production	2		

G1 (Administrative and Secretarial Techniques) | G2 (Quantitative Techniques)

G1 First Round	Coeff.	G2 First Round	Coeff.
General Education		*General Education*	
Written Examination		Written Examination	
French	4	French	4
Philosophy	2	Mathematics	3
Oral Examination		Philosophy	1
Foreign Language	3	Oral Examination	
Technical Education		Foreign Language	2
Written Examination		*Technical Education*	
Case Study	3	Written Examination	
Economics, Business Economics, Law	5	Case Study	6
Oral Examination		Economics, Business Economics, Law	5
Communication Tools and Techniques	3	*Second Round*	
Second Round		*General Education*	
General Education		Oral Examination	
Oral Examination		French *or* Mathematics	3
French	4	Knowledge of Contemporary Society	2
Knowledge of Contemporary Society	2	*Technical Education*	
Technical Education		Oral Examination	
Oral Examination		Economics, Business Economics, Law	5
Administrative Methods	3	Quantitative Techniques	3
Economics, Business Economics, Law	5		

G3 (Commercial/Sales Techniques) | H (Data Processing)

G3 First Round	Coeff.	H First Round	Coeff.
General Education		*General Education*	
Written Examination		Written Examination	
French	4	French	3

continued

Mathematics	2	Mathematics	3
Philosophy	1	Philosophy	1
Oral Examination		Oral Examination	
Foreign Language	3	Foreign Language	2

Technical Education

Technical Education

Written Examination
    Case Study   6
    Economics, Business
    Economics, Law   5

Second Round

General Education

Oral Examination
    Either French *or*   3
    Mathematics   2
    Knowledge of
    Contemporary Society   2

Technical Education

Oral Examination
    Commercial Techniques   3
    Economics, Business
    Economics, Law   5

Written Examination
    Case Study (Data
    Processing)   4
    Economics and
    Management Techniques   3
    Programming   2

Second Round

General Education

Oral Examination
    French *or* Mathematics   3
    Physics   2

Technical Education

Oral Examination
    Data Processing
    Technology   3
    Economics and
    Management Techniques   3

Grades on the *Baccalauréat*

Candidates who pass the *baccalauréat* on the first round are awarded their diplomas with *mentions* which are ratings of quality based on the overall average of the grades on the examination. *Très bien* (very good) is awarded for averages of 16 or higher; averages ranging from 14 to 15.99 earn a *bien* (good); 12 to 13.99 earn an *assez bien* (good enough); 10 to 11.99 earn a *passable* (satisfactory). If the average falls between 8/20 and 10/20, the candidate is required to submit to a validation oral examination, the *epreuve orale de contrôle*, which consists of two major subjects. The *baccalauréat* is awarded when the overall average of grades, on the first and second rounds combined, reaches 10/20. Candidates whose overall average falls short of 8/20 on the first round fail the examination and must repeat the *terminale*. A student who chooses to leave the *lycée* without passing the *baccalauréat* examination is issued a *certificat de fin d'études secondaires* (certificate of completion of secondary studies).

The results obtained on the 1985 examination at the Académie de Lille (see chart on page 27) are representative of the national situation; 65.2% of the candidates passed the *baccalauréat*. The median of grades awarded in these subjects, which are representative of the overall grading practices on the *baccalauréat*, falls in the 8-11 range. This demonstrates the severity of grading in France and must be taken into consideration in assessing *baccalauréat* results.

When a student has passed the *baccalauréat*, all subjects are regarded as having been passed regardless of individual scores. The following conversion

ELEMENTARY AND SECONDARY EDUCATION

Philosophy

Grades/20	Series	C	A	D	B
0–5		19.9%	19%	20.3%	21.8%
0–8		57%	59.5%	59.5%	60.4%
9–20		43%	40.5%	40.4%	39.5%
10–14		29.3%	27.4%	26.8%	26.7%
14–20		6.9%	7%	8.1%	8.5%
Overall Average Grade out of 20		8.28	8.26	8.10	8.05

Mathematics

Grades/20	Series	C	A1	D	B
0–5		21.3%	19.8%	10.7%	32.9%
0–8		48.2%	43.2%	31.3%	55.4%
9–20		51.7%	56.7%	68.6%	44.5%
10–14		32.2%	36.9%	45.6%	29.8%
14–20		15.3%	16.9%	20.7%	9.8%
Overall Average Grade out of 20		9.06	9.43	10.32	7.83

History/Geography

Grades/20	Series	C	A1	D	B
0–5		12.5%	15.2%	19%	14.8%
0–8		31.3%	36.3%	51.9%	35.6%
9–20		57.6%	52%	48%	50.9%
10–14		38.7%	36.2%	32.7%	34.6%
14–20		11%	8.8%	8.2%	7.7%
Overall Average Grade out of 20		9.2	8.8	8.7	8.5

scale is appropriate for the *baccalauréat* and has been approved by the National Council for the Evaluation of Foreign Educational Credentials.

French Grades	U.S. Grades
14-20	A
11-13	B
10	C
8-9	*
0-7	F

*These grades, which have no U.S. equivalent, may be considered as passing or failing, depending upon the student's overall performance.

Credit for the *Baccalauréat*

Advanced standing for the *baccalauréat* may be considered on a subject-by-subject basis in accordance with institutional policy on credit for college-level study completed in U.S. secondary institutions. It is recommended that the award of credit be based on a review of the *baccalauréat* program and the student's proposed course of study in the United States. Credit may be considered for subjects which carry a coefficient value of 4 or higher on the examination. These subjects were studied in greater depth in 1° and in *terminale* and constitute the fields of concentration of each section. For coefficients for all sections of the examination, see pages 18–26.

The following is a suggested sample credit conversion formula for determining advanced placement or transfer credit for a *baccalauréat* C (mathematics and physical science) program.

Subjects	Coefficients	U.S. Semester Credits
Written Examination		
Philosophy	2	-
Mathematics	5	6-8*
Physics	5	6-8*
History/Geography	2	-
Natural Sciences	2	-
Oral Examination		
Foreign Language I	3	-
French	3	-

*Institutions are advised to use their own course equivalents in assigning credit.

Vocational Education

Lower Secondary Programs

At the end of the observation cycle (end of 5°), students who have reached the age of 14 but whose academic performance is not satisfactory are encouraged to proceed toward vocational education. No student is required to accept placement in a vocational program and, indeed, many prefer to repeat the 5° in an attempt to remain in the academic track. Vocational programs at this level offer the following:

—*Classes Préprofessionnelles de Niveau*/CPPN (Pre-Vocational Remedial Classes)
—*Classes Préparatoires à l'Apprentissage*/CPA (Apprenticeship Training Classes)

A CPPN is a one-year remedial program for students who have reached the age of 14 but are not yet ready to undertake further vocational study and training. It provides remedial classes consisting of 12 weekly hours of instruction in French and mathematics and three hours of physical education. Students are subsequently streamed in a CPA or a 4° of a vocational *lycée*.

A CPA enrolls students who are 15 or older and can immediately begin vocational training. It offers a program where students alternate their time between school and apprenticeship training in business or industry. The 30-hour weekly schedule consists of eight hours of instruction in French and mathematics, the rest being devoted to vocational subjects. The program leads to a *Certificat d'Aptitude Professionnelle*/CAP (Certificate of Vocational Qualification) after two to three years of further apprenticeship training. Selected holders of a CAP can continue their studies by completing a bridge class designed to upgrade their general education for subsequent mainstreaming in programs leading to the *brevet de technicien* or the new *baccalauréat professionnel*.

Upper Secondary Programs

At the end of lower secondary education *(collège)*, one out of every four students is directed toward vocational education at a *lycée d'enseignement général et technique* (comprehensive *lycée*) or at a *lycée professionnel* (vocational *lycée*). Vocational programs integrate classroom instruction and apprenticeship training and lead, in two or three years, to a *Certificat d'Aptitude Professionnelle*/CAP (Certificate of Vocational Qualification) or to a *Brevet d'Enseignement Professionnel*/BEP (Certificate of Vocational Education), both qualifications for skilled workers.

The *baccalauréat professionnel* (vocational *baccalauréat)*, which was instituted in 1985, was designed to enhance the quality of vocational education and provide better employment opportunities. As a *baccalauréat*, it grants access to university. For holders of a CAP, the program is a three-year sequence which includes a one- year bridge class followed by two further years of study in 1° and *terminale*. Holders of a BEP complete two years of study including a bridge class known as *première d'adaptation* (adjustment 1°) and proceed to a *terminale* specific to the field of their choice. The program integrates classroom instruction with practical training. Five vocational sections were initially offered on the examination and additional ones are being considered.

Weekly hours are as follows: art education (2 hours), communication (3-4 hours), foreign language (3 hours), history/geography/civics (2 hours), physical education (3 hours), and vocational subjects (16-17 hours).

The *Brevet de Technicien*/BT (Technician's Certificate) is awarded following a three-year program offered in fields related to agriculture, manufacturing and service industries. Students begin the program by completing a 2° *de determination* although some fields require the completion of a *seconde* (2°) specific to the area of technical specialization. After the 2°, the BT requires the completion of two further years of study. A BT does not lead to university study but to nonuniversity technical programs leading to a *Brevet de Technicien Supérieur*/ BTS (Higher Technician's Certificate).

Section II. Higher Education in France

Higher education in France dates back to the Middle Ages with the founding of the Sorbonne in 1215. In the following centuries, several universities dedicated to law, medicine, and theology were founded in different cities by kings or the Church. From the beginning, academic and scientific research was carried out at special institutions distinct from the universities such as the Collège de France (College of France) founded in 1530; the Jardin des Plantes (Botanical Gardens) in 1626; the Observatoire de Paris (Paris Observatory) in 1672; the Ecole des Ponts et Chaussées (School of Bridges and Highways) in 1747; and the Ecole des Mines (School of Mines) in 1783.

Immediately after the French Revolution in 1793, the universities were abolished and replaced by specialized institutions, collectively known as *grandes écoles*. Established in 1794, the Ecole Polytechnique soon became a major institution for scientific education while schools such as the Ecole des Ponts et Chaussées (School of Highways and Bridges) and the Ecole des Mines (School of Mines) offered education in specific fields of engineering.

In 1806, Napoleon I recreated higher education in a new and reorganized fashion. The faculties of the former universities were accorded legal status and autonomy as schools of medicine, law and pharmacy and as faculties of science and letters, but were placed under the authority of a Grand Master in Paris. This highly centralized system of education, known as the Napoleonic University, was in force for most of the century and was unique in the uniformity of its curricula, teaching methods, and degree requirements. In 1808, Napoleon also founded the Ecole Normale Supérieure (Higher Normal School) to train teachers for the newly established elite secondary schools, the *lycées*.

The defeat of the French by the Germans in the Franco-Prussian War of 1870 was attributed to superior German technology and, as a result, the years following the war saw extensive educational reforms. An 1882 law instituted the separation of church and state in the area of education and simultaneously authorized the establishment of private schools under a legal framework set by the Ministry of Education. The private sector proceeded to establish highly selective business and engineering *grandes écoles* to train the manpower made necessary by the industrial revolution. In 1896, the existing *facultés* were merged into 23 universities, one per *académie*. Thus was born the dual system of higher education which is still in existence.

No major change took place in French higher education until 1966 when two-year technical institutions, known as *Instituts Universitaires de Technologie/* IUT (University Institutes of Technology), were established to train higher technicians. The post-war baby boom caused enrollment to soar and the universities became crowded. While many different reasons are cited for the student uprising of May 1968, one of its major causes was dissatisfaction with an overcrowded and rigid university system whose sole mission was the conservation and transmission of existing knowledge. Students demanded not only academic reform and the creation of professional programs, but also a democratic university in which the power of major professors would be curbed and where student and community concerns would be heard and addressed. The government heeded the calls for change and acted immediately. An extensive reform law (Loi d'Orientation de l'Enseignement Supérieur du 12 novembre 1968) was enacted and resulted in the creation of a new university system which gave institutions the autonomy to govern themselves. It also opened the way for universities to establish academic programs in business, engineering, applied science, and other curricula related to the needs of the employment market. French universities are still recovering from the upheaval of 1968 and several partial reforms have been implemented in the intervening 20 years.

Legal Basis of the Educational System

The Loi d'Orientation de l'Enseignement Supérieur (Higher Education Orientation Law) of November 12, 1968, as amended by the law of January 26, 1984, is the basis for all higher education administered by the Ministry of Education. The legal definition of an institution of higher education is *Etablissement Public à Caractère Scientifique, Culturel et Professionnel*/EPCSCP (Public Scientific, Cultural and Professional Institution). The various other institutions of technical and professional education operated by different ministries are governed by different laws and decrees.

Organization of Higher Education

Central Administration

The Ministry of Education has overall responsibility for higher education except for institutions operated by other agencies. From 1974 until 1981, higher education was administered by the now defunct Ministry of Universities. At the present time, higher education is overseen by a Secretary of State for Higher Education who reports to the Minister of Education and whose office is the Direction Générale des Enseignements Supérieurs/DESUP (General Directorate for Higher Education), composed of several divisions each responsible for a specific aspect of higher education—institutions of higher education; research; libraries, museums, scientific and technical information services; personnel; administration and finance. International relations are coordinated by the Direction de la Cooperation et des Relations Internationales/DCRI (Directorate for International Relations and Cooperation), a different bureau attached to the cabinet of the Minister of Education.

The Ministry of Education is assisted by the following permanent advisory bodies: the Conseil Supérieur de l'Education Nationale/CNES (Higher Council for National Education) which examines all regulations concerning education at all levels; the Conseil National de l'Enseignement Supérieur et de la Recherche/CNESER (National Council for Higher Education and Research), which advises the Minister on matters pertaining to higher education; the Comité National d'Evaluation (National Evaluation Committee) which monitors the administration, programs and curricula of higher education institutions and reports its findings and recommendations to the CNESER; the Conférence des Chefs d'Establissements Publics à Caractère Scientifique, Culturel et Professionnel (Conference of Heads of Public Scientific, Cultural and Professional Institutions), the assembly of the heads of institutions administered by the Ministry of Education, which represents their interests before the Ministry; and the Commission Interministerielle de Prospective et d'Orientation des Formations Supérieures (Interministerial Commission for Higher Education and Training), which coordinates with the Ministry of Education the activities of all the other ministries and agencies involved in higher education.

Regional Administration

The *recteur* (rector), who also bears the largely honorific title of *chancelier* (chancellor) of the university in his district and who is the representative of the Minister of Education, has limited direct powers over the universities. On budgetary matters the *recteur* can act on behalf of the Minister of Education.

Institutions of Higher Education

The largest number of institutions of higher education are administered by the Ministry of Education and are legally defined as *Etablissements Publics à Caractère Scientifique, Culturel et Professionel*/EPCSCP (Public Scientific, Cultural and Professional Institutions), a term which applies to all universities, research institutions, several *grandes écoles*, as well as university institutions of technology and elementary teacher training normal schools. The status of EPCSCP does not apply to institutions, including *grandes écoles*, administered by other agencies such as the Ministries of Agriculture, Culture, Defense, Health, Housing and Urban Affairs, Industry, Social Affairs, and Telecommunications—to name a few—and which account for a significant portion of professional and technical higher education.

Enrollment

In 1986–87, 1,240,200 students were enrolled at institutions operated by the Ministry of Education as follows: 923,800 students at universities (including 17,800 at private universities); 62,100 at university institutes of technology;

47,400 at *grandes écoles* of engineering including engineering schools operated by other ministries; 28,650 at business schools; 48,300 at postsecondary preparatory classes for *grandes écoles;* and 129,950 in two-year technical programs. An unspecified number were attending other public and private institutions of higher professional, technical or vocational education.

Student Life

Higher education at public institutions is free of charge even though students are expected to pay a nominal registration fee. Need-based government scholarships are available to cover the living expenses of eligible students. The government further provides a wide range of services for all students including loans, health insurance, subsidized housing and cafeterias. The Centre National des Oeuvres Universitaires et Scolaires/CNOUS (National Center for University and School Works), a national organization under the auspices of the Ministry of Education, has overall responsibility for student financial assistance, life and welfare. Through its regional affiliates, it administers residence halls and cafeterias.

Chapter II

University Education

History

French universities have a very long history and tradition; founded in Paris in 1215, the Sorbonne is their forerunner. Additional universities were established until 1793 when a decree of the revolutionary government abolished all of them because of their close identification with the Church. In lieu of universities, the government established specialized institutions of higher education such as the Ecole Polytechnique, the Conservatoire National des Arts et Métiers, the Ecole des Langues Orientales, and the Ecole des Beaux Arts.

In 1806, Napoleon created a university and appointed a *grand maître* (great master) to administer it. The Napoleonic university was not a teaching institution but a central administrative authority which had total monopoly over education at all levels, including primary and secondary schools. The law prohibited anyone from teaching outside the control of the university. Higher education was provided by independent faculties of law, letters, medicine, pharmacy, and science operated by the university.

An 1875 law abolished the Napoleonic university and established the freedom of teaching. Higher education was reorganized and faculties which were located in different cities were grouped into 23 universities, one in each newly created *académie*, a regional body in charge of educational administration. The system which emerged from this reform remained highly centralized since all universities were placed under the direct control of the Minister of National Education. Each university consisted of the same five faculties: law, letters, medicine, pharmacy, and science. The demise of the Napoleonic university and the reinstatement of the freedom of teaching permitted the establishment of private educational institutions. Thus several *grandes écoles* were simultaneously founded, primarily by the private sector, to educate students in engineering and business, fields not taught by the universities. (See Chapter IV for more information on the *grandes écoles*.)

French universities remained virtually unchanged until 1968 when a major student revolt forced the government to introduce fundamental structural and academic reforms.

The Reform of 1968

Enrollment at French universities grew quite substantially after World War II, increasing from 97,000 in 1945 to approximately 500,000 students in 1967. The universities were caught unprepared for an enrollment of this size. Their stated role—which had been the preservation and transmission of knowledge—no longer met the needs of the new generation of students who wanted professionally-oriented programs. In 1966, two-year technical institutions, known as the *instituts universitaires de technologie*/IUT (university institutes of technology), were created to offer young people an alternative route to a higher education diploma. The 60 IUT, however, did not relieve the overcrowding; the general malaise which had overcome the universities continued until it erupted in May 1968 into a major student uprising which was soon followed by a nationwide strike by workers. As a result of these events, a new Minister of Education was appointed and given the mandate to reform higher education. Within six months, in November 1968, the government introduced a major bill before the National Assembly which was enacted as Loi d'Orientation de l'Enseignement Supérieur (Higher Education Orientation Law). The new law changed French university education in a radical fashion.

The 1968 law was based on three main principles: autonomy; participation; multidisciplinary education. *Autonomy* — Universities were granted the right of self-government within a general legal framework enforced by the Ministry of Education. Even though since 1968 the Ministry no longer intervenes in the daily operation of universities, it continues to perform such major functions as determining university admission, conferring national diplomas, providing operating budgets, and hiring faculty and staff. *Participation* — The autocratic rule by senior professors over faculty was a major factor of the 1968 uprising. Under the 1968 law, universities are administered by an elected president assisted by various advisory councils whose membership includes representatives of students, faculty and staff. *Multidisciplinary Education* — Universities were reorganized in terms of *Unités d'Enseignement et de Recherche*/ UER (Teaching and Research Units) representing different disciplines, a structure designed to encourage interdisciplinary education.

The 23 universities which had existed until 1968 were first broken into 700 academic units corresponding to the departments of the former faculties. These units, newly named UERs, were subsequently organized into 70 multidisciplinary universities. Thus every old university yielded two or three new universities. See Appendix A for a list of French universities and institutions deemed to be universities.

The Reform of 1984

Throughout the 1970's, enrollment at French universities continued to grow very rapidly, reaching approximately 900,000 in the early 1980's. Universities continue to be at the center of national attention. Various governments have tried to implement reforms, some of which have led to confrontations with students, as in 1976 and in 1986. When the socialist government came to power in 1981, the issue of higher education was high on its agenda. After extensive consultation, in 1984 the Minister of Education successfully introduced in the National Assembly a major bill on university reform.

The reform had several objectives. To curb the high rate of attrition in the first year of university study, first cycle programs were revised to include orientation, guidance and testing of students. New programs and diplomas were created, primarily in technical fields, to make university study directly relevant to the job market and to encourage students to complete their education. Doctoral programs were totally revised with the introduction of a single *doctorat*. The law reinforced the notion of decentralization, which had been introduced in 1968 but had not been fully implemented. Universities were further encouraged to establish links with local government and the private sector in the development of new programs and research.

Current University Structure and Administration

Since 1968, French universities have exercised self-government under an elected president assisted and advised by various councils. In 1984, the former *Unité d'Enseignement et de Recherche*/UER was renamed *Unité de Formation et de Recherche*/UFR (Teaching and Research Unit). Universities are composed of UFR, research laboratories, and affiliated centers and institutes.

The President. The office of president was created by the 1968 law as the head of the university and its representative before the Ministry of Education. The president, a professor elected by the university general assembly for a five-year term which is not immediately renewable, chairs all three university councils and exercises full authority over academic, budgetary and personnel matters.

The Councils. The university is governed by three councils: the Administrative Council (Conseil d'Administration), the Scientific Council (Conseil Scientifique) and the Education and University Life Council (Conseil des Etudes et de la Vie Universitaire). Each council is composed of elected representatives of faculty, students and staff. Representatives of the local community are appointed to each council by the president. The Administrative Council acts on all matters pertaining to the operation of the university. The Scientific Council sets teaching and research policy. The Education and University Life Council deals with counseling and student life. On major issues, such as electing a new president or establishing a new UFR, all three councils act jointly as the Conseil de l'Université (University Council). That council determines the internal structure and by-laws of the institution. Any internal reorganization must be approved by the Ministry of Education.

Faculty and Staff. Faculty and staff are civil servants. When a vacancy occurs, the university receives a list of qualified candidates from which it may select a name. Final appointments are made by the Ministry of Education. In 1984, the law governing the status of university faculty was revised and all former classes of faculty were replaced by two categories: *Professeur* and *Maître de Conférence*. A *doctorat* is required for all university teaching positions. In addition, promotion to full professorship and the right to direct doctoral studies and dissertations requires the newly created *Habilitation à Diriger des Recherches* (Entitlement to Direct Research).

University Finance. Universities are funded by the Ministry of Education. Faculty and staff salaries are part of the national budget for all civil service employees. Each institution receives an operating budget calculated according to a complex formula which takes into account student enrollment, types of programs offered, and the size of the physical plant. The budget is allocated as a block grant by the Ministry of Education and the university administration determines specific expenditures. Additional revenue is generated from student registration fees, continuing education programs, grants and research contracts, and from education taxes levied from local businesses. The budget for research is allocated separately by the Ministry of Education which determines the amounts to be spent in specific areas. Overall financial control is exercised by the Ministry of Education and by the audit department of the Ministry of Finance. The Minister of Education and his local representative, the *Recteur* (Rector), who also bears the title of university chancellor, have veto power over any item in the budget.

Academic Organization

The Units of Teaching and Research

A teaching and research unit *(unité de formation et de recherche/*UFR) is an academic subdivision of a university, much like a school or faculty at a university in the United States. The UFR is composed of several academic departments or it may be devoted to a single discipline such as medicine. Most UFR are vertically integrated; that is, they encompass all levels of study. At some institutions, however, the UFR can be organized in terms of levels, i.e., First Cycle UFR, Second Cycle UFR, etc. Each UFR is administered by an elected council of 40 members, half of whom are external to the university. The directors of UFR are faculty members elected by the council for a five-year term which may be renewed only once. They report to the university president.

University-Affiliated Institutes and Schools

The Ministry of Education may attach institutes and schools to any university. Although these schools and institutes sometimes bear the designation of UFR *à Derogation* (Special UFR), they are fully independent from the university in terms of programs, diplomas, administration and budget. The directors of independent UFRs report directly to the Ministry of Education. University institutes of technology *(Instituts Universitaires de Technologie/*IUT) are examples of independent UFR attached to universities.

Libraries

Since 1970, libraries have been integrated into universities even though their budget is still directly controlled by the Ministry of Education. There are 60 university libraries in France—of which 21 are in Paris—whose total collection in 1980 was 17 million volumes. The best libraries and research facilities being in Paris, the overwhelming majority of doctoral students are enrolled at Parisian universities. Library collections at provincial universities tend to be modest. In addition to a central university library, each UFR maintains a specialized library.

University Admission

All holders of the *baccalauréat* by law are admissible to university to pursue the first university diploma, *Diplôme d'Etudes Universitaires Générales*/DEUG (Diploma of General University Studies). Holders of the DEUG have the right to continue their studies in traditional *licence* and *maîtrise* programs. Universities are barred from setting further requirements or imposing additional criteria which would restrict the enrollment of any student. Adults who do not hold the *baccalauréat* may be admitted by passing a university entrance examination (*examen spécial d'entrée à l'université*).

Academic Calendar

The standard academic year at French universities is twenty-five weeks long. It begins in September and ends in late June. The first semester usually ends in February.

National Diplomas of Higher Education

Diplômes Nationaux de l'Enseignement Supérieur (National Diplomas of Higher Education), which are conferred by the Ministry of Education, are the foundation of university education and most programs are designed accordingly. The Ministry of Education stipulates the length of all programs, up to 80% of curricular content, subject distribution and examinations leading to national diplomas. This system guarantees equality among institutions and parity among diplomas.

The following are the national diplomas of higher education:

Certificat de Capacité en Droit (Certificate of Qualification in Law). Although listed as a national diploma of higher education, the *certificat* is earned by two years of part-time evening study at universities and other private and public institutions. The sole requirement for admission is that applicants be

17 or older. Under special circumstances, holders of a *certificat de capacité en droit* may be admitted to the first year of university law programs.

Baccalauréat. As the foundation for all university study, the *Baccalauréat* is classified as a national diploma of higher education.

Diplôme Universitaire de Technologie/DUT (University Diploma of Technology)

Diplôme d'Etudes Universitaires Scientifiques et Techniques/DEUST (Diploma of University Scientific and Technical Studies)

Diplôme d'Etudes Universitaires Générales/DEUG (Diploma of General University Studies)

Licence

Maîtrise

Diplôme d'Etudes Supérieures Spécialisées/DESS (Diploma of Higher Specialized Studies)

Diplôme d'Etudes Approfondies/DEA (Diploma of Advanced Studies)

Doctorat

Habilitation à Diriger des Recherches (Entitlement to Direct Research)

The *Diplôme d'Etudes Supérieures Spécialisées*/DESS, the *Diplôme d'Etudes Approfondies*/DEA, the *Doctorat*, and the *Habilitation à Diriger des Recherches* bear the name of the institution where they were earned.

University Diplomas

As a result of the autonomy granted to universities since 1968 and strongly promoted under the 1984 reform, institutions have developed programs leading to internal diplomas known generically as *diplômes d'université*/DU (university diplomas). These programs do not duplicate those offered for national diplomas but reflect local or regional interests. Each institution establishes the requirements for admission, the length and content of programs, as well as the name of each internal diploma. Programs are highly specialized and are designed primarily for employment in the particular sector. Thus, for example, a university located in a region where tourism is important would offer programs in tourism, resort management, or similar professionally-oriented curricula. See document 2.1 for a sample *Diplôme d'Université*.

Teaching

The 1968 reform changed university instruction which had been based on the traditional *cours magistral* (lecture). Today, lectures are supplemented by small

UNIVERSITY EDUCATION

> **UNIVERSITÉ de REIMS CHAMPAGNE-ARDENNE**
>
> ## DIPLOME D'UNIVERSITÉ
>
> **ATTESTATION**
>
> Le Secrétaire Général de l'Université de Reims Champagne-Ardenne, soussigné, certifie que :
>
> Mademoiselle ....
>
> né le : ....1962....... à : ...THIEBLEMONT....... Départ. : .MARNE....
>
> a obtenu le ...Diplôme d'Université d'Informatique Appliquée à la Gestion des Entreprises (DUIAGE)........
>
> à la session de : ....Juin 1984.......
>
> Reims, le : ....
>
> Pour le Secrétaire Général
> Le Chef de la Scolarité
>
> R. MANIGLE

2.1. *Diplôme d'Université* (University Diploma) Awarded by the University of Reims (Note specific name, DUIAGE.)

group instruction *(travaux dirigés*/TD); and national diplomas require that at least one-quarter of instruction time be devoted to small group work. In the sciences, laboratory work *(travaux pratiques*/TP) is mandated. In the first two years of university study, students rely on professors' lecture notes, known as *polycopiés*, which may be purchased at a nominal cost. Research papers or significant reading assignments are not common until the second cycle.

Examinations

The tradition at French institutions is the year-end examination, usually held in June *(session de juin)*. A second examination takes place in September *(session de septembre)* for those who did not pass in June. Since 1968, classroom attendance may be monitored and continuous assessment *(contrôle continu)* has become common. Mid-year examinations, known as *examens partiels*, are taken, usually in February, and can account for one-half of the final grade. University examinations are prepared, administered and graded by teachers. Examinations consist of three- or four-hour written tests followed by orals before the professor.

Grading

Grades are awarded on a scale of 0–20 but the tradition is such that grades higher than 16 are seldom awarded. The passing grade for a single subject is usually 10/20 although grades of 8 and 9 indicate satisfactory performance. A student is considered to have passed the year *(admis)* when the combined average *(moyenne générale)* of grades is 10 or above. The relative weight of a subject is determined by its coefficient. The higher the value of the coefficient, the greater the importance of that particular subject. To obtain the *moyenne*, each grade is multiplied by the coefficient for the subject and the results are added. The total thus obtained is divided by the sum total value of coefficients. A student, for example, who obtained the results below would be regarded as passing even if the score on two subjects was less than 10. The grade of 12 in mathematics, which carried the heavier coefficient (5), compensated for the lower grades and raised the overall average above 10.

Subjects	Grades/20		Coefficient		
Mathematics	12	×	5	=	60
Biology	9	×	3	=	27
Chemistry	8	×	2	=	16
Sociology	14	×	1	=	14
Total			11		117

Average = 117 ÷ 11 = 10.63

There is no French equivalent for the U.S. "D." In making grade conversions, U.S. evaluators must make allowances for the particularly severe grading practices of French professors. The following U.S. grade equivalents have been approved by the National Council for the Evaluation of Foreign Educational Credentials.

French Grades	Mention*	U.S. Equivalents
16–20	très bien (very good)	A+ (seldom awarded)
14–15	bien (good)	A
12–13	assez bien (good enough)	B
10–11	passable (satisfactory)	C
8– 9	—	†
0– 7	ajourné (failed)	F

*The *mention* is an overall quality assessment based on grades earned.
†Is regarded as a passing grade if the entire year was passed.

Documentation

Universities issue records known as *relevé de notes* for each year of study. These records list the subjects studied, examinations taken and results obtained. When a student has completed a cycle or a given diploma program, a certificate of graduation and an overall transcript may be obtained. While official diplomas are not immediately issued, provisional certificates, known as *attestations*, are readily available. An *attestation* is a formal document bearing the signature of the secretary general and the seal of the university. Admissions officers should request annual records *(relevé de notes)* and *attestations*.

Transcripts often reflect courses as *unités de valeur*/UV (units of value). At some universities, courses are identified as *certificats* (certificates), particularly for second and third cycle programs. When that is the case, the *certificat* is not a credential but a subject or group of subjects which constitute the requirements for a particular diploma. See document 2.2a for a sample transcript for a DEUG and *licence*, and document 2.2b for a provisional *maîtrise*.

Program Structure

University programs are structured in three cycles. The requirements for admission to each cycle, which also constitute its definition, are mandated by law. The first cycle requires a *baccalauréat;* the second, a DEUG; and the third, a *maîtrise* or an equivalent.

First Cycle *(Premier Cycle)*

The first cycle, which constitutes the first two years of university study, leads to a *Diplôme d'Etudes Universitaires Générales*/DEUG, a *Diplôme d'Etudes Univ-*

```
UNIVERSITÉ   PAUL   VALÉRY   -   MONTPELLIER III
```

EN CONFORMITÉ AVEC LE PROCÉS-VERBAL SIGNÉ PAR LES MEMBRES DU JURY,
RELEVÉ DES UNITÉS DE VALEUR ANNUELLES OU CERTIFICATS OBTENUS PAR :

N° INSEE	NOM ET PRENOMS	DATE DE NAISSANCE	DEPARTEMENT
		31 08 55	99

CODE	*INTITULE DE L ENSEIGNEMENT*	S.AN.	MENTIONS
L1F	UV-ESPAGNOL - NON SPECIALISTES 2EME NIVEAU	J 78	PASSABLE
M3J	UV-1H30-LANGUE ITALIENNE POUR DEBUTANTS	J 78	PASSABLE
L1G	UV-ESPAGNOL-NON SPECIALISTES LITT.2EME NIVEAU	J 78	PASSABLE
R3H	UV-FRANCAIS- LITTERATURE COMPAREE 1ER CYCLE	J 78	PASSABLE
K3G	UV-ANGLAIS NON-SPECIALISTES - LITTERATURE	J 78	ASSEZ-BIEN
A1J	UV-LATIN 1ERE ANNEE-NON SPECIALISTES OPTION C	J 78	ASSEZ-BIEN
K3F	UV-ANGLAIS NON-SPECIALISTES - VERSION	J 79	PASSABLE
R3T	UV-3H-L EXPRESSION DRAMATIQUE I	J 79	ASSEZ-BIEN
L1E	UV-PANORAMA LETTRES & STE HISPANO-AMERICAINES	J 79	PASSABLE
22A	*** 1ERE ANNEE DE LETTRES MODERNES ***	J 79	ADMIS
A3C	UV-GREC NON SPECIALISTES 1ER DEGRE	O 79	ADMIS
R2H	UV-3H-GRAMMAIRE DU FRANCAIS MEDIEVAL MOD & CONTEMP.	J 80	ASSEZ-BIEN
P3X	UV-3H-PERSONNALITES ET MOUVEMENTS LITTERAIRES I	J 80	PASSABLE
P3U	UV-3H-LE RECIT ET SES TECHNIQUES I	J 80	PASSABLE
L1H	UV-LITTERATURE ESPAGNOLE MODERNE	J 80	ADMIS
22B	*** D.E.U.G. DE LETTRES MODERNES ***	J 80	ADMIS
22B	*** D.E.U.G. DE LETTRES MODERNES ***	O 80	ADMIS
A6L	C1-INITIATION A L ANTIQUITE	J 81	PASSABLE
R5M	UV-2H-LITTERATURE COMPAREE B	J 81	PASSABLE
K6P	C1-LANGUE LIT.CIVILISATION ANGLO-AMERICAINES	J 81	PASSABLE
R5J	C1-6H-LITTERATURE FRANCAISE I	O 81	PASSABLE
R6U	C1-LANGUE FRANCAISE 2E CYCLE	O 81	PASSABLE

Certifié conforme à l'original
qui nous a été présenté.

M... le 5 NOV. 1981

G. FRECHE

Qui lui ont permis d'obtenir :

LA LICENCE DE LETTRES MODERNES

(Application de l'arrêté ministériel du 16 Janvier 1976)

SIGNIFICATION DES ABREVIATIONS

UV: UNITE DE VALEUR   S: SESSION
C: CERTIFICAT   P: PARTIELS ET CONTROLE CONTINU
EA: ENSEMBLE ANNUEL   J: EXAMEN TERMINAL DE JUIN
EC: EPREUVE COMPLEMENTAIRE   O: EXAMEN TERMINAL D'OCTOBRE

NB Il n'est délivré qu'une seule attestation, l'intéressé peut faire
    de ce document toutes les copies ou photocopies qui lui sont
    nécessaires. Les copies devront être certifiées conformes à l'ori-
    ginal par le Maire ou le Commissaire de police de sa commune.

POUR ETRE VALABLE CETTE ATTESTATION DOIT PORTER LE SCEAU EN RELIEF DE L'UNIVERSITE

MONTPELLIER, LE 5 NOV. 1981

LE SECRETAIRE GENERAL DE L'UNIVERSITE

F. ROUQUAIROL

2.2a. Transcript of *Diplôme d'Etudes Universitaires Générales*/DEUG and *Licence* Courses from the University of Montpellier III

UNIVERSITÉ DE PARIS-SORBONNE (PARIS IV)

N°

COPIE CERTIFIEE CONFORME A L ORIGINAL
PRESENTEE CE JOUR 29/5/87

ATTESTATION DE MAITRISE

SECTION : PHILOSOPHIE

Paris, le 25 février 1986

Le Secrétaire général de l'Université de Paris-Sorbonne (Paris IV) certifie que
Mademoiselle
né(e) 1957
à PARIS 12°

est titulaire de la licence de Philosophie - novembre 1984 -

a obtenu :
C2 - Philosophie des sciences et de la connaissance - juin 1985 -

a soutenu à la session de NOVEMBRE 1985 un travail d'études et de recherches :
"LA THEORIE SCIENTIFIQUE SELON POPPER" (mention très-bien)

a été déclaré titulaire de la maîtrise de PHILOSOPHIE - NOVEMBRE 1985 -

Cette attestation, pour être valable, ne doit être ni surchargée, ni grattée. L'Université ne la délivre qu'une fois. Les Maires et les Commissaires de police français, les Agents diplomatiques ou consulaires de la France à l'étranger peuvent en délivrer des copies certifiées conformes.

Le Secrétaire général de l'Université.

jp

2.2b. Provisional *Maîtrise* Diploma Indicating Coursework and Thesis (University of Paris IV)

ersitaires Scientifiques et Techniques/DEUST and to various *Diplômes Universitaires*/DU. Students are expected to complete the first cycle within three years. The Ministry of Education stipulates the total minimum hours of instruction, core courses and electives for the award of the DEUG and the DEUST. Additional requirements may be set by each university.

The objectives of the first cycle are as follows:

1. to provide students with a solid grounding in a broad range of basic subjects and to teach them study skills;
2. to enable students to assess their interests and skills for further study; and
3. to prepare students for study at a higher level or for employment by giving them a useful qualification.

One of the principal objectives of the 1984 reform was to make the first cycle more relevant and attractive to students by creating programs with a professional bias and by making existing programs multidisciplinary and versatile. The newly created DEUST and most DU are terminal diplomas which do not necessarily permit students to continue their studies at the next stage. The popularity of two-year programs among students and employers has created a shortage of openings at university institutes of technology (*institut universitaire de technologie*/IUT). The creation of the DEUST is an attempt by the government to make more short programs widely available. Accordingly, the DEUST is patterned after programs offered at university institutes of technology and, though offered at universities, is designed to prepare students for immediate employment rather than further study. The first three semesters of a DEUST program are common with those of a DEUG in the same curriculum. In the final semester, DEUST students follow courses with a strong professional bias in preparation for employment.

ORIENTATION PROGRAMS

Since the 1984 reform, first cycle programs begin with an orientation period intended to help students adjust to university study. Orientation is conducted according to two models:

1st Model. The academic year begins with a short-term (a few days to one or two weeks) program of orientation to the university during which students participate in seminars describing different disciplines, meet with advisors, and take tests which will determine the fields in which they may be enrolled. This program, which is not included as an integral part of the total hours mandated for the DEUG, is preferred in liberal arts and social science disciplines.

2nd Model. Students begin the academic year in a one-term (usually 10 weeks) multidisciplinary program which also includes physical education and advisement sessions. At the end of the term, an examination determines the streams in which students are placed. The hours of instruction count toward the total requirements for the DEUG. This model is most often used in the sciences.

Students whose performance is found to be inadequate on placement examinations are enrolled in *baccalauréat*-level remedial programs for the remainder of the academic year. Those who complete the program successfully are mainstreamed into the first year of the DEUG or the DEUST at the beginning of the following academic year.

Sample Program

1. The orientation program at the University of Ste. Etienne requires that all students seeking a science DEUG complete an eight-week common program in science consisting of two hours of lecture and two hours of laboratory per week in each subject. The hours spent in this program are counted toward the total hours required for the DEUG. Students choose five of the following subjects: basic mathematical techniques, biology, chemistry, elementary and fundamental mathematics, geology, and physics. A final examination determines a student's subsequent placement. Each subject is graded out of 20 and the grades are added together. Depending upon the total of grades earned, a student is streamed as follows:

Total Grades	Placement
60 or above	The student may enroll in any science DEUG.
50 to 60	The examination committee will propose a DEUG program appropriate to the student's abilities.
40 to 50	The examination committee may propose a DEUG or a remedial program.
below 40	The student will be required to attend a remedial program for the remainder of the academic year.

2. The University of Ste. Etienne offers three types of remedial programs targeted at the type of DEUG which is sought. The program is set at *baccalauréat* level and must be completed successfully. Students who fail the remedial program must transfer to a non-science discipline at Ste. Etienne or to another university. In either case, the year spent in the remedial program is not counted toward the three-year limit for the DEUG.

DEUG PROGRAM DESCRIPTIONS

The subjects identified in the following description of programs reflect themes rather than actual course titles. Each university develops its curriculum following the national framework. Students' records will bear specific course titles. The distribution of courses and the minimum number of contact hours must be respected. The law mandates up to 80% of the curriculum with the remaining 20% reserved for each university to use for its own requirements.

DEUG diplomas are awarded in the following disciplines.

1. Law (900 hours)
2. Economics (900 hours)

3. Economic and Social Administration (900 hours)
4. Arts and Letters (700 hours)
   A. French Literature
   B. Foreign Languages, Literature and Civilization
   C. Applied Foreign Languages
   D. Plastic Arts
   E. Music
   F. Art History
5. Humanities and Social Sciences (700 hours)
   A. Philosophy
   B. Sociology
   C. Psychology
   D. History
   E. Geography
6. Sciences (1100 hours)
   A. Science and Structure of Matter (Physical Sciences)
   B. Science of Nature and Life (Life Sciences)
7. Mathematics Applied to Social Sciences (900 hours)
8. Science, Economy and Technology (1100 hours)
9. Health Sciences (1100 hours)
10. Communication and Language Science (900 hours)
    A. Culture and Communication
    B. Language Science
11. Theology (700 hours)
    A. Catholic Theology
    B. Protestant Theology
12. Sports and Physical Education Science and Techniques (1200 hours)
13. Elementary Education (700 hours)

1. LAW (900 Hours)

The law requires that 45% of core requirements be completed in the first year.

Required Subjects (45% of instruction—405 hours)

   Administrative Law and Public Administration
   Business Law
   Civil Law, Property and Contracts
   Constitutional Law and Political Institutions
   Economics
   Introduction to the History of Law
   Legal History and History of Legal Institutions
   Public Finance

Foreign Languages (5% of instruction—45 hours)

Electives (20% of instruction—180 hours chosen from the following):

   Accounting
   Contemporary Economic Problems
   Contemporary Political and Social History

Data Processing
Demography and Economic Geography
History of Political, Economic and Sociological Ideas
Introduction to Business Management
International Relations
Penal Law and Criminal Sociology
Political Science
Sociology and Philosophy of Law
Sociology and Social Psychology
Statistical Methods for Social Sciences

Introduction to Professional Practice (5% of instruction—45 hours)

Further Practice of Civil, Criminal and Business Law
Introduction to Business Enterprises (Social Law, Finances, Accounting and Financial Control)
Introduction to Civil, Criminal and Administrative Procedures
Introduction to Public Administrative Procedures (including Public Finance)
Orientation to the Structure and Operation of Trade Unions, Professional Associations, Media and Public Relations Organizations
Personnel Administration, Social Security

Free Electives (15% of instruction—135 hours)

2. ECONOMICS (900 Hours)

The law requires that 45% of core requirements be completed in the first year.

Required Subjects (45% of instruction—405 hours)

Economics
Quantitative Techniques

Foreign Language (5% of instruction—45 hours)

Electives (20% of instruction—180 hours chosen from the following):

Administrative Law and Administrative Institutions
Applied Data Processing
Business Law
Civil Law and Law of Contracts
Constitutional Law and Comparative Political Systems
Contemporary Economic Problems
Contemporary Political and Social History
Contemporary Social Problems
Demography and Economic Geography
Economic History and Contemporary Economic Problems
Financial Economics and Public Finance
History of Political, Economic and Social Ideas
International Economic and Political Relations
Introduction to Business Management
Labor Law and Sociology of Labor
Logic and Philosophy of Science
National Accounting
Political Science

continued

Private Accounting
Social Psychology and Sociology

Introduction to Professional Practice (5% of instruction—45 hours)

Introduction to Business Enterprise (Social Law, Finances, Accounting and Financial Control)
Introduction to Public Administrative Procedures (including Public Finance), Personnel Administration, Social Security
Orientation to the Structure and the Operation of Trade Unions, Professional Associations, Media and Public Relations Organizations

3. SOCIAL AND ECONOMIC ADMINISTRATION (900 Hours)

The law requires that 60% of core requirements (first and second group of subjects) be completed in the first year.

Required Subjects (80% of instruction—720 hours)

First Group (360 hours)

Contemporary History and Political Science
Economics
Law
Sociology and Social Psychology

Second Group (270 hours)

Applied Data Processing
Foreign Language
Mathematics and Statistics for Social Science

Third Group (90 hours)

Management and Accounting
Organization and Management of Labor

Free Electives (15% of instruction—135 hours)

4. ARTS AND LETTERS (700 Hours)

The law requires that 60% of core requirements be completed in the first year.

A. French Literature

Required Subjects (60% of instruction—420 hours)

Foreign Language and Literature
French Language and Literature from Its Origins to the Present
plus one of the following:
Ancient Greek Language and Literature
Archeology
Art History
Latin Language and Literature
Modern and Contemporary French History

Arts and Letters Electives (20%—140 hours)

B. Foreign Languages, Literature and Civilization

Required Subjects (60% of instruction—420 hours)

Contemporary French Language and Literature
Foreign Language, Literature and Civilization
Introduction to a Second Foreign Language, Literature and Civilization
 plus one of the following:
Art History
Contemporary French History
History of a Foreign Country
Third Foreign Language, Literature and Civilization

Arts and Letters Electives (20%—140 hours)

C. Applied Foreign Languages

Required Subjects (60% of instruction—420 hours)
First Foreign Language and Civilization
Introduction to Contemporary Society
Second Foreign Language and Civilization

Arts and Letters Electives (20%—140 hours)

D. Plastic Arts

Required Subjects (60% of instruction—420 hours)

History of Art and History of Music
Introduction to the Esthetics, Sociology and Semiology of Art
Oral and Written French
Plastic Art
 plus one of the following:
Experimental Psychology
Introduction to Dramatic Arts
Introduction to a Foreign Literature
Introduction to French Literature
Introduction to General Linguistics
Introduction to Industrial Design
Introduction to Mathematics and Computers
Introduction to Urbanism
Sociology and Ethnology

Required Studio Work (25% of instruction—175 hours)
Foreign Language (5% of instruction—35 hours)

E. Music

Required Subjects (60% of instruction—420 hours)

Communication (French)
History of Art and Music
Music Techniques
Practice of Music
 plus one of the following:
Introduction to Acoustics
Introduction to Experimental Psychology
Introduction to French or a Foreign Literature

continued

Introduction to General Linguistics and Phonetics
Introduction to History
Introduction to Mathematics and Computer Science
Introduction to a Second Foreign Language
Introduction to Sociology and Ethnology

Required Practice of a Musical Instrument or Voice Practice (25% of instruction—175 hours)

Foreign Language (5% of instruction—35 hours)

F. Art History

Required Subjects (60% of instruction—420 hours)

Communication (French)
History of Art and History of Music
Techniques and Methods of Art History and Archeology
  plus two of the following:
Introduction to Ancient and Medieval History
Introduction to Ancient Greek Language and Literature
Introduction to Contemporary and Modern History
Introduction to a Foreign Literature
Introduction to French Literature
Introduction to Latin Language and Literature
Introduction to a Second Foreign Language
Introduction to Sociology and Ethnology

Foreign Language (5% of instruction—35 hours)

Electives (20% 0f instruction—140 hours)

5. HUMANITIES AND SOCIAL SCIENCES (700 Hours)

The law requires that 55% of core requirements be completed in the first year.

A. Philosophy

Required Subjects (55%—385 hours)

General Philosophy
History of Great Philosophical Doctrines from Ancient Times to Present
Moral and Political Philosophy
Philosophy of Science (Logic, Epistemology and History of Science)
  plus one of the following:
Introduction to Biology
Introduction to Mathematics
Introduction to Physics
  plus one of the following:
Introduction to Economics
Introduction to History
Introduction to Psychology and Social Psychology
Introduction to Sociology and Political Science

Foreign Language (5% of instruction—35 hours)

Free Electives (20% of instruction—140 hours)

UNIVERSITY EDUCATION

B. Sociology

Required Subjects (55% of instruction—385 hours)

Contemporary and Modern History
Economics and Demography
Fundamentals of Sociology and Social Psychology
Introduction to Social Sciences and Introduction to Mathematical and Statistical Methods

Foreign Language (5% of instruction—35 hours)
Free Electives (20% of instruction—140 hours)

C. Psychology

Required Subjects (55% of instruction—385 hours)

Biology, Genetics and Pathological Psychology
Fundamentals of Psychology and Social Psychology
Introduction to Mathematical and Statistical Methods
Introduction to Social Sciences

Foreign Language (5% of instruction—35 hours)
Free Electives (20% of instruction—140 hours)

D. History

Required Subjects (55% of instruction—385 hours)

Ancient History
Contemporary History
Introduction to Mathematical and Statistical Methods
Introduction to the Science of History
Medieval History
Modern History
  plus one of the following:
Introduction to Archeology and Art History
Introduction to Economics and Demography
Introduction to Geographical Science
Introduction to Sociology and Social Psychology

Foreign Language (5% of instruction—35 hours)
Free Electives (20% of instruction—140 hours)

E. Geography

Required Subjects (55% of instruction—385 hours)

Introduction to Mathematical and Statistical Methods
Introduction to Natural Science
Introduction to Social Sciences
Physical and Human Geography, including Regional Analysis
  plus one of the following:
Fundamental Aspects of Historical Science
Introduction to Demography and Economics
Introduction to Sociology and Social Psychology

Foreign Language (5% of instruction—35 hours)
Free Electives (20% of instruction—140 hours)

continued

6. SCIENCES (1100 Hours)

The law requires that 70% of core requirements be completed in the first year. The discipline is divided into two sections: Physical Sciences (A), and Life Sciences (B).

Required Subjects (60% of instruction—660 hours)

	A	B
Biological Techniques and Methods	–	*
Computer Science—Programming	*	*
Graphics	*	–
Methods and Techniques of Chemical Analysis and Separation	*	*
Numerical Methods	*	*
Physical Measurements	*	*
or		
Earth Science: Geological Methods and Techniques	–	*

University Electives (chosen from the following):

	A	B
Applied Mathematics	*	*
Astronomy	*	–
Biochemical Methods and Techniques	*	*
Biochemistry	*	*
Biological Methods and Techniques	*	*
Biology	*	*
Chemical Analysis	*	–
Chemical Techniques Applied to Biology	*	–
Chemistry	–	*
Computer Science	*	*
Earth Science	*	*
Electromagnetism, Optics, Electronics, Electrotechniques, Automatic Control	*	*
Geological Methods	*	*
Graphics (Engineering Drawing)	*	*
Mathematical Statistics	*	–
Measurement Techniques Applied to Biology	–	*
Mechanical Technology	*	*
Mechanics	*	*
Metrology (Measurement Techniques)	*	–
Numerical Analysis	*	–
Physical Technology	*	*
Physics	*	*
Programming	*	*
Statistical Techniques	*	*

Free Electives (10% of instruction—110 hours chosen from the following):

Accounting, Business Law and Management Economics
Economics
Introduction to Written and Oral Communication
Philosophy and History of Science
Political and Administrative Institutions

UNIVERSITY EDUCATION

7. MATHEMATICS APPLIED TO SOCIAL SCIENCES (900 Hours)

The law requires that 40% of core requirements and 25% of mandated electives be completed in the first year.

Required Subjects (40% of instruction—360 hours)

    Applied Statistics and Computer Science
    Mathematics

Foreign Language (5% of instruction—45 hours)

Electives (25% of instruction—225 hours chosen from the following):

    Economics
    Geography, History, and History of Science and Technology
    Management, Accounting
    Psychology, Sociology and Linguistics

Free Electives (15% of instruction—135 hours)

8. SCIENCE, ECONOMICS AND TECHNOLOGY (1100 Hours)

Required Subjects (60% of instruction—660 hours)

    Computer Science
    Economics
    Electronics
    Law
    Mathematics, Statistics, Probability
    Physics and General Chemistry
    Technology

Foreign Language Instruction (25% of instruction—275 hours)

Free Electives (5% of instruction—55 hours)

9. HEALTH SCIENCE (1100 Hours)

Required Subjects (60% of instruction—660 hours)

    Human Biology
        Biochemistry
        Embryology
        Formal and Physiological Genetics
        General Anatomy
        General Biology
        General Physiology
        Histology
    Introduction to Law and Economics
        Administrative Institutions
        Economics
        Legislation
    Introduction to Professional Practice
        Ergonomics
        Health
        Health Care

continued

Social Sciences
   Ethnology
   Psychology
   Social and Cultural Anthropology
   Sociology

Foreign Language (5% of instruction—55 hours)

Free Electives (10% of instruction—110 hours)

10. COMMUNICATION LANGUAGE SCIENCE (1100 Hours)

This discipline is divided into two sections: Culture and Communication (A), Language Science (B).

Required Subjects (50% of instruction—450 hours)

	A	B
Analysis and Production of Texts and Documents	*	—
Communication, Cultures, Societies	*	—
Data Processing	*	*
Languages	*	*
Linguistics	—	*
Psychology	—	*
Theoretical and Practical Approaches to Communication	*	—

Foreign Languages (5% of instruction—55 hours)
Free Electives (20% of instruction—180 hours)

11. THEOLOGY (700 Hours)

The law requires that 60% of core requirements be completed in the first year.

Required Subjects (60% of instruction—420 hours)

A. Catholic Theology
Biblical Languages
Biblical Science
Christian Ethics
Dogmatic Theology
History of the Church
Philosophical Questions

B. Protestant Theology
History of Religions and History of Christianity
Languages, Literature and Civilizations of the New Testament
Languages, Literature and Civilizations of the Old Testament
Philosophy of Religion and Systematic Theology
   plus one of the following:
Musicology and Hymns
Practical Theology
Sociology of Protestantism

Foreign Language (5% of instruction—35 hours)

Free Electives (20% of instruction—140 hours)

12. SPORT AND PHYSICAL EDUCATION SCIENCE AND TECHNIQUES
(1200 Hours)

The law requires that 70% of core requirements be completed in the first year.

Required Subjects (60% of instruction—720 hours)

    General Knowledge of the History and Techniques of Sports and Physical Education
    Introduction to Mathematical and Statistical Methods and Introduction to Mechanics
       plus
    Biological Sciences
      General Biology
      Human Anatomy and Physiology
       plus
    Social Sciences
      Fundamental Aspects of Psychology
      Social Psychology
      Sociology
       plus
    Supervised Practice of Sports and Physical Education (at least ⅓ of the total core program—240 hours)

Foreign Language (5% of instruction—60 hours)

University Electives (chosen from the following):

    Biomechanics and Physiology of Human Movement
    Biotypology and Anthropology
    Computer Science
    Ecology
    Economics and Management Science
    Education
    Genetics
    History of Sports and Physical Education
    Oral and Written Communication
    Practice of Sports and Physical Education

Free Electives (10% of instruction—120 hours chosen from the following):

    Audiovisual Methods and Techniques
    Biochemistry
    Documentation Techniques
    Ergonomics and Physiology of Work
    Foreign Languages
    History of Civilization
    Introduction to Group Activities
    Music (Voice and Instrument)
    Philosophy and History of Science and Technology
      or other subjects taught at university

continued

13. ELEMENTARY EDUCATION (700 Hours)

This program is structured in terms of units. Each unit consists of 70 hours of instruction and includes theory and practice. The DEUG requires the completion of 6 core units and 4 electives. The distribution of courses between the two years is determined locally.

Required Units (70 hours each)

    Physical and Psychological Development of Children
        The Major Themes of Development
        Factors Affecting Development
        Problems of Development
    General and Educational Philosophy
        Education Doctrines and Systems
        General Philosophy
        Philosophical Foundations of Education
        Professional Ethics
    Introduction to the Political, Economic, Social and Cultural Environment
        Contemporary Economic Problems
        Contemporary Social and Cultural Problems
        Political and Administrative Institutions
    French Language and Literature
    Mathematics
    Foreign Language, Literature and Civilization

Electives (70 hours each)

    Experimental Science: Biology, Physics
    History and Geography:
        History
            European and French History
            Introduction to Historical Science
            Main Features of Modern and Contemporary History
              plus
        Geography
            Elements of World Geography
            Physical and Human Geography of France
    Art and Music
        Music: History of Music, Practice of Music
            plus
        Art: History of Art, Practice of a Plastic Art
    Supervised Practice of Sports and Physical Education
    French Language and Literature
    Further Study of Child Development
    Further Study of Mathematics
    Further Study of a Foreign Language, Literature and Civilization

See Tables 2.1 and 2.2 for sample DEUG curriculums in social sciences, and analytical and physical sciences, respectively. Table 2.3 presents a sample DEUST program in music professions. Sample document 2.3 is a DEUG diploma from the University of Aix-Marseille.

Table 2.1. Sample DEUG Program in Social Sciences, University of Lyon II

DEUG in Sociology

The diploma calls for the completion of 14 *unités de valeur*/UV (units of value). Each UV represents 50 hours of coursework.

Major (8 UV)

Economics & Social Sciences
Historical Demographics
History of Social Sciences
Introduction to Fields of Investigation in Social Sciences
Introduction to Research Techniques
Research & Investigation in Sociology
Social & Economic History
Statistics
Study of Communication & Interaction (Interpersonal Relations, Interviews; Discussion Groups)
Study of Ideologies
Textual Analysis

plus

1 UV of Foreign Language *and* 1 UV of French

plus

4 UV of additional study in Sociology *or* 4 UV chosen from another discipline

Total: 700 Hours

Table 2.2. Sample Program in Analytical and Physical Sciences (DEUG A), University of Lyon I (Claude Bernard)

First Year (24 weeks)

1st Semester (13 weeks)
Four-Week Orientation

plus

Nine Weeks (25 hours/week)
  Computer Science
  English
  Mathematics
  Mechanics
  Physics
  Professional Orientation

2nd Semester (11 weeks)
  Chemistry (44 hours)
  Computer Science (22 hours)
  Mathematics (99 hours)
  Physics & Mechanics (99 hours)

Second Year (25 weeks)

1st Semester
  Computer Science (52 hours)
  English (13 hours)
  Mathematics (130 hours)
  Mechanics (39 hours)
  Physics (78 hours)

2nd Semester
  English (13 hours)
  Mathematics (130 hours)
  Mechanics (26 hours)
  Physics (78 hours)
  Science Elective (78 hours)

Optional Subjects
  Physical Education (50 hours)
  Free Elective (25 hours)

Total: 1252 Hours

Table 2.3. Sample DEUST Program in Music Professions, University of Lyon II

25 *unités de valeur*/UV (units of value) are required: 24 UV of coursework (8 UV of general education, 6 UV of fundamental languages, 10 UV of professional subjects) and 1 UV of practical internship. Each UV represents 50 hours of instruction.

General Education (8 UV)	Professional Subjects (10 UV)
Choir Practice	Audiovisual Techniques
History of Music	Dance
Principles of Electro-Acoustics	Organization of Cultural Activities
Voice Practice	Pedagogy
Fundamental Languages (6 UV)	Principles of Management
Accompaniment	Stage Production
Harmony	*Practical Training* (1 UV)
Solfeggio	Total: 1240 Hours

Second Cycle *(Second Cycle)*

The second cycle begins after the DEUG and leads to the *licence* in one year, the *maîtrise* in two years and the new *magistère* in three years. It builds upon the basic education acquired in the DEUG and provides students with the knowledge required for professional practice or further study. Traditional and professional programs are offered in the second cycle.

TRADITIONAL *LICENCE* AND *MAÎTRISE* PROGRAMS

Disciplines traditionally taught by the university such as arts and letters, economics, law, mathematics, pure sciences, and social sciences constitute this category and lead primarily to secondary school teacher recruitment examinations, such as the CAPES and the *agrégation* (see Chapter VII, "Teacher Training"), or to doctoral studies and research. Students who intend to sit for teacher examinations enroll in the *enseignement* (teaching) section of the program and complete specific courses required for teacher examinations. Those enrolled in the *libre* (free) section do not have such requirements. Both programs are equal in length and level. At the end of the first year, all students earn a *licence* which is a prerequisite for admission to the second year of the second cycle leading to a *maîtrise*. A *maîtrise* in science is earned by coursework whereas in literature and humanities a *maîtrise* usually requires a thesis *(mémoire)* as well. The program of instruction ranges between a minimum of 350 hours and a maximum of 550 hours in each year. The specific number of hours for each course and program structure are determined by each university. See Tables 2.4 and 2.5 for sample *licence* and *maîtrise* programs in sociology and mathematics, respectively. See also documents 2.4 and 2.5 for a sample *licence* and *maîtrise*, respectively.

UNIVERSITY EDUCATION 61

2.3. *Diplôme d'Etudes Universitaires Générales*/DEUG Diploma Awarded by the University of Aix-Marseille

2.4. *Licence* Awarded by the University of Montpellier III

Table 2.4. Sample *Licence* and *Maîtrise* Programs in Sociology, University of Lyon II

***Licence* in Sociology**

Admission to the program requires a DEUG in Humanities and Social Sciences—Sociology Option (5.B), a DEUG in Mathematics Applied to Social Sciences (7), or a DEUG in Communication Language Science (10). The curriculum is structured in terms of *certificats* (certificates) which consist of three courses each. The *licence* requires two *certificats* as follows:

Certificat C1

Social Sciences
  History and Demography *or* Economics (2 hours/week)
  Quantitative Methods (2 hours/week)
Elective (one of the following [2 hours/week])
  Advanced Sociology
  Data Processing
  Ethnology
  Labor Sociology
  Linguistics
  Social Psychology

Certificat C2

Required Subjects
  Fundamental Aspects of Industrial Societies (5 hours/week)
  Research Methods in Sociology (1 hour/week)
  Theory of Sociology (2 hours/week)

    Total: 350 Hours

***Maîtrise* in Sociology**

Admission to the program requires a *licence* in sociology.

Coursework
  Mathematics (1 hour/week)
  Sociology of Industrial Societies (1 hour/week)
Electives (3 hours/week) including the following:
  Course in Sociology or Related Field
  Seminar on Research
Thesis (topic identified in research seminar)

    Total: 150 Hours of Coursework + Thesis

PROFESSIONAL *MAÎTRISE* PROGRAMS

Professional programs are two-year curricula which lead directly to a *maîtrise* **without a** *licence* being awarded in the first year. Such programs tend to have a narrow focus, a strong applied bias, and include practical training in industry. They lead to a *Maîtrise des Sciences et Techniques*/MST (*Maîtrise* of Science and Technology), a *Maîtrise des Sciences de Gestion*/MSG (*Maîtrise* of Business Science) and a *Maîtrise d'Informatique Appliquée à la Gestion*/MIAG (*Maîtrise* of Computer Science Applied to Business). Admission to professional programs is selective. In addition to a DEUG, applicants must complete specific prerequisites, as mandated, for each program.

A *Maîtrise des Sciences et Techniques*/MST is awarded following a two-year (minimum of 60 weeks) program. The curriculum requires between 1500 and 1800 hours of instruction over the two years, supplemented by a period of practical training of at least 10 weeks. See Table 2.6 for a sample MST program.

The *Maîtrise des Sciences de Gestion*/MSG is awarded after a two-year program which follows the same general pattern as the MST. It requires at least 1000 hours of instruction and two months of practical training over two years. Initially offered solely at the University of Paris IX-Dauphine, it has now been extended to several other universities. Admission is selective and the completion of the following subjects is a prerequisite: economics, English, mathematics, psychology, sociology, and statistics. See Table 2.7 for an MSG program from the University of Paris IX - Dauphine. Document 2.6 shows a sample MSG.

Table 2.5. Sample *Licence* and *Maîtrise* Program in Mathematics, University of Lyon I

***Licence* in Mathematics**

Admission to the program requires a DEUG in Science—A (6).

Required Subjects

Differential Calculus & Numerical Analysis (330 hours)
  plus one of the following:
Engineering Mathematics (256 hours)
Pure Mathematics (256 hours)
  Total: 586 Hours

***Maîtrise* in Mathematics (Engineering Mathematics Option)**

Admission requires a *licence* in mathematics.

Required Subjects

Automatic Data Processing (128 hours)
Optimization (64 hours)
Statistics & Data Analysis (128 hours)
  plus
Electives (three of the following):
Numerical Analysis (64 hours)
Operations Research (64 hours)
Random Phenomena A (64 hours)
Random Phenomena B (64 hours)
  Total: 512 Hours

Table 2.6. Sample MST Program in Applied Biological and Medical Science, University of Lyon I

This MST is designed to train highly skilled professionals in the development, manufacturing, distribution and maintenance of sophisticated medical equipment and supplies. Admission requires prior completion of a DEUG in science and a 500-hour preparatory program specific to the MST. The courses of the preparatory program are concurrent with, and *in addition to,* those required for a DEUG.

Preparatory Program for the MST

First Year	Hours	*Second Year*	Hours
Additional Physics	40	Additional Mathematics	30
Communication (French)	30	Communication (French)	30
Electrical Technology	30	Electrical Technology	30
Human Physiopathology	60	Human Physiopathology	60
Mechanical Technology	80	Introduction to Electronics	30
Totals:	240 Hours		260 Hours

MST Program

First Year	Lect.	Lab	*Second Year*	Lect.	Lab
Analytical Chemistry	60	30	Administrative & Business		
Biomedical Captors	60	30	Law	30	–
Biophysical Monitoring	60	30	Automatic Control	30	15
Data Processing	20	–	Biochemical Analysis	30	15
Economics	30	–	Biomechanics, Prosthetic &		
Electricity	45	–	Orthotic Devices	30	15
Electronics	75	30	Business Economics	30	–
English	60	–	Cardiological Techniques	30	15
General Accounting	40	–	Data Processing	10	10
German	60	–	Electrical Technology	30	25
Law	40	–	Electronics &		
Logic	20	–	Instrumentation	90	45
Marketing	30	–	English	60	–
Mathematics	60	–	Financial Management &		
Mechanics	30	–	Forecasting	40	–
Physics	60	60	German	60	–
Radiology	60	15	Human Relations	20	–
Respiratory Assistance &			Labor Law & Personnel		
Exploratory Devices	30	15	Management	20	–
Totals:	840	180	Mechanical Technology	40	40
			Medical Data Processing	10	10
Practical Training in a			Microbiological Techniques	20	10
Hospital	(5 weeks)		Microprocessors & Logical		
			Circuits	30	25
			Neo- & Post-Natal		
			Monitoring	10	10
			Physics & Chemistry of		
			Materials	60	10

Safety	10	10
Sales Techniques	30	–
Surgical Supplies & Equipment	20	10
Urological Techniques	30	15
Totals:	770	280

Industrial Practical Training (5 weeks)

Table 2.7. Sample MSG Program, University of Paris IX—Dauphine

This MSG is structured in terms of *unités de valeur*/UV (units of value). Each UV represents 28–30 hours of instruction (1 hour/week/academic year or 2 hours/week/semester). Students are expected to take all 12 UV in required subjects in the first year and to devote the second year to remaining subjects, an internship report and a project.

First Year (360 hours)

Required Subjects

Business Economics
Business English
Evolution of Business Administration
Introduction to Data Processing
Introduction to Finance (Taxation)
Introduction to Financial Management

Required Subjects (continued)

Introduction to Management Models I & II (Operations Research)
Labor Relations & Personnel Management
Law
Marketing Management
Sociology & Psychology

July–October: Mandatory 8-week practical internship in a private or public business enterprise. An internship report must be submitted and defended before two faculty members.

Second Year (300 hours)

a. UV of Integration (1 UV × 30 hours) requiring *either:*

Business Policy & Structure   Public Administration

b. Electives (3 UV × 30 hours) requiring three of the following:

Accounting & Financial Aspects of Business
Advanced Technologies
Economic Aspects of Business
English
Entrepreneurship
Human Relations in Business
Legal & Financial Aspects of Business

c. Optional Subjects (6 UV × 30 hours) requiring six of the following:

Business Law
Data Processing & Management
Employee Relations
English for International Relations
Finance
Financial Control
Inventory Control
Marketing
Methods of Public Administration
Production Management
Psychology & Sociology of Labor Organizations
Taxation & Financial Management

continued

or one of the following three tracks (comprising 6 UV × 30 hours each):

a. *Public Administration Track*

Foundations & Principles of Public Sector Accounting
Management & Economics of the Public Sector
Management of Public Enterprises
Public Sector Financial Control
   plus two of the following:
Non-Commercial Organizations
Planning
Political Economics
Public Finance

b. *Marketing Track*

Communication Policy
Consumer Behavior & Qualitative Market Study
Distribution Policy: Pricing & Sales
Market Research
Marketing of Services & International Marketing
Product & Marketing Policy

c. *Financial Track*

Accounting & Financial Markets of International Groups
Financial & Stock Market Analysis
Financial Forecasting & Fund Management
Financial Planning
Financial Policy & Business Strategy
French Financial Markets
International Financial Markets
International Business Management
Long Term Financial Management & Capitalization
Portfolio Management & Financial Markets
   plus two of the following:
Financial Accounting
Synthesis & Financial Practice— Diagnostic & Forecasting
Taxation

d. Project

2.5. Traditional *Maîtrise* Diploma Awarded by the University of Montpellier III

2.6. Professional *Maîtrise* (*Maîtrise des Sciences de Gestion*/MSG) Awarded by the University of Lyon III

The *Maîtrise de Methodes Informatiques Appliquées à la Gestion*/MIAG is awarded upon completion of a two-year curriculum patterned after the MST and the MSG. The total hours of instruction range between 1400 and 1600 over two years, including at least 300 hours of coursework in foreign languages, humanities, and social sciences. The MIAG, when set up with a strong mathematical bias, is directly accessible to holders of the scientific DEUG. Applicants who hold a DEUG in economics or business must undergo a preparatory program in mathematics. The MIAG program includes courses in algorithms, COBOL, data analysis, data base, economics, financial analysis, graph theory, linear programming, operations research, programming language, statistics and probability, thematic models, and theory of data processing. In addition, courses in accounting, business management, communication, English, information systems, and production management are required.

THE *MAGISTÈRE*

The *magistère* was created in 1985 and the first degree will be awarded in 1988 as the university equivalent of a diploma from a *grande école* (see Chapter IV for more information on the *grande école*). This program requires three years of study beyond the DEUG and is offered by individual universities, jointly by several universities and by universities in cooperation with *grandes écoles*. The creation of the *magistère* is an attempt by the Ministry of Education to make university education attractive to talented students who otherwise would attend *grandes écoles*. Admission to the *magistère* is by examination after the DEUG and is highly selective. The *magistère* is not a national diploma of higher education but has been labeled as a *diplôme accrédité*, a university diploma accredited by the Ministry of Education. It has been conceived as a terminal qualification which leads to employment.

The following *magistère* programs were accredited by the Ministry of Education for 1986-87.

Universities	Programs
University of Aix-Marseille I	Political Science of the Non-Western World
University of Aix-Marseille III	Business Law, Finance and Accounting, Economics for Engineers
University of Angers	Tourism
University of Clermont-Ferrand I	Economic Development and Policy
University of Grenoble I	Mathematical Applications, Physics
University of Grenoble II	Business Management
University of Lille I	Labor Sociology
University of Lyon I	Cell and Molecular Biology
University of Montpellier I	Business Law Practice
University of Nancy I	Microbiology and Enzymology
University of Nice and Ecole Nationale Supérieure des Mines de Paris	Computer Science
University of Orléans	Industrial Material and Minerals
Ecole Normale Supérieure and Universities of Paris VI and XI	Earth Sciences
University of Paris I	Economics, International Relations
Universities of Paris I and VIII	Environmental Studies
University of Paris II	Business Law Practice
University of Paris III	Industrial Economics, Simultaneous Translation
University of Paris IV	Communication
University of Paris V	Social Sciences
Universities of Paris V, VI, XI	Computer Science
Universities of Paris VI, VII, IX, XI, XIII and Ecole Normale Supérieure	Fundamental and Applied Mathematics and Computer Science, Physics, Chemistry
Universities of Paris VI, VII, XI and Ecole Normale Supérieure	Biology
University of Paris VII	Linguistics
University of Paris IX and Ecole Nationale de la Statistique et de l'Administration Economique	Economics of the Banking and Financial Industries

University of Paris IX	Management Science
University of Poitiers	Communication Law
University of Rennes I	Mathematical Models and Computer Methods
University of Strasbourg I	Chemistry and Biology
Universities of Toulouse I and III	Statistics for Economists

DIPLÔME d'ETUDES POLITIQUES

Unique to the *Instituts d'Etudes Politiques*/IEP (Institutes of Political Studies), the *Diplôme d'Etudes Politiques* (Diploma of Political Studies) is earned after three years of study beyond the *baccalauréat*. There are seven institutes of political studies: one in Paris and six in major provincial cities—Aix, Bordeaux, Grenoble, Lyon, Strasbourg, and Toulouse. The Institut d'Etudes Politiques de Paris is an independent private institution enjoying the special status of *Grand Etablissement* (Major Institution) granted by an act of the National Assembly. The remaining six are public institutions and are designated as UFR of universities.

Admission to an institute of political studies is by entrance examination open to holders of a *baccalauréat*, although the majority of applicants complete a one-year preparatory program before attempting that examination. Further selection takes place at the institute of political studies at the end of the first year of study known as *année préparatoire* (preparatory year). Students who hold a *licence* are admitted directly into the second year of IEP. The overwhelming majority of students who graduate from an institute of political studies already hold a *licence* or another university diploma. A *diplôme d'études politiques* leads to employment in the public and private sectors. It is also the most favored route for access to the Ecole Nationale d'Administration/ENA (National School of Administration), a prestigious institution which trains upper-echelon civil servants. Graduates who have written a thesis in history, law, or political science in their second or third year of study at the institute may be admitted to the third cycle of university study. Institutes of political studies offer programs in four specialties: economics and finance, international relations, public service, and social and economic policy. Table 2.8 presents a program from an institute of political studies. See Document 2.7 for a sample diploma awarded by the Institute of Political Studies of Grenoble.

Table 2.8. Sample *Diplôme d'Etudes Politiques* Program, Institut d'Etudes Politiques de Lyon (Institute of Political Studies of Lyon)

First Year (20 hours/week)	**Third Year** (28 hours/week)
Required Core Courses	*Required Core Courses for All Sections*
Contemporary History (1789-1939)	International Economics
Economics	Major Problems of Contemporary Society
Introduction to Third World Problems	

continued

Political Doctrines
Political Institutions &
  Constitutional Law
Political Sociology
Required Methodology Lectures
Economics
Political Doctrines
Political Institutions &
  Constitutional Law
Political Sociology
Foreign Language Practice
Physical Education

Second Year (30 hours/week)

Required Core Courses for All Sections
History of Economic Doctrines
Methods & Techniques in Social
  Sciences
20th Century French History
Methodology Lecture
20th Century French History

*Political & Public Administration
Courses*

Required Core Courses
Administrative Institutions, Law, &
  Public Administration
Economic Geography
Political Economy
Public Finance
Methodology Lectures
Methods & Techniques in Social
  Sciences
Administrative Institutions, Law, &
  Public Administration

Business & Economics Courses

Required Core Courses
Administrative Institutions
The Business Enterprise
Economic Policies
Economic & Industrial Policy
Social Law/Business Law
Methodology Lectures
Economic Policies
Financial Analysis: Introduction to
  Management Accounting

Information & Media Courses

Required Core Courses
Administrative Institutions

Social & Economic Interventionism
World History Since 1945

*Political & Public Administration
Courses*

Required Core Courses
European Community Law &
  Institutions
  or
Political Systems of the Arab World
Sociology & International Legal
  Relations
Methodology Lectures
Public Law & Regional
  Development
International Legal Relations

Business & Economics Courses

Required Core Courses
Business Management
European Economy
  or one of the following:
The Economy of the Arab World
Financial Analysis
Organizational & Labor Sociology
Methodology Lectures
Financial Analysis II
International Economics
Organizational & Labor Sociology

Information & Media Courses

Required Core Courses
Communication & Advertising
Information & Media Law
Media Economics
Social & Business Law
Methodology Lectures
Media Economics
News & Media

The complete program represents 1950 hours of instruction.

Communication & Information
   Theory
Economic Policies
Psychology & Sociology of
   Communication
Public Finance
Socio-Semiology of Information
Methodology Lectures
   Information & Communication
      Theory
   Methodology & Techniques of
      Social Sciences

Third Cycle *(Troisième Cycle)*

The final stage of university study, the third cycle, requires a *maîtrise* or an equivalent for admission. Graduates of *grandes écoles* and students enrolled in the final year of programs leading to a *diplôme d'ingénieur* (diploma of engineer) at selected *grandes écoles* are also admissible. Although different types of programs and diplomas are offered at this level, instruction is essentially based on research. The third cycle is the only level of university study where applicants undergo selection for admission. Application is made to the relevant teaching and research unit and the decision is endorsed by the university president. To be admitted, an applicant must hold strong second cycle records and show potential for success in the proposed program of study.

The research required in third cycle programs often takes place at independent laboratories which work closely with universities. Faculty and graduate students constitute a major portion of the fulltime staff of national research centers such as the Centre National de la Recherche Scientifique/CNRS (National Center for Scientific Research) and the Institut National de la Santé et de la Recherche Médicale/INSERM (National Institute of Health and Medical Research). Research also takes place at institutions of higher learning and research classified as *Grands Etablissements Littéraires et Scientifiques* (Major Institutions of Letters and Science).

THE *DIPLÔME D'ETUDES SUPÉRIEURES SPÉCIALISÉES*

The *Diplôme d'Etudes Supérieures Spécialisées*/DESS (Diploma of Higher Specialized Studies) requires one year of study beyond the *maîtrise*. It is a terminal diploma and does not lead to further study. Thus, the holder of a DESS who wishes to continue studies towards a *doctorat* must first complete a DEA (see below). Each DESS program is designed for a specific occupation and is developed in consultation with the relevant professional organizations. Programs include coursework and practical training with the relative length determined by the university. In general, a DESS represents 300 to 600 hours of coursework and at least three months of practical training.

2.7. Diploma Awarded by the Institute of Political Studies of Grenoble

There are three major categories of DESS:

1. DESS designed to provide professional training in the field of specialization of the *maîtrise* (e.g., DESS in clinical psychology for psychology *maîtrise* holders);
2. Highly specialized DESS providing advanced training in a very specific field (e.g., DESS in Quality Control for the Chemical and Pharmaceutical Industries);
3. DESS designed to provide advanced technical and professional skills for students from a liberal arts background (e.g., DESS in computer science or business administration for holders of any *maîtrise*).

THE *DIPLÔME D'ETUDES APPROFONDIES*

Awarded in one year of study beyond the *maîtrise*, the *Diplôme d'Etudes Approfondies*/DEA (Diploma of Advanced Studies) constitutes the first year of a doctoral program. Students who are in the final year of specific engineering schools (*écoles d'ingénieur*) may be simultaneously enrolled in a DEA program. Admission to a DEA is authorized by the university president upon consultation with the director of doctoral programs.

The program consists of 300 hours of coursework divided between the field of specialization (100 hours) and research techniques (200 hours) (see Table 2.9). The Ministry of Education recommends that a DEA be taught in the

Table 2.9. Sample DEA Program in Social Psychology and Etiology, University of Paris X–Nanterre

Admission to this program requires a *maîtrise* in psychology including coursework in social psychology. Applicants undergo an interview designed to assess their qualification and suitability for the program.

Subjects Common to all DEA in Psychology (four of the following):

Human & Ecological Etiology (30 hours)
Introduction to Experiments (37 hours)
Introduction to Laboratory & Field Work (37 hours)
Introduction to Research (37 hours)
Research in Developmental Psychology (37 hours)
Theory of Psychological Pathology & Clinical Methodology (37 hours)

Subjects Specific to Social Psychology and Etiology

    Attitude Changes (25 hours)
    Group Dynamics (37 hours)

        plus one of the following:

    Analysis of Discourse (37 hours)
    Interviewing (30 hours)
    Workshops & Case Studies (37 hours)

Electives (one of the following):

    Applied Statistics & Multivariant Analysis (25 hours)
    Bibliography (25 hours)

        plus one or more of the following:

    Concepts of Applied Psychoanalysis (25 hours)
    Epistemology of Social Sciences (30 hours)
    Family Group Dynamics (30 hours)

        Total: 302 Hours + Thesis

context of doctoral programs and offered jointly by academic institutions and research laboratories.

In addition to examinations in all the coursework, candidates for a DEA must defend a thesis accompanied by an extensive annotated bibliography. For candidates who propose to continue their studies toward a *doctorat*, the thesis usually constitutes a dissertation proposal. Although conceived as the first year of doctoral studies, the DEA is a national diploma of higher education in its own right. Many students prefer not to continue their studies beyond it.

THE *DOCTORAT*

The *doctorat* created by the 1984 reform law is seen as a major innovation in French higher education. Prior to its advent, three types of doctorates were awarded: *Doctorat de Troisième Cycle* (Third Cycle Doctorate), *Doctorat d'Etat* (State Doctorate) and *Diplôme de Docteur Ingénieur* (Diploma of Doctor of Engineering). (See discussion below for details on these doctorates.) The multiplicity of doctoral diplomas posed many problems, notably in terms of their recognition abroad. The new degree is said to be patterned after the Ph.D. in the United States and is designed for international recognition in order to promote the exchange of faculty and researchers.

A *doctorat* must be earned in a minimum of three years and a maximum of five years beyond the *maîtrise*, including the first year which is devoted to a DEA. An application is made after completion of the DEA and requires approval of the university president on the recommendation of a dissertation director. Candidates are expected to conduct research, preferably at a national center for research such as the Centre National de la Recherche Scientifique/CNRS (National Center for Scientific Research) and prepare a dissertation under a qualified director. In the sciences, candidates belong to a research team working under the dissertation director. A *doctorat* can be prepared at an institution other than the one where the DEA was earned.

Doctoral dissertations may be directed by the following:

—faculty or researchers entitled *(habilités)* to direct research;
—holders of a *doctorat d'Etat* who have been authorized to direct research by the university president on the advice of the scientific council;
—qualified persons (usually distinguished professionals) appointed by the president on the recommendation of the scientific council.

Completed dissertations are read by two readers, one of whom is external to the institution. The readers' comments are submitted in writing to the jury which presides over the defense. The jury is composed of at least three members appointed by the president and includes the dissertation director and one outside person, either French or foreign, who is recognized in the field. At least half of the members of the jury must be holders of the *Habilitation à Diriger des Recherches* (see below). A *doctorat* is awarded with the following quality assessments: *très honorable* (very high honors); *honorable* (honors); and *passable* (satisfactory). The degree bears the name of the awarding institution. The jury reserves the right to refuse the award of the degree.

When a dissertation is the result of a team effort, the candidate's contribution must be carefully outlined in the form of a short thesis and submitted as part of the dissertation.

THE *HABILITATION À DIRIGER DES RECHERCHES* (ENTITLEMENT TO DIRECT RESEARCH)

Established in 1984, this qualification is open to holders of a new *doctorat* or a *doctorat d'Etat*. The *Habilitation* qualifies its holders for consideration for promotion to full professorship and to direct doctoral dissertations. Candidates submit an application to the university president and proceed to compose a dossier of research, publications and other contributions to the field. The

UNIVERSITY EDUCATION 75

degree is awarded after a review of the dossier by a panel and an oral presentation by the candidate. There is no deadline for completing the process.

While the diploma enables the holder to direct doctoral dissertations, it does not automatically result in a promotion to full professorship, which is an administrative decision of the Ministry of Education. Document 2.8 shows a sample DESS from the University of Strasbourg III; Document 2.9, a DEA from the University of Lille III; and 2.10, a provisional certificate for a new *doctorat* from the University of Paris 7.

DOCTORAL DEGREES PRIOR TO THE REFORM OF 1984

During this period of transition, French candidates may submit doctoral degrees earned under the pre-1984 regime. In Raymond E. Wanner's volume *France* (1975), French doctoral degrees were described as follows.

1. The *Doctorat de Troisième Cycle*—3° Cycle. Sometimes referred to as the *Doctorat de Spécialité,* this doctorate of the third cycle was awarded after a period of advanced academic study of two to three years in length. The *Doctorat de 3° Cycle* was designed to develop a candidate's knowledge of the specialty as well as methods of research and logic necessary for a career in scientific

2.8. *Diplôme d'Etudes Supérieures Spécialisées*/DESS **Awarded by the University of Strasbourg III**

UNIVERSITY EDUCATION

2.9. *Diplôme d'Etudes Approfondies*/DEA Awarded by the University of Lille III

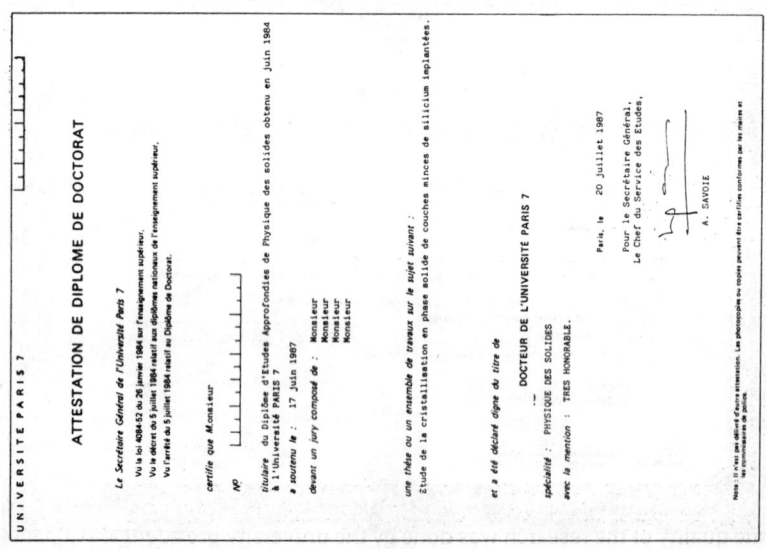

2.10. Provisional Certificate of New *Doctorat* Awarded by the University of Paris 7 (Note dates [1984] indicating applicable laws.)

research, higher education, government, industry and commerce. The *Maîtrise* or an equivalent was required for applicants who were admitted by the university president or director of the university-affiliated institution after consultation with the candidate's advisor.

The two-part program included studies leading to the *Diplôme d'Etudes Approfondies*/DEA and a research project. The candidate who successfully undertook the DEA in the first year of the *troisième cycle* progressed to the second year of study under a research director chosen by the university president from among full professors *(professeurs)* or associate professors *(maîtres de conférences)*. The research project could appear as a doctoral thesis, a collection of articles, contributions to group reports, or reports on experiments. When the research was part of a group project, the candidate's individual role was clearly defined. The degree was awarded upon the candidate's successful defense of the thesis in a public session before a university-sponsored examining board.

2. The *Diplôme de Docteur-Ingénieur*. Applicants for the diploma of doctor in engineering—like those enrolled in the doctorate of the third cycle program—completed the DEA and research study (see above). Those whose *Diplôme d'Ingénieur* was earned at a high level engineering school identified by the Ministry of Education were not required to earn the DEA but immediately began their two-year fulltime research. Students required to earn the DEA spent three years in doctoral studies.

3. The *Doctorat d'Etat*. The state doctorate—France's most prestigious academic degree—demonstrated the candidate's ability to do original research of very high quality. Admission to the program required a *maîtrise* or the equivalent. Doctoral candidates studying in those areas not covered by the *maîtrise* (economics, law, some management programs, and political science), had to have the *Diplôme d'Etudes Approfondies*/DEA or the *Diplôme d'Etudes Supérieures Spécialisées*/DESS or an equivalent determined by the university. University officials also determined on an individual basis any candidate's need to complete additional advanced study prior to submitting research work.

Work on the state doctorate was directed at a university-related institution by a research director with full or associate professor rank. Candidates formally registered their topics with the university which, in turn, set limits on the scope of the proposed research to be completed within a five-year period. Programs were offered in Catholic theology, economics, law, letters and humanities, management science, political science, Protestant theology, and science. Those who worked on a private basis enrolled in a university when they were ready to submit their research for evaluation and defense, unless a judgment was called for on the scientific merit of the research. Initial screening of the quality of the research was done by the university president and a panel of experts. Research completed for the *Doctorat de Troisième Cycle* or the *Diplôme de Docteur-Ingénieur* or for foreign doctoral degrees could be used as part of the required research. A précis of the thesis accepted for defense was given to all those holding the *Doctorat d'Etat* at the university.

The candidate earned the doctorate by successfully defending a doctoral thesis or significant original research before a university-appointed doctoral board. The five-member board took into account not only the breadth of the candidate's knowledge of the specialty but the applicant's ability to present the research in general scientific and cultural contexts. The doctoral board could specify on the diploma the specialized part of the academic programs addressed by the research or thesis. The diploma included the names and titles of doctoral board members, the thesis or research title, and bibliographic data. (Wanner 118-121)

In 1975, the Council on Evaluation of Foreign Student Credentials approved the following placement recommendations for the *doctorat*. (Wanner 182)

- The *Doctorat d'Etat* may be considered to be of Ph.D. level for purposes of academic exchange and staffing.

- The *Doctorat de Troisième Cycle* and *Doctorat de l'Université* represent a level of advanced training beyond the U.S. master's degree and, in some instances, approach Ph.D. level. These doctorates should always be evaluated on an individual basis with particular attention paid to the quality of the doctoral dissertation submitted.

- The *Diplôme de Docteur-Ingénieur* should be considered as a *Doctorat de Troisième Cycle*.

International Education

The 140,000 foreign students enrolled at French universities constitute approximately 12% of the total university enrollment. The largest number of students (60%) are from former French colonies in Africa. The remaining 40% are from Europe, the Middle East, Asia and the United States.

Admission

Foreign students who wish to study in France submit a preliminary application to the Embassy of France located in their country of origin and take a French language proficiency test administered by the Embassy. The Embassy forwards the application and results of the language test to the universities chosen by the student. The final admission and placement determination is made by each university.

Language Proficiency Assessment

Since 1985, the Ministry of Education has instituted two standard tests to assess the language proficiency of foreign students. Tests are administered by universities, approved French language programs and French embassies abroad. The diplomas thus earned are the *Diplôme Elémentaire de Langue Française*/DELF (Elementary Diploma in French Language) and the *Diplôme Approfondi de Langue Française*/DALF (Advanced Diploma in French Language). The DELF represents basic proficiency in the language and the DALF, the level of proficiency required to undertake a program of study at a French university. The DELF examination has six separate components which may be taken at any time and in any order except for the sixth and final examination which must be taken after the first five have been passed. The DALF consists of four examinations which are taken at any time and in any sequence. To become eligible for the DALF examinations, candidates must hold a DELF or must have been exempted from it by an equivalent examination. Although there are no formal course requirements, the Ministry of Education estimates that each examination represents 100 hours of preparation; thus the DELF represents 600 hours and the DALF 400 hours.

French Language and Civilization Programs for Foreigners

Universities and several university-affiliated programs offer French language and civilization programs for foreigners during the academic year and during the summer. Programs range in length from one semester to one full year and are validated by various diplomas and certificates. Although institutions may award internal certificates and diplomas, there are three certificates, established in 1961, recognized by the Ministry of Education. They are as follows: *Certificat Pratique de Langue Française (1° Degré)* (Practical Certificate in French); *Diplôme d'Etudes Françaises (2° Degré)* (Diploma of French Studies); and *Diplôme Supérieur d'Etudes Françaises (3° Degré)* (Higher Diploma of French Studies).

Each certificate or diploma requires approximately one year of fulltime study. The *certificat pratique de langue française* is an introductory program designed for beginners. The *diplôme d'études françaises* offers seven options (art history, demography, economics, geography, history of ideas, literature, and political institutions) and is designed to prepare students to undertake studies at a French university. The *diplôme supérieur d'études françaises* is an advanced program which provides the student with skills such as composition, textual analysis, translation, and writing. Foreign students who are otherwise eligible for admission to a French university may be exempted from the first year of university study in foreign languages or French literature on the basis of a *diplôme supérieur d'études françaises*.

Diplomas in Teaching French as a Foreign Language

Teaching French as a foreign language *(français langue étrangère)* is taught at several universities in programs leading to a *licence, maîtrise, diplôme d'études approfondies*/DEA (diploma of advanced studies), *diplôme d'études supérieures spécialisées*/DESS (diploma of higher specialized studies) and a *doctorat*.

Short programs for experienced teachers of French from foreign countries are organized by the Centre International d'Etudes Pédagogiques de Sèvres/ CIEP (International Center for Pedagogical Studies at Sèvres) and the Bureau pour l'Enseignement de la Langue et de la Civilisation Françaises/BELC (Bureau for Teaching French Language and Civilization) in cooperation with different universities. Programs vary in length and content; however, they are always designed for qualified and experienced teachers who hold university degrees from their home countries.

Chapter III

Short Higher Technical Education

In the past ten years, short (two-year) higher technical education has become very popular in France because it offers better opportunities for employment. Short higher technical education was initially designed for students who graduated with a technical *baccalauréat*. Present day applicants, however, tend to be holders of an academic *baccalauréat*. The two main types of short technical programs are those offered at *Instituts Universitaires de Technologie*/IUT (University Institutes of Technology), leading to the *Diplôme Universitaire de Technologie*/DUT; and programs leading to the *Brevet de Technicien Supérieur*/BTS (Higher Technician's Certificate).

The *Diplôme Universitaire de Technologie*/DUT

The *Diplôme Universitaire de Technologie*/DUT (University Diploma of Technology) requires the completion of two years of study at a university institute of technology (IUT). The DUT is classified as a national diploma of higher education and is equivalent to a first cycle university degree (DEUG). Admission to an IUT requires a *baccalauréat* and has become increasingly competitive as the job prospects for graduates are excellent. Holders of a DEUG may be admitted to a special one-year program and earn a DUT. Although the DUT was initially conceived as a terminal degree, approximately 30% of the graduates continue their studies at a university or at a *grande école* of engineering where they may sit for the entrance examination after at least three years of professional experience. See document 3.1 for a sample DUT diploma.

Established in 1966, 67 IUT offer programs in applied sciences, business, engineering and technology, and social services. Although fully independent in terms of administration and budget, each IUT is designated as a special unit (UFR *à dérogation*) of the local university. The typical IUT is composed of one to six departments and annually enrolls between 60 and 160 students. Programs are offered in 19 major fields which are further divided into 36 specializations.

The first year of the program in each major field is common for all students. Specialization occurs in the second year. The academic year is 32 weeks and students are required to attend 35 hours of class each week. The curriculum stresses small group instruction and laboratory work—50% of the instructional hours—while one-third of the time is spent in lectures and one-fifth in communication (writing). Eight weeks of practical training and a written report are required for graduation. A sample curriculum in civil engineering is presented in Table 3.1.

Table 3.1. Sample Curriculum in Civil Engineering Offered at an IUT (in Annual Hours)

Subjects	Lectures	Tutorials	Lab
First Year			
Applied Mathematics	32–48	64–96	18
Building Construction & Design	57	96–144	63
Building Materials	58	6	56
Communication (French)	–	70	10
Physics & Construction Equipment	62–70	68–76	63
Site Organization & Supervision	20	28	3.5
Structures	64	54	49
Totals:	293–317	386–474	262–30
Grand Total: 941.5 to 1053.5 Hours			
Second Year (Building Construction and Public Works Option)			
Applied Mathematics	17	17	18
Communication Methods	–	70	10
Design & Construction	–	70	17.5
Geotechniques	28	56	24.5
Physics & Construction Equipment	54	46	35
Site Organization & Supervision	8	84	10.5
Structures	87	95	108.5
Project	–	–	120
Totals:	194	438	344
Grand Total: 976 Hours			

Programs offered at IUT are as follows:

Major Fields	Specializations
Applied Biology	Agronomy, Biological and Biochemical Analysis, Dietetics, Environmental Engineering, Food and Biological Industries
Business Administration and Management	Accounting and Finance, Small Business Management, Personnel Management
Chemistry	Material Science, Textiles
Chemical Engineering	Bio-Industries, Chemical Industries
Civil Engineering	Building Construction and Public Works, Building Materials and Climates
Computer Science	None
Electrical Engineering	Automatic Control and Systems, Computer Science for Industry, Electronics, Electrical Technology and Power, Electronics
Energy and Heat Engineering	None

Health and Safety	Occupational Hygiene and Safety, Public Health and Safety
Industrial Maintenance	None
Information and Communication Professions	Communication (advertising, journalism and public relations), Documentation
Legal Professions	None
Mechanical and Industrial Engineering	None
Physical Measurements	Instrumentation Techniques, Physical and Chemical Measurements and Control
Sales and Marketing	None
Social Services Professions	Social and Cultural Activities Worker, Social Worker, Special Education Teacher
Statistics, Economics and Quantitative Management Techniques	None
Transportation and Logistics	None

The *Brevet de Technicien Supérieur*/BTS

The *Brevet de Technicien Supérieur*/BTS (Higher Technician's Certificate) is a state diploma *(diplôme d'Etat)* awarded by the Ministry of Education following two-year programs in 70 fields of specialization including agriculture, applied science, business and commerce, engineering technology, graphic art and health professions. The BTS is offered in *Sections de Technicien Supérieur*/STS (higher technician sections) located on the premises of *lycées* and at private institutions approved by the government. Admission requires a *baccalauréat* or a *brevet de technicien*/BT (technician's certificate). As the BTS is a marketable credential, there is growing demand for admission and programs have become increasingly selective.

The curriculum in each discipline and the final examination are set by the Ministry of Education. Tables 3.2 and 3.3 present BTS curriculums for assistant engineering technician, and marketing and distribution programs, respectively. Class organization and teaching resemble that of the *lycée*. Attendance is mandatory and closely monitored. In addition to classroom instruction, practical training of four weeks during the summer (between the first and second years) is required.

The final examination is administered in the same manner as the *baccalauréat*. In order to pass, a candidate must earn an overall grade of 12/20. When the average falls between 8/20 and 10/20, a second round of examinations is required. A candidate whose average is below 8/20 as a result of the first round of examinations is considered to have failed and must repeat the second year. Only 55% of the students who attempt the examination in any given year pass. See Chapter I for more details on grades on the *baccalauréat*. See document 3.2 for a sample BTS.

BTS in Graphic Art. A two-year program designed for F-12 *baccalauréat* holders, the BTS in graphic art can be earned in three years by students who hold another *baccalauréat*. The first year is spent in a preparatory program.

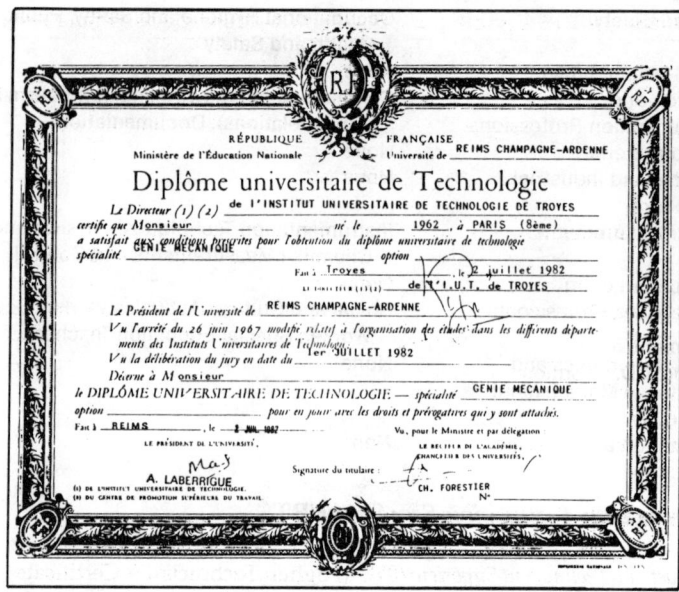

3.1. University Diploma of Technology Awarded by the IUT of Troyes

Table 3.2. Sample BTS Curriculum for Assistant Engineering Technician
         (Assistance Technique Ingénieur)

Subjects	Weekly Hours*	
	First Year	Second Year
Required Subjects		
Automation	1 + (3)	(2)
Construction; Applied Mechanics; Technology	3 + (8)	5 + (8)
Electrical Technology; Applied Electronics	3 + (3)	3 + (3)
Foreign Language	(2)	(2)
French	3	3
Introduction to Business	(1)	1 + (1)
Mathematics	3 + (2)	3 + (2)
Typing	(2)	(2)
Total:	35	35
Optional Subject		
Foreign Language II	(2)	(2)

NOTE: Students are required to complete four weeks of practical training during the summer between the first and second years.
*Hours between parentheses indicate tutorials or laboratory work.

SHORT HIGHER TECHNICAL EDUCATION

Table 3.3. Sample BTS Marketing and Distribution *(Action Commerciale)* Program

Subject	Weekly Hours* First Year	Second Year
Applied Marketing & Distribution	(6)	(6)
Data Processing	1	1
Economics & Organization of Business	2	2
Foreign Language I	4	4
French & General Studies	2	2
Mathematics Applied to Business	2	1
General Economics	2	2
Law	2	2
Management Tools	3	3
Marketing & Distribution	7	7
Total:	31	30
Electives		
Foreign Language II	3	3
Physical Education	2	2
Typing	2	2

NOTE: Students are required to complete four weeks of practical training during the summer between the first and second years.
*Hours between parentheses indicate practical work.

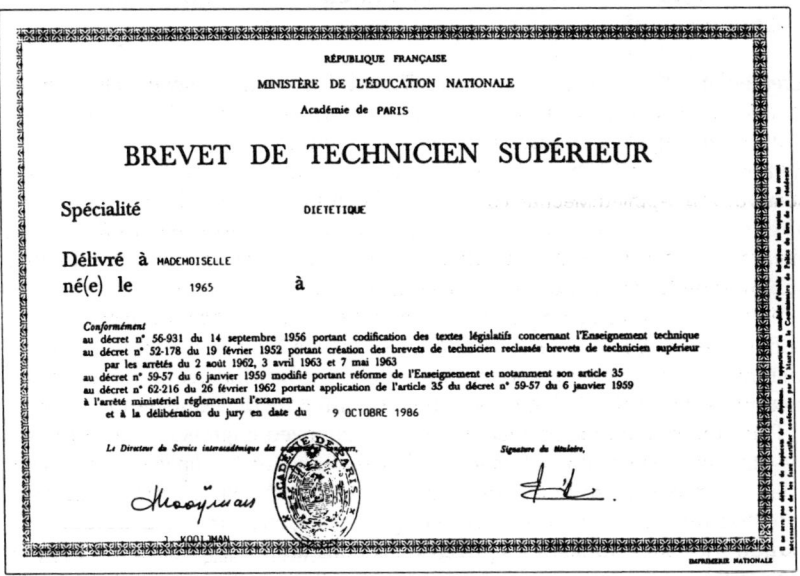

3.2. Higher Technician's Certificate

Chapter IV

Engineering Education

Introduction

French engineering education today is offered primarily at *grandes écoles*, national institutes of applied science, university schools of engineering and at the Conservatoire National des Arts et Métiers/CNAM (National Conservatory of Arts and Crafts) which offers part-time continuing education. Since engineering institutions are highly selective, they enroll less than 5% of the students in higher education. Of the 164 institutions which are currently in operation, more than half were founded after 1945. In the last twenty years, engineering programs have been introduced at several universities, a trend which is developing very rapidly in keeping with the government's desire to increase the number of engineering graduates from the current 260,000 to 400,000 by the year 2000.

The Commission des Titres d'Ingénieur/CTI (Engineering Titles Commission)

Created in 1934, the Commission des Titres d'Ingénieur/CTI controls teaching at all engineering institutions and grants them the right to award the *diplôme d'ingénieur* (diploma of engineer). Diplomas indicate the name of the institution which awarded them. The CTI has the mandate to define and direct the education and training of engineers at all institutions regardless of affiliation; to determine whether private institutions may be authorized to award the *diplôme d'ingénieur*; to act in an advisory capacity regarding public institutions; and to monitor all institutions awarding engineering diplomas.

The commission is composed of 24 members: 12 members representing the public higher education sector (appointed by the Minister of Education); six members representing employers (appointed by the Minister of Industry); six members representing the profession (appointed by the Minister of Labor).

The commission maintains a list of all recognized engineering institutions by category. There are 164 schools that may award the *diplôme d'ingénieur*. They are public institutions, including university schools of engineering; private technical institutions recognized by the State; and private institutions. In addition to being ranked, engineering schools are categorized according to their admission procedures and the nature of the programs offered. See Appendix B for a list of institutions awarding the *diplôme d'ingénieur*.

Institutions can be grouped as follows:
1. traditional *grandes écoles*,
2. institutions which offer five-year integrated programs (including university programs in engineering),
3. institutions which offer four-year programs,
4. institutions which offer continuing education programs, and
5. institutions which offer post-diploma programs.

Special Features

Engineering schools are small in size, ranging in enrollment from a few hundred to one or two thousand students. The largest institution, the Institut National des Sciences Appliquées de Lyon (National Institute of Applied Science of Lyon), has an enrollment of 3000. Limited enrollment permits teachers to know their students and to follow their progress closely. The physical plant at *grandes écoles* is usually well maintained, attractive, and offers many amenities, such as sports facilities, which are not available at universities. Entering classes, known as *promotions*, are kept together and graduate at the same time. There is tremendous loyalty to the institutions and alumni associations are very strong. Graduates, who often end up in leadership positions in every sector of French life, promote the interests of their alma mater, protect it from undue outside interference, and see to it that a steady supply of funds is provided by the government even in periods of budgetary retrenchment.

In the past twenty years, as French higher education was undergoing continuous upheaval and change, *grandes écoles* have remained untouched by the turmoil and have actually flourished. Their stability has further strengthened their position and prestige in the eyes of the public. The government spends three to four times more annually on each student enrolled at a *grande école* than on a university student. The discrepancy in subsidies is not questioned because it is part of the tradition and is entirely compatible with French meritocracy. The *concours* (see below) and the other hurdles that students have to overcome to enter a *grande école* justify all the benefits and privileges that graduates will derive for the rest of their lives. Once admitted, virtually all students graduate with a *diplôme d'ingénieur* and proceed to fairly successful careers in business or government.

Traditional *Grandes Ecoles (Baccalauréat + 2 + 3)*

Engineering education offered in *grandes écoles* dates back to the eighteenth century when the first specialized institutions of higher education were established by the government to train the engineers and technicians needed to build roads, bridges and equipment required for military campaigns. The tradition was strengthened when the universities were abolished during the

French Revolution and more *grandes écoles* were established instead. During the nineteenth century, additional *grandes écoles* were created by business and industry to meet the manpower needs of the industrial revolution.

Admission to a traditional *grande école* of engineering requires the completion of two years of postsecondary preparatory study in a *classe préparatoire* (preparatory class) and the passing of a competitive examination known as *concours*. The engineering program lasts three years and leads to a *diplôme d'ingénieur* (diploma of engineer) bearing the name of the awarding institution. A diploma issued by a traditional *grande école* does not usually indicate the student's major; institutions will issue a detailed transcript which lists all subjects studied and grades earned.

Pre-Engineering Education *(Classes Préparatoires)*

Orientation toward *grandes écoles* begins as early as lower secondary school where promising students are encouraged to excel in mathematics in order to enter the scientific stream of a *lycée* and pass the *baccalauréat* C with very good grades. The first and most stringent selection takes place at the end of the *lycée* when students apply to *classes préparatoires* (two-year preparatory programs) leading to the examinations for admission to *grandes écoles*. Only students with very high grades on the *baccalauréat* are actually eligible for these classes.

Classes préparatoires are offered at selected urban *lycées* throughout France. The two-year program is dedicated exclusively to preparing students for the entrance examination to *grandes écoles*. A common first year, known as *mathématiques supérieures* (higher mathematics), leads to a second year known as *mathématiques spéciales* (special mathematics). There are seven types of *classes préparatoires*, classified according to the type of *baccalauréat* required for admission and the type of *école d'ingénieur* (school of engineering) to which they lead (see Table 4.1). The curriculum stresses mathematics, physical sciences and quantitative methods.

Table 4.2 lists the curriculum for the mathematics and physics ('M' and 'P') type of *classe préparatoire*. The program further requires a total of 40 minutes be spent weekly in oral examinations in foreign languages, French, mathematics, and physics. In addition to classroom work, students must spend six or more hours daily on homework assignments and outside preparation.

Records from *classes préparatoires*, which resemble those issued by *lycées*, can be obtained by U.S. admissions officers. The grading system used in *lycées* applies to *classes préparatoires*, as well.

Traditionally, access to most *grandes écoles* was through the 'M' and 'P' types of *classes préparatoires*. In recent years, special classes have been created to accommodate students who hold technical *baccalauréats* (F). All *classes préparatoires* do not give access to all the *concours*, nor to all *écoles d'ingénieur*. Students who have completed the 'M' and 'P' type of class are eligible to take almost any *concours* except for the ones that require preparation in biological sciences

Table 4.1. Types of Classes Préparatoires Classified by Baccalauréat

Baccalauréat Type	Classe Préparatoire Type	Grandes Ecoles
1. C & E	Mathematics (M, M') Physics (P, P') Technology (T)	Engineering
2. E only	Technology (T')	Engineering
3. F1–F10	Technical (TA)	Engineering
4. F5 & F6	Technical (TB)	Engineering
5. F7, F7', F8	Technical (TB')	Engineering
6. C & D	Biology (C)	Agronomy
7. D'	Biology (TD'1, TD'2)	Agronomy

for admission to schools of agronomy. Only classes #6 and #7 lead to *grandes écoles* of agronomy (see Table 4.1).

Admission to *Grandes Ecoles*

In May and June of the second year of a *classe préparatoire*, entrance examinations *(concours)* for admission to *grandes écoles* are administered. Each institution (or groups of institutions) administers its own examinations which are based on the curriculum of the *classes préparatoires*. Students take at least two different *concours* to improve their chances of admission. Candidates who pass the written portion are regarded as *admissibles* (eligible for admission) and are invited to take the oral examination which is administered separately by each institution. The oral examination determines whether a candidate is definitively admitted to a particular *grande école*. The *concours* is not a traditional examination designed to demonstrate mastery of a subject matter. It is specifically devised to select students and results are interpreted by individual institutions according to their own criteria. Accordingly, students who may have failed to enter one institution may very well be admitted to their second choice. Candidates who pass the examination are ranked according to their results and receive offers according to their rank. Those who do not secure admission to the institution of their choice often repeat the second year of the *classe préparatoire* for a second attempt at the *concours*. Only one repetition is allowed.

Out of 100 students admitted in the first year of a *classe préparatoire*, 71% pass to the second year, 27% transfer to another type of higher education institution, and 2% are allowed to repeat the year in exceptional circumstances only. In the second year, of 100 students admitted, 44% pass the *concours* and enter a *grande école*, 47% repeat the second year (only one repetition allowed), and 9% transfer to another type of institution, usually a university.

Table 4.2. Sample *Classe Préparatoire* Program, Mathematics (M) and Physics (P)

Subject	Lectures	Weekly Hours Tutorials	Laboratory
First Year (Mathématiques Supérieures)			
Foreign Language I	2	–	–
Foreign Language II	1	–	–
French	2	–	–
Industrial Design	–	–	2
Latin (optional)	1	–	–
Mathematics	12	2	–
Physical Education	2	–	–
Physics	9	–	2
Second Year (Mathématiques Spéciales)			
Mathematics Section			
Chemistry	2	–	1
Foreign Language	2	–	–
French	2	–	–
Industrial Design	–	–	2
Mathematics	11	3	–
Physical Education	2	–	–
Physics	6	–	1
Physics Section			
Chemistry	3	–	2.5
Foreign Language	2	–	–
Industrial Design	2	–	–
Mathematics	8	3	–
Physical Education	2	–	–
Physics	7	–	2.5

The three most selective *concours* are the *Concours de l'Ecole Polytechnique*, the *Concours Mines-Ponts* and the *Concours Centrale-Supélec*, all accessible to students who have completed the 'M' and 'P' types of preparatory classes.

The *concours Mines-Ponts* is administered jointly by the following institutions. See Table 4.3 for the 1983 results of the *concours Mines-Ponts* and Table 4.4 for 1985 admissions.

Ecole Nationale de l'Aéronautique et de l'Espace
Ecole Nationale de Techniques Avancées
Ecole Nationale des Télécommunications de Bretagne
Ecole Nationale des Télécommunications de Paris
Ecole Nationale Supérieure de la Métallurgie et de l'Industrie des Mines de
  Nancy

ENGINEERING EDUCATION

Ecole Nationale Supérieure des Mines de Paris
Ecole Nationale Supérieure des Mines de Sainte Etienne
Ecole Nationale Supérieure des Ponts et Chaussées
Ecole Polytechnique (Although it participates in this *concours*, the Polytechnique admits most of its students by its own *concours*.)

Table 4.3 shows the relative selectivity of these institutions. In looking at these figures, one must bear in mind that all institutions do not receive the same number of applications and do not admit the same number of students.

The *concours Centrale-Supélec* is administered jointly by the following institutions:

Ecole Centrale de Lyon
Ecole Centrale des Arts et Manufactures
Ecole Nationale Supérieure d'Electronique et de ses Applications
Ecole Supérieure d'Electricité
Ecole Supérieure d'Optique
Institut d'Informatique d'Entreprise
Institut Industriel du Nord de la France

Table 4.3. 1983 Results of the *'Concours Mines-Ponts'*

Candidates	Types of *Classes Préparatoires*		
	M	P'	TA
Candidates Taking the *Concours*	3662	2200	239
Candidates Passing and Ranked	862	496	12

Table 4.4. 1985 Admissions on the *'Concours Mines-Ponts'*

| | | Types of *Classe Préparatoire* | | | |
| | | M | | P | |
Schools	Rank:	Highest	Lowest	Highest	Lowest
Ecole des Mines (Paris)		1	181	9	61
Mines/Nancy		641	871	–	–
Mines/Ste. Etienne		346	806	–	–
Ponts & Chaussées		186	476	85	257
SupAéro		166	546	49	221
Techniques Avancées		271	611	157	281
Télécommunication/Bret.		341	686	–	–
Télécommunications		86	291	125	137

Program Structure

The program offered at traditional *grandes écoles* stresses applied sciences, economics, mathematics, mathematical methods, and social sciences. The broad-based curriculum is designed to ensure versatility and allow for the subsequent specialization of graduates in a variety of scientific or administrative disciplines. Indeed, graduates of institutions such as the Ecole Polytechnique or the Ecole Nationale Supérieure des Mines de Paris, to name a few, are regarded as scientists in the broadest sense of the term rather than engineers. See Table 4.5 for a traditional *grande école* program. Students who graduate in the top 10% of their class are generally recruited by the government to join the Corps d'Ingénieurs de l'Etat (State Corps of Engineers) or to attend the Ecole Nationale d'Administration/ENA (National School of Administration), after which they become high-level civil servants assigned either to government agencies or to one of the state owned and operated corporations. The private sector also recruits graduates for executive positions. See document 4.1 for a sample Diploma of Engineer from the Ecole Centrale de Lyon.

Five-Year Integrated Programs

Integrated programs of engineering were established beginning in the 1950's and were initially offered at institutes of applied science. Since the mid-1970's, five-year engineering programs have also been offered at selected universities. A *diplôme d'ingénieur* is awarded after the completion of a five-year program organized in two cycles. The two-year first cycle is common for all students and constitutes the pre-engineering stage. It leads to a second (engineering)

4.1. *Diplôme d'Ingénieur* Awarded by Ecole Centrale de Lyon

ENGINEERING EDUCATION 93

Table 4.5. Sample Traditional *Grande Ecole* Program, Ecole Nationale Supérieure des Mines de Paris

School Profile—Founded in 1783, the Ecole Nationale Supérieure des Mines de Paris is one of the oldest and most prestigious *grandes écoles* of engineering. It is often placed second only to the Ecole Polytechnique even though many graduates of the Ecole Polytechnique continue their advanced studies at the Ecole des Mines after they join the national corps of mining engineers or one of the other state corps. The institution has extensive research laboratories in mining, geological engineering, applied geology, marine science, chemical engineering, metallurgy, mathematics, automatic control, and engineering management. It has the authority to grant the *diplôme d'études approfondies*/DEA (diploma of advanced studies) and the *doctorat*. The institution has an enrollment of 250 students with 94 graduating each year.

The program is divided into three components: a core curriculum of 1100 hours of lectures, recitations and laboratory; 375 hours of electives; 120 days of optional activities and projects.

Subject	Length	Hours	Subject	Length	Hours
First Year			**Second Year**		
Core Curriculum			Automation	–	25
Computer Science	–	30	Econometrics	–	23
Crystallography	–	28	Electronics	–	12 + 35 (lab)
Descriptive Economics	–	18	Engineering Internship	1 mo.	–
Electronics	–	15 + 20 (lab)	Fluid Mechanics	–	55
Factory Internship	1 mo.	–	Foreign Languages	–	100
Foreign Language	–	100	Machines	–	36
Geology Field Work	6 days	–	Mathematics	–	22
Introduction to Geology	–	34	Probabilities	–	25
Introduction to Mechanical			Social Sciences	–	19
Technology	–	10	Statistics	–	20
Material Science	–	25	Thermokinetics	–	25
Mathematics	–	48	*Specialized Studies* (to be		
Mechanics	–	62	chosen from)		
Oral Communication	–	15	Atoms & Molecular Lasers	–	38
Physics	–	56	Biotechnology	–	38
Sociology	–	17	Computer Science	–	18
Thermodynamics	–	40	Cost Analysis	–	15
Workshop	5 days	–	Ecology	–	23
					continued

Specialized Studies (to be chosen from)
- Electronics — 25
- Industrial Internship — 6 days, –
- Macroeconomics — 15
- Mathematics — 38
- Sociology — 15

Core Curriculum
- Commercial & Labor Law — 25
- Foreign Languages — 50
- General & Business Accounting — 25
- Legislation — 20

Specialized Studies (to be chosen from)
- Atomic Engineering — 25
- Automatic Control — 38
- Dynamics of Structures — 38
- Economic Analysis & Planning — 38
- Electrochemistry — 15
- Geodynamics & Deformation of Rocks — 38

- Economics of Mineral Resources — 20
- Fluid Mechanics & Mass Transfer — 38
- Geology Field Work — 4 wks., –
- Geophysics — 38
- Material Transformation Processes — 38
- Mathematics — 22
- Mechanics of Solids — 23
- Metallurgy — 38
- Operations Research — 18
- Physics & Chemistry — 30 (lab)
- Scientific Calculations — 25
- Sociology — 25
- Statistics — 15
- Structural Measurements — 38

*Electives*¹ — 40 + 4 wks.

Third Year

Specialized Studies (continued)
- Marine Geology — 25
- Mathematical Programming — 20
- Mineralogy — 15
- Nuclear Physics — 25
- Political Institutions — 15
- Sociology of Social Classes — 15
- Stochastic Processes — 25
- Thermal Machines — 25
- Western Economies — 12
- World Economics — 19

*Electives** — 22 days + 12 wks.

Electives: Applied Mathematics (automatic control, computer science, mathematical morphology), Atomic Engineering, Biotechnology, Chemical Engineering, Earth Science, Energy Mechanics, Materials Science & Engineering, Mining Infrastructure, Scientific Management, Sociology, Thermodynamics

cycle which is three years in length. Admission to the second cycle is by *concours*. See document 4.2 for a Diploma of Engineering from INSA/Toulouse. The Institut National de Sciences Appliquées de Rennes/INSA (National Institute of Applied Sciences of Rennes) offers an integrated five-year program (see Table 4.6).

French universities have gradually introduced engineering programs in the last twenty years. The rate at which programs are developed has recently increased in accordance with the government's objective of doubling the number of engineers by the end of the century. In 1985-86 alone, programs were implemented at 17 universities. Admission is open to holders of a scientific *baccalauréat* but, prior to undertaking the engineering curriculum, students must complete a first cycle university program in mathematics and physical science *(Diplôme d'Etudes Universitaires Générales/*DEUG) or a *Diplôme Universitaires de Technologie/*DUT from a university institute of technology and

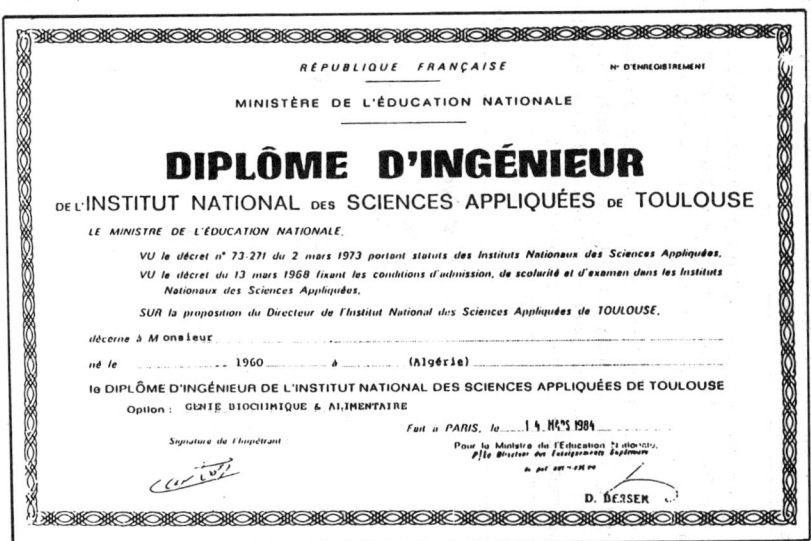

4.2. Diploma of Engineer Awarded by the INSA/Toulouse

undergo an entrance *concours*. University engineering programs lead to a *diplôme d'ingénieur* after three years of study and are similar in structure to those offered at national institutes of applied science. The unique feature of university engineering programs is that they allow holders of relevant *maîtrises*, preferably a *maîtrise* of science and technology, to enter the third year of the engineering curriculum and to graduate with a *diplôme d'ingénieur* after one year of study.

Table 4.6. Sample Integrated Five-Year Program, Institut National de Sciences Appliquées de Rennes/INSA (National Institute of Applied Sciences of Rennes)

School Profile—The INSA/Rennes trains civil engineers, applied physicists, electrical engineers, and computer engineers. With extensive research laboratories, it is authorized to award the DEA and the *doctorat*. INSA/Rennes has an enrollment of 700 students (including those in pre-engineering) and graduates 164 each year. The institution also offers continuing education programs for holders of the BTS and the DEUG.

The academic program is divided into two cycles. The two-year first cycle is common for all students and constitutes the pre-engineering component. The second cycle lasts three years with students enrolled in one of four departments: civil engineering, electrical engineering, applied physics, or computer science. While in the final year, students may concurrently prepare a DEA in automatic control, civil engineering, material science, or computer science.

Subject	First Cycle					
	First Year			Second Year		
	Lect.	Recita.	Lab	Lect.	Recita.	Lab
Additional Mathematics*	24	—	—	—	—	—
Chemistry	32	32	80	64	44	64
Computer Science	—	—	—	48	—	—
English	32	—	—	32	—	—
French	24	—	—	32	—	—
German (optional)	112	128	—	—	128	—
Mathematics	16	32	—	112	32	—
Mechanics	64	—	—	16	—	—
Physical Education	64	64	96	64	64	64
Physics	24	—	—	64	—	—
Spanish (optional)	—	—	—	32	96	24
Strength of Materials	128	—	—	128	—	—
Technology						
Workshop/Technology/Graphics						

*For students with a technical *baccalauréat*.

ENGINEERING EDUCATION

Second Cycle

Civil Engineering

First Year

	Lect.	Recita.	Lab
Computer Science	10	36	—
Concrete	32	96	128
Engineering Design	96	—	—
English	64	—	—
Fluid Mechanics & Hydraulics	48	96	128
Mathematics	16	64	—
Mechanics of Deformable Solids	48	192	128
Mineralogy	48	32	180
Numerical Analysis	16	48	—
Physical Education	64	—	—
Statistics	16	16	—
Strength of Materials	24	—	—

Second Year

	Lect.	Recita.	Lab
Computer Science	18	30	—
English	128	—	—
Geology	48	116	128
Ground Water/Coastal Hydraulics	24	48	—
Highway Engineering	32	32	256
Reinforced Concrete	48	96	—
Resistance of Materials	16	—	256
Soil Mechanics	64	112	128
Structures	48	102	—
Studio	—	128	—
Thermal Heating of Buildings	16	16	—
Topography	16	126	—

Electrical Engineering

First Year

	Lect.	Recita.	Lab
Electronics	56	80	128
English	32	—	—
Logic	48	48	64
Mathematics	16	16	—
Microwave Circuits	40	24	16
Numerical Analysis & Programming	24	56	—
Physical Education	64	—	—
Physics of Components	48	56	32

Second Year

	Lect.	Recita.	Lab
Automatic Control	48	48	64
Discrete Systems	16	16	—
Economics	64	—	—
Electrical Systems & Functions	64	64	128
English	72	—	—
Mathematics	16	16	—
Microcomputers	48	16	16
Physical Education	64	—	—
Probabilities	24	24	—
Sensors & Activators	16	16	32
Signals Theory	16	16	—

Third Year

	Lect.	Recita.	Lab
Artificial Intelligence	16	—	—
Computer Science	24	16	24
English	32	—	—
Microcomputers	24	24	—
Optimization & Automation	32	32	—

continued

Third Year

Subject			
Building Acoustics	15	—	—
English	30	7½	—
Finished Products	15	—	—
Heat	75	—	—
Heating & Air Conditioning	15	—	—
Industrial Electricity	15	—	—
Law & Management	30	—	—
Management & Contracts	30	—	—
Measurement/Reinforced Concrete	64	—	—
Prestressed Concrete	22½	22½	—
Project	—	—	—
Site Visits	32	—	—
Soil Works	15	—	—
Steel Construction	50	25	—
Urbanism & Architecture	15	—	—
Wood & Prefabricated Structures	8	—	—
Project (16 weeks)	—	—	—
Robotics	8	24	8
Signal Processing	32	24	—
Telecommunication Systems	32	16	16

Department of Computer Science

First Year

Subject			
Algorithms	—	12	16
Applied Probabilities	30	30	—
Calculation of Predicates	16	16	—
Computer & System Architecture	60	60	60
Construction of a Compiler	15	15	—
English	60	—	—
Graphics	30	30	—
Logic	30	45	—
Machine Languages	—	12	16
Mathematics	23	—	—
Programming	—	45	30
Programming Methods	30	—	—
System Functions & Utilization	30	30	30
Trees & Backtracking	30	30	—

Department of Applied Physics

First Year

Subject			
Applied Physics	32	—	—
Electronic Circuits	32	40	258
English	54	—	—
German	32	—	—
Mathematics	40	40	—
Numerical Analysis	24	32	—
Physical Education	32	40	—
Propagation	32	40	—
Programming	24	—	—
Quantum Mechanics	3	56	—
Solid State Electronics	48	64	258
Statistics & Probability	24	24	—

Second Year

Course			
COBOL	8	6	6
Grammars & Semantics	30	30	–
Mathematics	23	–	–
Programming Methods	30	30	15
Statistics	15	15	–
Systems	60	30	30
Theory of Languages	30	30	16
plus one of the following:			
A. Data Base Architectures	60	–	–
Computer Graphics	60	–	–
B. Artificial Intelligence	60	–	–
Compilation	60	–	–
Project	90	–	–
VLSI	60	–	–

Third Year

Course			
Algorithm of Distribution	37½	–	–
Artificial Intelligence (Expert Systems)	37½	–	–
Parallelism & Sequential Distribution	37½	–	–

Options (one of the following):

Lectures

Course			
Computer Graphics *or* Databases *or* Parallel Architectures *or* Software Engineering	37½	–	–

Second Year

Course			
Automatic & Logical Circuits	32	32	64
Economics	144	–	–
Electronic Functions	32	32	256
English	54	–	–
German	32	–	–
Metallurgy	64	64	512
Physical Education	32	–	–
Theory of Solid State Electronics	64	64	512

Third Year

Course			
Ceramic Materials	16	16	–
Economics	32	–	–
Electrical & Logical Circuits	24	32	256
English	27	–	–
German	16	–	–
Metallurgy	32	48	–
Physical Education	16	–	–
Power Systems	16	–	–
Theory of Solids	24	32	–
Final Project (1 semester)	–	–	–

continued

Seminars
Case Study of Software Systems:
- ADA — 12 —
- ENCHERE — 18 —
- Public & Business Networks — 12 —
- Robotics — 12 —
- CONCERTO — 3 —
- UNIX — 3 —
- VSLI — 12 —
- Software Production in a SSCI — 6 —

General Studies
- Additional Mathematics — 24 —
- Economics — 24 —
- English — 24 —

Professional Internship (15 weeks)

Four-Year Programs

There are two types of four-year programs. The first type requires the completion of one year of *classe préparatoire* and the passing of a *concours*. It is followed by a three-year engineering curriculum. Until 1985, five institutions, known as *Ecoles Nationales d'Ingénieurs*/ENI (National Schools for Engineers) and located in Belfort, Brest, Metz, Ste. Etienne and Tarbes, offered four-year programs in engineering after the *baccalauréat*. Since 1985, the programs at Ste. Etienne and Tarbes have been extended to five years and the 1990 graduates from these two institutions will have completed a five-year integrated program.

Admission to a four-year program is by *concours* for holders of C and E *baccalauréats*. Four-year programs are still offered at three of the schools: Belfort, Brest, and Metz. See Table 4.7 for a sample program.

Continuing Education Programs

The *diplôme d'ingénieur* can also be earned through continuing education programs run by the Conservatoire National des Arts et Métiers/CNAM (National Conservatory of Arts and Crafts). The CNAM is open to all persons who are 18 or older and who are employed. The program is organized in terms of three sequential cycles composed of a series of units known as *valeurs* (values). Each *valeur* represents 80 hours of lecture or 60 hours of laboratory work.

The first cycle is composed of seven *valeurs* and leads to the *Diplôme de Premier Cycle Technique*/DPCT (Diploma of First Technical Cycle). Although the *baccalauréat* diploma is not required for admission, the program requires applicants to have reached the level of the *baccalauréat*. The DPCT is formally regarded as the equivalent of a DEUG (two years of university study).

The second cycle is composed of six *valeurs* and leads to the *Diplôme d'Etudes Supérieures Techniques*/DEST (Diploma of Higher Technical Education). Holders of a DEST may attempt the entrance *concours* for *grandes écoles* of engineering.

The third (complementary) cycle leads to a *diplôme d'ingénieur*. Candidates for the *diplôme* must be holders of the DEST and must pass a qualifying examination *(examen probatoire)* after which they complete supplementary courses and prepare a thesis.

Post-*Diplôme d'Ingénieur* Programs

Several options are available for *ingénieurs diplômés* who wish to pursue their studies.

a. DEA and doctoral studies at a *grande école* or at a university;
b. a second *diplôme d'ingénieur* in a specialization at another *grande école* or at special institutions which offer programs designed for holders of a previous *diplôme d'ingénieur*;
c. a *mastère*.

Table 4.7. Sample Four-Year Engineering Curriculum, Ecole Nationale d'Ingénieurs de Belfort

School Profile—Founded in 1962, this institution is dedicated to training engineers specializing in mechanical construction. It has a total enrollment of 300–400 students and graduates 80–100 annually.

Subjects	Total Hours					
	Lect.	Tutor.	Lab	Lect.	Tutor.	Lab
	First Year			**Second Year**		
				First Semester		
Chemistry	32	16	16	–	–	–
Communication (Writing)	32	32	–	–	–	–
Computer Science	32	16	32	–	–	4
Construction	32	128	38	32	64	–
Economics	–	–	–	16	16	–
Electricity	–	–	–	32	16	16
Foreign Languages	32	32	–	16	–	–
Manufacturing	32	160	–	32	–	48
Mathematics	160	64	–	32	16	–
Mechanics	64	48	–	64	16	16
Metallurgy	–	–	–	32	16	16
Organization & Methods	32	32	32	32	32	32
Physical Education	(64 hours)			(32 hours)		
Physics	16	8	16	–	–	–
Totals:	464	536	134	288	176	132
				Second Semester Practical Training in Industry		
	Third Year			**Fourth Year**		
	First Semester					
Automatic Control	–	–	–	64	64	48
Construction	32	64	–	32	96	–
Economics	16	16	16	32	–	–
Electricity	32	16	16	–	–	–
Electronics/Electrical Technology	–	–	–	64	64	48
Foreign Languages	16	–	–	32	–	–
Manufacturing	32	–	16	32	–	96
Mathematics	32	16	–	32	16	–
Mechanics	64	32	16	64	32	48
Organization & Methods	32	16	16	32	32	32
Physical Education	(32 hours)			(32 hours)		
Physics	32	16	16	16	–	–
Final Thesis	–	–	–	100	–	–
Totals:	288	176	96	500	304	272
	Second Semester Practical Training in Industry					

DEA and Doctoral Studies

Studies toward the *Diplôme d'Etudes Approfondies*/DEA (Diploma of Advanced Studies) or the *doctorat* can be undertaken at *grandes écoles* or at a university with which there exists an articulation agreement. DEA and doctoral degrees awarded by *grandes écoles* are equivalent in all aspects to those awarded by universities. Students enrolled at some *grandes écoles* can earn a DEA simultaneously with a *diplôme d'ingénieur* by completing additional coursework and a thesis in their third year. The DEA program provides training in research techniques lacking in the traditional engineering curriculum. As of 1984, the following *grandes écoles* have been granted the right to award doctoral degrees independently:

Conservatoire National des Arts et Métiers/CNAM
Ecole Centrale des Arts et Manufactures
Ecole Centrale de Lyon
Ecole Nationale des Ponts et Chaussées
Ecole Nationale Supérieure de l'Aéronautique et de l'Espace
Ecole Nationale Supérieure des Mines de Paris
Ecole Nationale Supérieure des Télécommunications
Ecole Polytechnique
Ecole Supérieure de Physique et de Chimie Industrielle de la Ville de Paris/
  ESPCI
Institut National des Sciences Appliquées de Lyon
Institut National des Sciences Appliquées de Rennes
Institut National des Sciences Appliquées de Toulouse
Université de Technologie de Compiège

Studies at Specialized Institutes

Graduates of the Ecole Polytechnique can obtain specialized training by enrolling in the second year at another *grande école*, designated as *école d'application* (school of application/specialization), and earn a second *diplôme d'ingénieur* with a specific major. The Ecole Nationale des Mines de Paris, and the Ecole Nationale des Ponts et Chaussées are examples of application schools.

Institutions attached to specific sectors of the economy offer specialized training accessible only to graduates who hold a three-year *diplôme d'ingénieur*. These programs are fashioned to train persons for employment in the sector with which they are linked. They last from one to two years and lead to a second *diplôme d'ingénieur*. See Table 4.8 for a sample program from the Institut Textile de France.

The *Mastère*

In 1986, the *grandes écoles* created a new qualification called *mastère*, in order to provide a common identity for different post-diploma programs offered at

Table 4.8. Sample Specialized Program, Institut Textile de France

School Profile—Founded in 1948, the institution offers a one-year program in textiles for *ingénieurs diplômés*. A three-month practical training and a project lead to the award of a *Diplôme d'Ingénieur de l'Institut Textile de France*.

Subjects	Hours	Subject	Hours
Fabrics	41	Productivity, Economics & Management	46
General Introduction	27		
Creation & Innovation	17	Spinning & Weaving	35
Industrial Physics	12	Textile Fibers	44
Product Control & Application	39	Treatment of Fabrics	43
		Total:	304
		Laboratory	68
		Site Visits	135
		Grand Total:	507
		Practical Training (3 months)	

various institutions. The *mastère* (abbreviated 'MS') is a post-*diplôme d'ingénieur* qualification designed to complement the broad-based training provided at most *grandes écoles*. The title, *mastère*, is a registered trademark *(label)* held by the Conférence des Grandes Ecoles, the association of *grandes écoles*. Admission into a *mastère* program requires either a *diplôme d'ingénieur* or a DEA from a university. The program consists of 12 months of highly specialized study which includes 250 hours of classroom work, laboratory and applied work, a 4-6 months' internship, and a project. Candidates must also prepare and defend a short thesis. See Table 4.9 for a sample *mastère* program.

Table 4.9. Sample *Mastère* Program in Electronics, Ecole Centrale des Arts et Manufactures de Paris

School Profile—The program is designed to provide students with professional skills for employment in industries related to automation, electronics, and microelectronics. The curriculum stresses basic concepts and industrial applications, including recent developments, in each field. Classroom instruction constitutes 30% of the total time period. The remaining 70% is divided between laboratory work (38%) and a project (32%). The program includes a six-month internship in an industrial concern, which is also the basis for the project.

Subject	Hours Lect.	Lab	Subject	Hours Lect.	Lab
Basic Theory & Analysis & Processing of Signals	54	15	Microelectronics	25.5	6
			Microprocessors	19.5	9
			Semiconductors	24	6

Computer-Assisted Design	9	6	Sequential Automatic Control for Industry	12	–
Electronic Accounting	9	3	Synthesis	21	–
High Level Frequency	33	9	Total:	252	64.5
Telecommunications	21	–			
Industrial Electronics & Electrical Technology	24	10.5	Practical Experience & Project (40 half-days)		

The following *mastère* programs were in operation in 1987.

Institutions	Programs
Centre d'Enseignement et de Recherches Appliqués au Management/Centre d'Enseignement et de Recherches en Informatique, Communication et Systèmes (Sophia-Antipolis)	Software Engineering
Centre d'Etudes Supérieures Industrielles (Paris)	Industrial Computer Science
Conservatoire National des Arts et Métiers (Paris)	Strategies and Techniques of Organizing Processes
Ecole Centrale de Lyon	Electrical Engineering; Energy; Mechanical Engineering
Ecole Centrale des Arts et Manufactures (Paris)	Aerospace and Aeronautical Engineering; Applied Mathematics; Bioengineering; Building Engineering; Chemical Engineering and Food Sciences; Civil Engineering (Public Works); Computer Science; Economics and Management Science; Electronics; Geomechanics and Mechanical Modelling of Structures; Heat Transfer; Industrial Engineering and Management of Technological Innovation; Materials Science and Engineering; Ocean; Physics; Quality Control and Management; Real Time Data Processing; Robotics; Urban Planning
Ecole Nationale d'Ingénieurs de Tarbes	Automated Production; Materials Engineering

continued

Ecole Nationale des Ponts et Chaussées (Paris)	Civil Engineering (Bridges and Tunnel Design); Civil Engineering (Highways and Transportation); Civil Engineering (Operational Urban Planning); Civil Engineering (Sciences and Building Design)
Ecole Nationale des Travaux Publics de l'Etat (Vaulx-en-Velin)	Building Construction; Civil Engineering; Computer Science; Geotechniques and Structures; Hydraulics and Environment; Regional and Urban Development; Rehabilitation of Industrial Architecture
Ecole Nationale du Génie Rural des Eaux et des Forêts (Paris)	Forestry Science; Water Science and Development
Ecole Nationale Supérieure d'Arts et Métiers (Paris)	Quality Control Management
Ecole Nationale Supérieure d'Electrotechnique, d'Electronique; d'Informatique et d'Hydraulique de Toulouse	Advanced Computer Science Applications; Automatic Control; Computer Science; Electrical Engineering—Power Electronics; Electronics; Energy Engineering;
Ecole Nationale Supérieure d'Ingénieurs de Constructions Aéronautiques (Toulouse)	Aeronautical Maintenance; Data Processing Systems; Helicopter Engineering
Ecole Nationale Supérieure d'Ingénieurs de Génie Chimique (Toulouse)	Chemical Engineering
Ecole Nationale Supérieure de Chimie de Lille	Chemical Technology
Ecole Nationale Supérieure de Chimie de Montpellier	Artificial Intelligence and Biological Macromolecules; Fine Organic Chemistry and New Materials; Plastic Materials and Their Processing
Ecole Nationale Supérieure de l'Aéronautique et de l'Espace (Toulouse)	Advanced Automatic Control Systems; Aeronautical and Space Techniques; Aerospace Electronics; Aerospace Mechanics; Computer Science; Propulsion Systems
Ecole Nationale Supérieure de Physique de Marseille	Optoelectronics and Guide Waves; Semiconductor Devices; Signal Processing and Computer Engineering

Ecole Nationale Supérieure de Télécommunications de Bretagne	Image and Artificial Intelligence
Ecole Nationale Supérieure des Industries Agricoles et Alimentaires (Massy)	Food Chemical Engineering; Food Products Quality Control; Food Technology for Mediterranean and Tropical Products; Industrial Management for Food Industry; Microbial Technology
Ecole Nationale Supérieure des Ingénieurs des Travaux Ruraux et des Techniques Sanitaires (Strasbourg)	Irrigation, Drainage and Small Dams Engineering; Water Supply and Sanitation Engineering
Ecole Nationale Supérieure des Mines de Paris	Applied Geology for Mining; Forming of Metals and Materials; Geostatistics
Ecole Nationale Supérieure des Mines de Sainte-Etienne	Automatic Control; Software Engineering
Ecole Nationale Supérieure des Techniques Avancées (Paris)	Computer Aided Design; Computer Aided Manufacturing and Robotics
Ecole Nationale Supérieure des Techniques Industrielles et des Mines de Douai	Robotics
Ecole Nationale Supérieure des Télécommunications (Paris)	Components of Telecommunication Devices; Design of Integrated Circuits; Design and Architecture of Computer Systems; Design of Transmission Systems; Image Processing; Image and Sound Processing; Information Systems and Local Area Networks; Man-Machine Interaction and Artificial Intelligence; Signal Processing; Software Engineering; Telecommunications and Aerospace Systems; Telecommunications and Remote Data Processing Networks
Ecole Spéciale de Travaux Publics du Bâtiment et de l'Industrie (Paris)	Civil Engineering/Rehabilitation of Public Buildings; Quality Control and Management
Ecole Supérieure d'Electricité (Gif-sur-Yvette)	Advanced Computer Networks; Artificial Intelligence and Productivity; Automatic Control Systems; Communication Systems; Computer Science and Communication; Computer System Engineering; Control Engineering

continued

	and Automation; High Speed Electronics; Instrumentation and Metrology; Microelectronics—Design and Technology; Power Electronics; Power Systems; Signal and Image Processing; Solid State Electronics
Ecole Supérieure d'Ingénieurs de Marseille	Building and Civil Engineering; Heating and Refrigeration Engineering; Industrial Data Processing; Materials and Structures; Offshore Engineering; Power Electronics Engineering; Heat
Ecole Supérieure du Cuir et des Peintures, Encres et Adhésifs (Lyon)	Leather; Paints, Ink and Adhesives; Plastic Processing
Hautes Etudes Industrielles (Lille)	Electrical Engineering and Power Device Electronics; Information Technology Applied to Industry
Institut Catholique d'Arts et Métiers (Lille)	International Business Engineering
Institut Industriel du Nord (Lille)	Automation; Automated Production; Chemical Engineering Processing; Civil Engineering; Electrotechnics; Industrial Data Processing; Management Data Processing; Mechanical Engineering; Regional Development; Transportation
Institut National des Sciences Appliqués (Lyon)	CAD in Architecture, Construction and Urban Engineering; Industrial Automation and Robotics; Computer Science
Institut Supérieur d'Electronique du Nord (Lille)	Acoustic Systems Design
Institut Supérieur du Béton Armé (Marseille)	Construction and Civil Engineering
Université de Technologie de Compiègne	Biomedical Equipment

Chapter V

Agricultural Education

Agricultural education is offered primarily at institutions which operate under the control of the Ministry of Agriculture. Postsecondary programs vary in length from two years in the higher technician sections *(section de technicien supérieur*/STS) at *lycées agricoles* (agricultural *lycées*) to four or five years at institutions classified as *grandes écoles* of agriculture. Programs in biology or chemistry applied to agriculture are also offered at university faculties of science and lead to regular university degrees.

Short Programs

Two-year programs in agriculture lead to the *Brevet de Technicien Supérieur Agricole*/BTSA (Higher Technician's Certificate in Agriculture) and are offered in the higher technician section of agricultural *lycées*. Admission requires a *baccalauréat* D' (agricultural option) or a *Brevet de Technicien Agricole* (Agricultural Technician's Certificate). Students who hold a scientific *baccalauréat* are admitted by special examination. The structure of programs leading to a BTSA is identical to that of other *brevet de technicien supérieur*/BTS (higher technician's certificate) programs and includes four weeks of practical training between the first and second years (see Chapter III, "Short Higher Technical Education"). The BTSA is offered in the following areas:

Agricultural Biology and Biotechnology
Agricultural Machinery
Agricultural Techniques and Business Administration
Animal Husbandry
Crop Protection
Dairy Production
Environmental Protection
Equestrian Science
Farm Management (for women)
Food Production
Forestry
Horticulture
Irrigation and Water Resources Management
Plant Husbandry
Production and Marketing of Wines and Spirits
Transformation, Distribution and Marketing of Agricultural Products
Tropical Agriculture
Winemaking and Oenology

Special Program in Winemaking

The *Diplôme National d'Oenologie* (National Diploma of Oenology) is awarded following a two-year program designed to train specialists in all aspects of winemaking, including viticulture, production, marketing and distribution. The program, which includes four months of practical training, is offered at six universities located in Bordeaux, Dijon, Montpellier, Reims and Toulouse. Admission requires a BTSA in winemaking, a *diplôme d'études universitaires générales*/DEUG (diploma of general university studies) in biological sciences, or a *diplôme universitaire de technologie*/DUT (university diploma of technology) in applied biology or chemistry.

Long Programs

Several institutions, categorized as *grandes écoles*, offer programs leading to the title of *Diplôme d'Ingénieur Agronome* (Diploma of Agricultural Engineer). As for all *grandes écoles*, admission is by competitive entrance examination *(concours)* following a preparatory class *(classe préparatoire)*. (See *grandes écoles* in Chapter IV, "Engineering".)

Institutions are grouped as follows:

a. traditional *grandes écoles*
b. institutions which offer five-year integrated programs
c. institutions which offer four-year programs
d. institutions which offer post-*diplôme d'ingénieur* programs

Traditional *Grandes Ecoles*

Several institutions, including those known as a group as *Ecoles Nationales Supérieures d'Agronomie*/ENSA (Higher National Schools of Agriculture), constitute this category. Admission to a traditional *grande école* of agriculture requires the completion of a two-year *classe préparatoire biologique* (preparatory class in biology) and the passing of an entrance *concours*. The organization and administration of the *concours* are identical to those for engineering *grandes écoles*. The five ENSA administer a joint examination. Admission to a particular institution depends on the results obtained on the *concours*. See Table 5.1 for the weekly hours for preparatory courses in the first year *(biologie-mathématiques supérieures)* and the second year *(biologie-mathématiques spéciales)*.

PROGRAM STRUCTURE

The training offered at *grandes écoles* of agriculture lasts three years. The first two years are common for all students and lead to a *Diplôme d'Agronomie*

Table 5.1. Sample Curriculum for a *Classe Préparatoire Biologique*

Courses	First Year Lecture	Lab	Second Year Lecture	Lab
Biological Sciences	6	3	6	3
Chemistry	3	1	2	1
Foreign Language I	2	–	2	–
Foreign Language II (optional)	(1)	–	(1)	–
French	2	–	2	–
Geography	1	–	1	–
Mathematics	7	2	7	2
Physical Education	2	–	2	–
Physics	3	1	4	1
Totals	26 (27)	7	26 (27)	7
Grand Total	33/34		33/34	

Générale (Diploma in General Agriculture). The final year is spent studying a speciality and ends with the award of a *Diplôme d'Ingénieur Agronome* (Diploma of Agricultural Engineer) which is recognized by the Engineering Titles Commission (Comission des Titres d'Ingénieur/CTI). A sample program at the Ecole Nationale Supérieure d'Agronomie et des Industries Alimentaires de Nancy/ENSAIA is presented in Table 5.2. See document 5.1 for a Certificate of Diploma of General Agriculture and document 5.2 for a Certificate of Diploma of Agricultural Engineer.

Table 5.2. Sample Program, Ecole Nationale Supérieure d'Agronomie et des Industries Alimentaires de Nancy/ENSAIA

School Profile—ENSAIA was created in 1970 by the amalgamation of three existing institutions: Ecole d'Agronomie, Ecole de Brasserie, and Ecole de Laiterie. It trains specialists for the agricultural and food production industries and has a total enrollment of 330. In addition to the *diplôme d'ingénieur*, ENSAIA is authorized to award the *diplôme d'études approfondies*/DEA (diploma of advanced studies) and the *doctorat*.

Courses	Hrs.	Courses	Hrs.
First Year		**Second Year**	
Accounting & Business		*Common for All Tracks*	
Management	18	Business Management	55
Agricultural Science	120	Computer Science	45
Basic Industrial Engineering	55	Foreign Languages	60
Chemistry & Biochemistry	112	Legal & Social Aspects	25
Ecology	20	Physical Education	60
Economics	36	Statistics	30

continued

Farm Practice (7 weeks)	–	*Optional*	
Foreign Language	50	*Agricultural Track*	
Humanities	26	Agricultural Engineering	60
Industrial Practice (4 weeks)	–	Animal Husbandry	70
Introduction to Food &		Crop Protection	60
Agricultural Systems	25	Economics	50
Mathematics	36	Food Science	30
Microbiology	63	Genetics	15
Physical Education	50	Soil Science & Fertilizers	60
Physiology	36	Vegetable Production	60
Practical Training	–	Electives	105
Thermodynamics	36	*Food Industry Track*	
		Food Production Industrial	
		Engineering	365
		Food Science	190
		Practical Training Abroad	(8 weeks)
		Science for Engineers	315

Third Year*

Specializations	*Practical Training*
Animal Science	Depending upon specialization,
Applied Economics	3 to 6 months in industry or a
Beer Making	research laboratory.
Crop Fertilization & Production	
Dairy Production	
Food Science & Production	
Plant Science	
Water Resources Management	

*Students may also attend the final year at another ENSA.

Integrated Five-Year Programs

Students are admitted directly with the *baccalauréat* to the Ecole Supérieure d' Agriculture d'Angers/ESA, the Institut Supérieur Agricole de Beauvais/ISAB, and the Ecole Supérieure d'Agriculture de Purpan, three institutions offering five-year programs leading to the *diplôme d'ingénieur agronome* (diploma of agricultural engineer). See Table 5.3 for a sample five-year integrated program. The first two years are spent in a preparatory program leading to a *concours* which determines admission to the second three-year stage. Holders of a DEUG may also be admitted to the second stage by passing an examination. All three institutions award a *diplôme d'ingénieur agronome* which is recognized by the engineering titles commission.

Four-Year Programs

Known as *Ecoles Nationales d'Ingénieurs des Travaux Agricoles*/ENITA (National Schools for Agricultural Work Engineers), five institutions located in Angers,

AGRICULTURAL EDUCATION

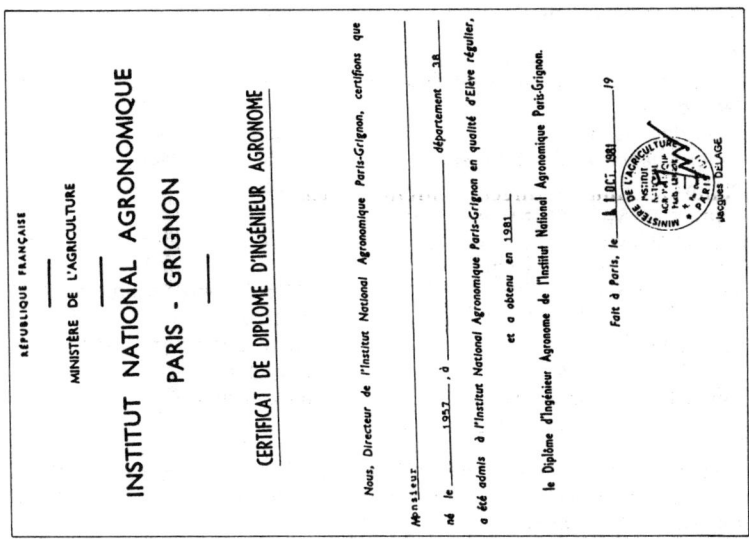

5.1. Certificate of Diploma of General Agriculture Awarded by the Institut National Agronomique, Paris-Grignon

5.2. Certificate of Diploma of Agricultural Engineer Awarded by the Institut National Agronomique, Paris-Grignon

Table 5.3. Sample Five-Year Integrated Program, Institut Supérieur Agricole de Beauvais/ISAB

School Profile—Founded in 1854, the ISAB trains specialists in agricultural science and technology.

First Cycle (Two Years)

The first two years are patterned after the *classes préparatoires biologiques* (described above) and the *Diplôme d'Etudes Universitaires Générales*/DEUG (first cycle of university study) in natural sciences. In addition to studies in the classroom, students are expected to complete 14 weeks of practical training in France or abroad.

Second Cycle (Three Years)

Course	Lectures	Tutorials	Laboratory
Third Year			
Agricultural & Food Industry Engineering	70	30	–
Agricultural Crop Production	65	20	–
Animal Husbandry	95	–	10
Computer Science	22	–	12
Economics & Accounting	100	24	–
English	60	–	–
Law	25	–	–
Plant Pathology	65	–	60
Soil Science	32	20	–
Statistics	40	–	12
Miscellaneous			
Agricultural Chemistry Lab, Professional Associations, Visits	100	–	–
Fourth Year			
Agriculture & Production of Cattle Feed	44	6	–
Applied Genetics	55	–	–
Business Management	145	40	–
Computer Science & Data Analysis	55	40	–
Labor Law	65	–	–
Rural Economics, Commerce & Agricultural Markets	60	15	–
Electives (one of the following)			
Agricultural Crop Production	100 total hours including laboratory		
Animal Husbandry	100 total hours including laboratory		
Personnel Management	100 total hours		

Fifth Year

The year is divided into two segments: 6 months of practical training (preceding May to October) followed by a 6-month (November–May) program which includes the following:

Business Management	240 total hours
Technical Seminars on Current Issues Related to Agricultural Policy	–

Electives
International Commerce, Management
of Cooperatives, Agricultural & Rural   180 total hours
Development

Bordeaux, Clermont-Ferrand, Dijon, and Nantes offer programs in agricultural engineering, applied economics, and in technologies related to agriculture and food production. Admission to ENITA is by *concours* following the completion of a special one-year *classe préparatoire*. Students who have passed the written part of the ENSA *concours* or holders of a DEUG are also eligible for admission. The ENITA program is three years in length (see Table 5.4 for a sample program) and leads to a *diplôme d'ingénieur des techniques agricoles* (diploma of engineer of agricultural technology) which is recognized by the engineering titles commission.

Table 5.4. Sample Four-Year Program, Ecole Nationale d'Ingénieurs des Travaux Agricoles de Bordeaux

Courses	Lecture	Lab	Courses	Lecture	Lab
First Year			**Second Year**		
Agricultural Zoology	20	18	Agricultural Zoology	20	18
Agriculture	44	36	Agronomy	36	36
Analytical Chemistry &			Animal Husbandry	62	24
Biochemistry	–	24	Chemistry & Technology	32	33
Applied Biochemistry	24	6	Economics	27	–
Botany	17	12	English	30	–
Crop Harvesting Equipment	9	–	Finance	18	–
Data Processing	15	20	Genetics	9	–
English	30	–	Management	62	–
General Economics	18	–	Mathematics	10	12
Industrial Food Production	12	6	Mechanics	32	12
Law	9	–	Physical Education	45	–
Metabolic Biochemistry	16	–	Physics	15	3
Microbiology	12	–	Plant Pathology	20	27
Physical Education	45	–	Sociological Research	12	–
Plant Pathology	20	9	Statistics	66	–
Plant Physiology	12	–	Topography	–	18
Rural Economics	20	52	Veterinary Hygiene	18	–
Statistics	54	–	Viticulture	24	15
Thermal Engines & Tractors	28	24	*Practical Training*	1 month	
Viticulture	12	6	(during summer)		
Zootechnology	40	78			
Farm Practical Training (during breaks)	8 weeks				

continued

Third Year (Specialization)

Available Specialities

Agriculture & Fertilizers	Economics & Social
Animal Husbandry	Sciences
Crop Protection	Viticulture, Winemaking

Practical Training
From April to the following September, students are expected to complete 6 months of practical training and prepare a thesis which is required for graduation.

Specialized and Post-*Diplôme d'Ingénieur* Programs

Known as *écoles d'application* (application schools) or *écoles spécialisées* (specialized schools), these institutions admit students who have completed the first two years at a traditional *grande école* of agriculture and hold a *diplôme d'agronomie générale* (general diploma in agriculture); or graduates who hold a *diplôme d'ingénieur agronome* (diploma of agricultural engineer). The two-year program which is offered leads to a highly specialized *diplôme d'ingénieur*. There are eight such institutions in the field of agriculture and agribusiness.

- Centre National d'Etudes Agronomiques des Régions Chaudes (National Center for the Study of Agriculture in Hot Regions)
- Ecole Nationale du Génie Rural et des Eaux et Fôrets (National School of Rural Engineering, Waters and Forests) This school admits graduates of the Ecole Polytechnique as well.
- Ecole Nationale Supérieure d'Horticulture (Higher National School of Horticulture)
- Ecole Nationale Supérieure de Meunerie et Industries Céréalières (Higher National School of Milling and the Cereal Industries)
- Ecole Nationale Supérieure des Sciences Agronomiques Appliquées (Higher National School of Applied Agricultural Science)
- Ecole Supérieure d'Application des Corps Gras (Higher School of Shortening)
- Institut d'Etudes Supérieures d'Industrie et d'Economie Laitiére (Institute of Higher Studies of Economics of the Dairy Industry)
- Institut Français du Froid Industriel (French Institute of Industrial Refrigeration)

Veterinary Medicine

Veterinary medicine is offered at four national schools which are classified as *grandes écoles*. They are the Ecole Nationale Vétérinaire de Lyon, Ecole Nationale Vétérinaire de Maisons-Alfort, Ecole Nationale Vétérinaire de Nantes, and the Ecole Nationale Vétérinaire de Toulouse. Admission to veterinary schools requires the completion of a specific one-year *classe préparatoire* and the passing of a common *concours*. The number of spaces at veterinary schools is limited and admission is extremely competitive.

The veterinary medicine program is four years in length. A *Diplôme d'Etat de Docteur Vétérinaire* (State Diploma of Veterinary Doctor) is conferred after the completion of studies and the submission of a thesis. The diploma is awarded by the medical schools of the Universities of Lyon, Nantes and Toulouse, respectively, for the schools of veterinary medicine located in those cities, and by the University of Paris for the school located in Maisons-Alfort. Graduates of schools of veterinary medicine may continue their studies in several fields of specialization offered at two institutions.

The Institut d'Elevage et de Médecine Vétérinaire des Pays Tropicaux (Institute of Tropical Animal Husbandry and Veterinary Medicine) offers several specialities: animal science and economics (one year); microbiology, serology and veterinary hygiene (one year); and veterinary medicine for tropical countries (one year).

The Ecole Nationale des Services Vétérinaires de Maisons-Alfort (National School of Veterinary Services of Maisons-Alfort) offers a two-year training program for state veterinarians and food and animal health inspectors. Admission is by *concours* after the third year of study in veterinary medicine.

Chapter VI

Business Education

Since the 1970's, business education has become increasingly popular among French students. It is presently offered at different institutions with programs varying in length from two years at technical schools, two to five years at universities, and *grandes écoles de commerce et de gestion (grandes écoles* of business administration), and three to four years at other private institutions.

Short (Two-Year) Programs

Two-year programs in business and commerce are offered at *Instituts Universitaires de Technologie*/IUT (University Institutes of Technology), in the *Séctions de Technicien Supérieur*/STS (Higher Technician Section) of selected *lycées* and at private institutions. Programs at IUT lead to the *Diplôme Universitaire de Technologie*/DUT (University Diploma of Technology). The *Brevet de Technicien Supérieur*/BTS (Higher Technician's Certificate) is awarded after the completion of studies in a higher technician section or at a private institution authorized by the Ministy of Education. Programs are offered in accounting, business administration, computer science, marketing, secretarial science, and statistics. (See Chapter III for more information on higher technical education.)

Long Programs

Long programs are offered at *grandes écoles de gestion (grandes écoles* of business) or institutions of similar standing; at other private institutions; and at university and university-affiliated institutions. *Grandes écoles* and institutions which are comparable in status award diplomas endorsed by the Ministry of Education. The remaining institutions award diplomas and certificates which have varying degrees of academic recognition in France. University programs lead to traditional university degrees.

Recognition of Institutions

All business schools which are not affiliated with a university are private. Their recognition by the government, therefore, becomes significant in determining their status. There are two levels of recognition.

The right to award *diplômes revêtus du visa officiel* (diplomas bearing the official seal) is the highest form of recognition that the government can bestow upon a school and its diploma. To become eligible, institutions must have been in existence for five years and have undergone an extensive review by the Ministry of Education. At such institutions, the admissions committee and the final examination jury are chaired by a delegate of the Ministry of Education. Admission to a program leading to a *diplôme visé* (sealed diploma) requires the completion of *classes préparatoires* and a selective entrance examination *(concours)*. The *Diplôme d'Etudes Supérieures Commerciales, Administratives et Financières*/DESCAF (Diploma of Higher Studies in Commerce, Administration and Finance) awarded by the 17 *Ecoles Supérieures de Commerce et d'Administration des Entreprises*/ESCAE or *'Sup de Co'* (Higher Schools of Commerce and Business Administration) requires the completion of four years of study including a one year pre-business program comparable to a *classe préparatoire* and an entrance *concours*. For professional purposes, a *diplôme visé* from a *grande école* of business is regarded as comparable to a *diplôme d'ingénieur* awarded by an engineering school and entitles graduates to apply for admission to the third cycle of university study. See document 6.1a for a sample diploma from the Ecole Supérieure de Commerce de Paris. Document 6.1b is a DESCAF.

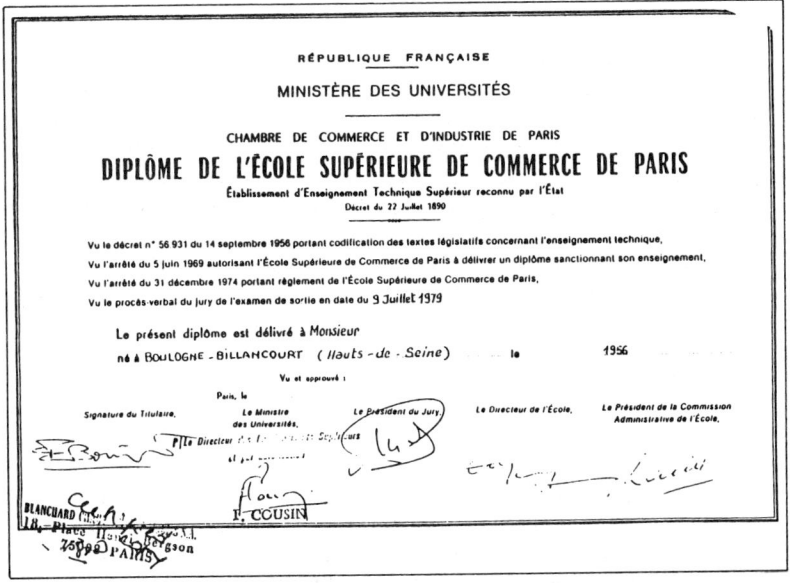

6.1a. Diploma Awarded by the Ecole Supérieure de Commerce de Paris

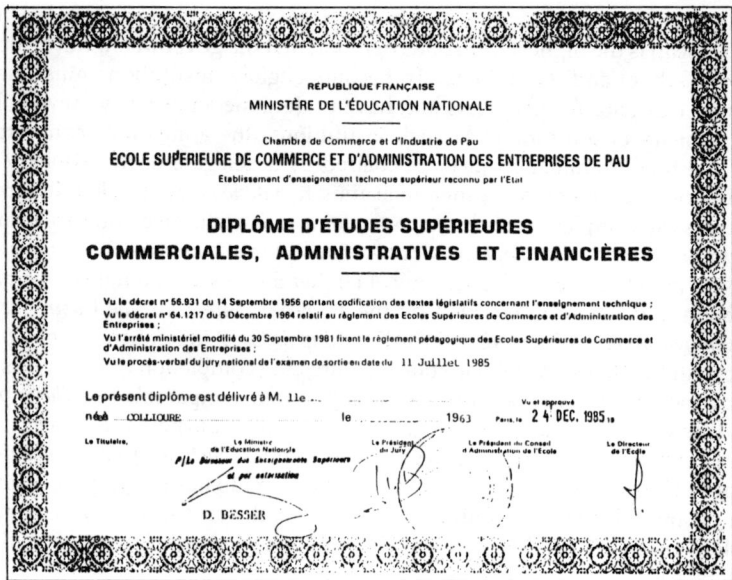

6.1b. *Diplôme d'Etudes Supérieures Commerciales, Administratives et Financières/ DESCAF* Awarded by the ESCAE of Pau

Etablissements reconnus par l'Etat (institutions recognized by the state) refers to private institutions recognized by the government whose diplomas and certificates have not yet been endorsed. An institution is granted recognition after it has been established that it meets the standards for private technical higher education. Application for recognition can be made immediately after an institution has been established, usually as a first step toward the *diplôme visé*. Students attending recognized institutions are eligible for government financial assistance. The diplomas and certificates awarded by these institutions do not grant the same legal rights as a *diplôme visé*. Graduates are eligible for admission to universities in France with possible advanced standing determined on a case-by-case basis by each university.

Credentials

Credentials awarded by nonuniversity business schools do not have a specific name; they are identified as *Diplôme de (name of institution)* or as *Certificat de Fin d'Etudes* (Certificate of Completion). Diplomas and certificates awarded by business schools indicate the legal status of the school. When the diploma is endorsed by the Ministry of Education, the name of the Ministry and its seal appear on the document. When an institution is recognized but the diploma is not endorsed, this factor will also be indicated on the document as *établissement reconnu par l'Etat*. See document 6.2 for a sample *Certificat de Fin d'Etudes* from a recognized institution. Document 6.3 is a bachelor of science in international management from a nonrecognized institution.

Grandes Ecoles

The history and development of *grandes écoles de commerce et de gestion* (*grandes écoles* of business) parallel those of *grandes écoles* of engineering. Business *grandes écoles* were first founded in the nineteenth century by chambers of commerce in response to the needs of the business community for trained managers. Until the 1950's, when universities began offering programs in business, private schools were the sole purveyors of business education in France.

There are three categories of *grandes écoles* of business that award diplomas endorsed by the Ministry of Education. The first category consists of the oldest and most selective institutions: the Ecole des Hautes Etudes Commerciales/HEC (Higher School of Commerce), the Ecole Supérieure des Sciences Economiques et Commerciales/ESSEC (Higher School of Economics and Commerce), the Ecole Supérieure de Commerce de Paris/ESCP (Higher School of Commerce in Paris), and the Ecole Supérieure de Commerce de Lyon/Sup de Co - Lyon (Higher School of Commerce of Lyon). The second category comprises 17 institutions known as *Ecoles Supérieures de Commerce et d'Administration des Entreprises*/ESCAE or *'Sup de Co'* (Higher Schools of Commerce and Business Administration). Finally, the third category consists of several other institutions which also award diplomas endorsed by the Ministry of Education.

Traditional programs are three years in length, preceded by a one-year preparatory class *(classe préparatoire)* and an entrance *concours* (competitive examination). The *classe préparatoire* is offered at selected *lycées* or at private institutions. At the ESCAE, however, it is offered at the business school.

CLASSES PRÉPARATOIRES

Business preparatory classes *(classes préparatoires)* are offered in three tracks: general, economics and technical. The general track is designed for students who hold a scientific (C) *baccalauréat*; the economic track, for students with an economic (B) or a literary (A) *baccalauréat*. The technical track is designed for students holding a technical (G or H) *baccalauréat*. Preparatory classes are one year in length except for the technical track which requires two years and is intended for students whose backgrounds are not as strong in mathematics as those of students in the other tracks. See Table 6.1 for sample preparatory class programs.

6.2. *Certificat de Fin d'Etudes* (Certificate of Completion) Issued by the Institut de Préparation à l'Administration et à la Gestion (Recognized Institution)

6.3. Degree from MBA Institute (Nonrecognized Institution)

BUSINESS EDUCATION

Table 6.1. Classes Préparatoires Programs

Course	Weekly Hours Lectures	Tutorials	Course	Weekly Hours Lectures	Tutorials
General Track			**Technical Track**		
Foreign Language I	3.5	–	*First Year*		
Foreign Language II	2.5	–	Business Methods	3	–
French	2.5	–	Economics	3	–
History & Geography	6	–	Foreign Language I	3	2
Mathematics	7	2	Foreign Language II	4	2
Philosophy	2	–	French	3	–
Physical Education	2	–	Mathematics	7	–
Economics Track			Philosophy	3	–
			Physical Education	2	–
Foreign Language I	3.5	–			
Foreign Language II	2.5	–	*Second Year*		
French	4.5	–	Business Methods	–	2
History & Economic Analysis of Contemporary Societies	6	–	Economics	3	2
			Foreign Language I	3	–
			Foreign Language II	4	–
Mathematics	7	2	French	3	–
Physical Education	2	–	Mathematics	7	2
			Philosophy	3	–
			Physical Education	2	–

ADMISSION TO BUSINESS *GRANDES ECOLES*

Each institution administers its own *concours* based on the curriculum of the *classe préparatoire*. On passing the written examination, students undergo orals which determine their final admission. Out of 2654 candidates who took the 1982 *concours* for admission to the ESSEC, 508 passed the written examination and were eligible for the orals, which only 223 passed. Of the students who were admitted, 222 came from the general track of the *classes préparatoires*, one from the economic track and none from the technical track. Although ESSEC is one of the highly selective institutions, these figures are representative of the admission practices of these institutions. Candidates who plan to enter one of the three major schools of business—Ecole des Hautes Etudes Commerciales/HEC, Ecole Supérieure des Sciences Economiques et Commerciales/ESSEC, or Ecole Supérieure de Commerce de Paris/ESCP—generally spend two years in *classes préparatoires* because of the competitiveness of the entrance examinations. Plans are under consideration to extend the business *classes préparatoires* to two years.

Parallel Admission. A limited number of students who hold a previous university diploma (*maîtrise* or higher), or a diploma from one of the *instituts d'études politiques* (institutes of political studies) are admitted to the second year of a *grande école* of business by passing a special entrance examination. Institutions admit no more than a dozen students through this means. See Table 6.2 for a sample HEC curriculum.

Table 6.2. Sample Program, Ecole des Hautes Etudes Commerciales/HEC

School Profile—The HEC is regarded as the most selective of the French business schools. It was created in 1881 by the business community to train managers in finance and trade. The first year of the three-year curriculum is devoted to basic studies with specialization occuring in the last 2 years. Classes are 80 minutes long and meet twice a week. In addition to classroom instruction, students are required to complete 3 periods of practical training in the summer of the first and second years, and in the second term of the third year. The second internship may be spent abroad.

Since 1973, an international management program has been offered at HEC. Selected students spend the third year of the program at institutions in Canada, Brazil, Japan, the United States, and Western Europe. Each year, 30–35 students participate in the program.

First Year

First Semester	Second Semester
Analytical Accounting	Corporate Law & Finance
Business & Labor Law	Culture & Society
Culture & Society	English (Foreign Language I)
Data Processing & Modelling	Finance
Economics	Foreign Language II
English (Foreign Language I)	Information Systems
Financial Accounting	Marketing
Foreign Language II	Production
Introduction to Business	Statistics

Second Year (Three Terms)

Students take a common core of 8 required subjects, 7 optional subjects chosen from a list of 150, and 3 foreign language courses.

Core Courses	Core Courses (continued)
Advanced Accounting	Human Resources Management
Business Strategy	International Business
Economics	Management Control
Finance	Marketing

Third Year (Three Terms)

The first and last terms are spent on campus and the second term in practical training in a business concern. Students must take 7 or 8 courses in their major and 3 courses in the minor. A common course in "Business Policy" and a research project are also required.

Majors	Minors*
Accounting	Business Strategy
Business Economics	Computerization
Entrepreneurship	Culture & Communication
Finance	Finance
International Business	Geopolitical Considerations
International Fiscal & Legal Strategies	Individual Productivity
International Management Program	International Business
Management Control	Marketing
Marketing	Public Policy

*In lieu of a minor, students have the option of taking the following advanced courses in their major: Accounting, Business Economics, Entrepreneurship, International Business, International Business & Legal Strategies, Marketing.

Other Business Schools

This category refers to institutions which offer three or four-year business programs and award various diplomas and certificates, including some bachelor's and master's degrees. A number of these institutions have achieved the status of *établissements reconnus* (recognized institutions) while others have no recognition by the Ministry of Education (see "Recognition of Institutions" above).

Admission requires the *baccalauréat* and, at some schools, a written or oral entrance test. However, since many institutions already offer two-year programs leading to the *brevet de technicien supérieur*/BTS (higher technician's certificate), their internal diplomas and certificates in business can be earned following one or two years of study beyond the BTS.

Admissions officers in the United States are advised to consider records from such institutions carefully to determine whether the institution has been granted recognition. A detailed syllabus, which includes the number of contact hours for each subject, should be required to properly assess the level and content of each program. Furthermore, as most programs include substantial amounts of practical training, the amount of time spent in classroom instruction can vary a great deal; hence the number of years of study should not be the sole indicator of the amount of work completed. For nonrecognized institutions, a prospectus of the school which includes entrance requirements, faculty, administrative personnel, enrollment, library facilities, etc. should be requested.

Post-*Diplôme* Programs

The *Mastère*

The *mastère* (abbreviated as 'MS') is a new qualification introduced in 1986 and designed to complement the basic training provided at *grandes écoles* of business. The program is offered solely at institutions which award *diplômes visés* and are members of the Conférence des Grandes Ecoles (Association of *Grandes Ecoles*). The *mastère* is a registered trademark *(label)* of the Conférence des Grandes Ecoles. Admission into the program requires a *diplôme* from a *grande école* of business, a *diplôme d'ingénieur* or a DEA awarded by a university. The program consists of 12 months of highly specialized study including 250 hours of classroom work, a 4-6 months' internship and a project. Candidates must also prepare and defend a short thesis. Document 6.4 is a sample *mastère*.

The Master of Business Administration

The Institut Européen d'Administration des Affaires/INSEAD (European Institute of Business Administration), located in Fontainebleau, is a private international business school which offers a one-year program leading to a Master of Business Administration degree. The institution was developed in cooperation with the business school of Harvard University. Admission to INSEAD requires a first university degree (earned after four or more years of study) and at least three years of professional experience. French applicants must hold a *diplôme* from a *grande école* or a university *maîtrise*. The degree awarded by INSEAD is not recognized by the Ministry of Education but the institution is well-regarded and attracts students from all over the world.

6.4. *Mastère* **Awarded by the Centre d'Enseignement et de Recherche Appliqués au Management/CERAM**

University Business Education

Universities have introduced business programs since the 1970's. The *Maîtrise des Sciences de Gestion*/MSG (*Maîtrise* of Management Science), the *Maîtrise d'Informatique Appliquée à la Gestion*/MIAG (*Maîtrise* of Computer Science Applied to Management), the *Maîtrise des Sciences et Techniques*/MST (*Maîtrise* of Science and Technology) and the *Diplôme d'Etudes Supérieures Spécialisées*/DESS (Diploma of Higher Specialized Studies) are the main university qualifications in business. (See Chapter II for details on university degrees.)

Created in the 1950's, *Instituts d'Administration des Entreprises*/IAE (Institutes of Business Administration) are special public institutions which offer programs in business in affiliation with 20 universities. The one-year curriculum leads to a *Certificat d'Aptitude à l'Administration des Entreprises*/CAAE (Certificate of Qualification in Business Administration), which is equivalent to a university DESS. The CAAE is designed for holders of a *maîtrise*, a *diplôme d'ingénieur* or equivalent qualifications. (See Chapter II for details on the DESS.) See document 6.5 for a CAAE awarded by the IAE of Aix-Marseille.

Professional Accounting Programs

French professional accountants bear the title of *expert comptable* (accounting expert), a qualification earned after seven or more years of study. The title is

6.5. *Certificat d'Aptitude à l'Administration des Entreprises*/CAAE **Awarded by the IAE of Aix-Marseille**

awarded by the Ministry of Education after candidates have undergone training, practical experience and national examinations organized in three stages. Although no postsecondary education is required to begin the process, a large majority of the candidates for the *diplôme d'expert comptable* are university graduates or graduates of a *grande école* of business.

STAGE I

Certificat Préparatoire aux Etudes Comptables et Financières/CPECF (Preparatory Certificate for Studies in Accounting and Finance). The certificate is earned by passing five examinations and is designed for holders of the *baccalauréat* who have not had any previous training in accounting. Although no formal studies are required to sit for the CPECF examinations, students usually attend part-time preparatory classes for at least one year.

The subjects are as follows:

1. Law
2. Economics
3. Quantitative Methods (Mathematics and Data Processing)
4. Accounting
5. Communication

STAGE II

Diplôme d'Etudes Comptables Supérieures/DECS (Diploma of Higher Studies in Accounting). The diploma is earned by passing 11 additional examinations organized in two series. To be eligible, candidates must hold either a CPECF, a higher technician's certificate (BTS), or a university diploma of technology (DUT) in business. As for the CPECF, formal studies are not mandated although students participate in preparatory programs lasting from three to five years. The first DECS examination consists of seven subjects and four subjects are required for the second examination. In order to sit for the second series (14, 15 and 16), candidates must have passed all the examinations in the first series or must have been exempted from them. Exemptions are granted on a subject-by-subject basis to graduates of *grandes écoles* and university programs in business. The *maîtrise* of science and technology (MST) with specialization in accounting *(Maîtrise des Sciences et Techniques Comptables et Financières*/MSTCF) is the only qualification which permits candidates to proceed directly to the third stage by granting them full exemption from the DECS. (For a description of the MST, see Chapter II.) See document 6.6 for a sample DECS.

First DECS examination subjects include:

6. Law II (Business and Corporate Law)
7. Law III

8. Economics II
9. Economics III
10. Quantitative Methods
11. Accounting II (Auditing)
12. Accounting III and Management Control

Second DECS examination subjects include:

13. Synthesis of Economics and Accounting
14. Synthesis of Law and Accounting
15. Major Case Study
16. Oral Presentation of a Project (based on practical experience)

STAGE III

Diplôme d'Expert Comptable (Diploma of Accounting Expert). To become eligible for the third and final stage, candidates must hold a DECS or an equivalent. The program consists of three years of professional internship under the supervision of a senior accountant qualified by the Ordre des Comptables (Order of Accountants) to train interns. In the course of their internship, candidates participate in 800 hours of professional seminars each year. The final examination, which consists of three parts, legal and contractual auditing, an oral examination and the defense of a thesis, must be taken at one sitting.

6.6. *Diplôme d'Etudes Comptables Supérieures*

Chapter VII

Teacher Training

Except for elementary school teachers who attend normal schools *(écoles normales)*, the training of teachers in France takes place on-the-job. Prospective secondary school teachers pass comprehensive examinations in their field of specialty but their actual training in pedagogy takes place during the first year of employment and consists of observing experienced teachers and participating in part-time seminars at a *Centre Pédagogique Régional*/CPR (Regional Pedagogical Center). The CPR is not a teaching institution and does not have a fulltime staff. It is a center which coordinates and oversees the practical training of new teachers and assesses their performance. All teachers in France are civil servants. Elementary school teachers are recruited, trained and employed locally. Secondary school teachers are recruited by means of national examinations and may be assigned to teach nationwide.

Elementary School Teacher Training

Until 1986, elementary school teachers were recruited by competitive examination after the *baccalauréat* and underwent two years of training at a normal school *(école normale)*. The professional training offered in the two-year program included French, mathematics and general education, with emphasis on linguistics and modern mathematics. Instruction in art, drawing and physical education was also emphasized. On completion of the program, students were awarded the *Certificat de Fin d'Etudes Normales*/CFEN (Certificate of the Completion of Normal School Studies). The *Certificat d'Aptitude Pédagogiques*/CAP (Certificate of Pedagogical Aptitude) was granted upon demonstration of teaching ability usually during the new teacher's first trimester of teaching. Full teacher status and the title *instituteur* were then granted on January 1 following completion of normal school studies.

In 1986, in an effort to upgrade the qualification of primary school teachers, the entrance requirement to the *école normale* became the *Diplôme d'Etudes Universitaires Générales*/DEUG (Diploma of General University Studies) which represents two years of university study.

Student teachers undergo four semesters of training at an *école normale* that includes eight weeks of practice teaching in the final semester and graduate with a *Diplôme d'Etudes Supérieures d'Instituteur* (Elementary School Teacher Education Diploma). The instruction at *écoles normales* is conducted by experienced teachers who have qualified as *instituteurs maîtres formateurs* (master teachers) by examination, following at least five years of teaching practice. Student teachers are regarded as employees of the state and earn a salary.

The current elementary teacher education curriculum is divided into three main areas of study.

I. Theory and Practice of Education
A. Philosophy (100 hours); History and Sociology of Education (25 hours); General Pedagogy (55 hours); Psychology (70 hours)
B. The Kindergarten (Knowledge of Children from Infancy to 6 or 7 Years, Knowledge of the Kindergarten) (70 hours)
C. Introduction to Student Adjustment and Integration (42 hours)
D. The Schooling of Foreign and Immigrant Children (27 hours)
E. Internship in a Kindergarten (81 hours)
F. Internship in a Primary School (162 hours)
G. Internship in a Lower Secondary School (27 hours)
H. Final Teaching Practice (216 hours)

II. Curricular Studies (including Methodology and Didactics)
A. French (150 hours)
B. Mathematics (135 hours)
C. Science and Technology (Biology - Geology [40 hours], Physics [40 hours], Technology [40 hours], Computer Science [70 hours])
D. History and Geography (100 hours)
E. Civics (20 hours)
F. Physical Education and Sports (100 hours)
G. Music (50 hours)
H. Plastic Arts (50 hours)

III. Administration
A. Knowledge of the Educational System (History, Rules and Regulations, Ethics) (39 hours)
B. Effects of Economic, Social and Cultural Problems on Education (54 hours)
C. Introduction to Continuing and Adult Education (27 hours)
D. Electives (one of the following—Further Study of One of the Subjects of Category I, Foreign Language and Culture, Regional Language and Culture, The Kindergarten) (100 hours)

Special Education Teachers

Teaching of the Handicapped

Teachers and counselors for the educationally handicapped require a *Certificat d'Aptitude à l'Education des Enfants et Adolescents Déficients ou Inadaptés* (Certificate of Qualification to Teach Deficient or Maladjusted Children and Adolescents), a qualification earned by an examination which is open to elementary school teachers who are not older than 45 years and who have had at least two years of teaching experience. The preparation for the examination lasts one year and is conducted at two specialized national centers, Suresnes and Beaumont-sur-Oise, or at *écoles normales* located in provincial capitals. Candidates who are admitted to the program must serve for at least five years after becoming qualified.

Specializations are offered in teaching the hearing-impaired, blind and visually handicapped, physically (motor) handicapped, and those with learning handicaps or behavioral difficulties.

School Psychologists

School psychologists must hold a *Diplôme de Psychologue Scolaire* (Diploma of School Psychologist), a qualification earned by two years of training and open to elementary school teachers who have taught for at least five years and who are not older than 40. Training takes place at five universities: Aix, Besançon, Bordeaux, Grenoble, and Paris. Upon completion of the program, graduates are required to serve for five years.

Vocational Education Teachers

Teachers of vocational subjects in lower secondary programs qualify by a *Certificat d'Aptitude à l'Enseignement dans les Lycées Professionnels*/CAELP (Certificate of Qualification to Teach in Vocational Secondary Schools). They are technicians in their fields and teach practical skills such as carpentry, gardening, hairdressing, etc.

Admission to vocational teacher training programs is by examination for holders of technical qualifications such as a *Diplôme d'Etudes Universitaires Générales*/DEUG (Diploma of General University Studies), *Diplôme Universitaire de Technologie*/DUT (University Diploma of Technology), or a *Brevet de Technicien Supérieur*/BTS (Higher Technician's Certificate) which represent two years of postsecondary education, supplemented by at least two years of work experience.

Student teachers undergo two years of training at an *Ecole Normale Nationale d'Apprentissage*/ENNA (National Normal School of Apprenticeship). Since prospective teachers are already proficient in their technical field, their teacher training consists of pedagogy and practice teaching in a vocational school.

Secondary School Teachers

Lower Secondary School *(Collège)* Teachers

Until 1986, teachers at *collèges* (lower secondary schools) were known as *Professeurs d'Enseignement Général des Collèges*/PEGC (Lower Secondary School

Teachers). Student teachers were recruited regionally by an examination set at the level of the DEUG (two years of university study) and selected candidates underwent three years of further training and internship at regional pedagogical centers to earn a *Certificat d'Aptitude au Professorat de l'Enseignement Général des Collèges*/CAPEGC (Certificate of Qualification for Teaching in Lower Secondary Schools). PEGC were required to teach at least two subjects as follows: French and Art, French and Foreign Languages, French and History/Geography, French and Latin, French and Music, French and Physical Education, Mathematics and Art, Mathematics and Music, Mathematics and Physical Education, Mathematics and Physics, Natural Sciences and Physical Education, Natural Sciences and Physics, and Technical Education and Technology.

In 1986, the PEGC was abolished in order to create a single body of secondary school teachers, all holders of the CAPES (see below).

Upper Secondary School *(Lycée)* Teachers

The *Certificat d'Aptitude au Professorat de l'Enseignement Secondaire*/CAPES (Certificate of Qualification to Teach Secondary Education) is a professional qualification earned by national *concours* which enables its holders to teach in secondary schools. In order to sit for the examination, candidates must hold a *licence d'enseignement* (teaching). The examination itself requires one or more years of further preparation in the discipline. Most candidates do not pass the examination on their first attempt.

The first part of the CAPES examination is dedicated entirely to the subject of specialization. After passing the first part, successful candidates are assigned for one year to a *collège* or a *lycée* as interns under the supervision of a regional pedagogical center. In addition to practice in the classroom, student teachers attend lectures, seminars and pedagogical workshops. In the course of their internship, student teachers are assigned to three different senior teachers, at different levels of secondary education, and spend nine weeks with each one in observation and practice teaching. The comments of supervising teachers constitute an important part of the practical training and are taken into account in the final assessment. At the end of the year of internship, student teachers take the practical part of the CAPES examination which consists of teaching an actual class before an examination panel. Following the class, candidates undergo an oral examination on educational theory. Fully qualified teachers are required to serve for five years.

Students who have passed the first (theory) part of the CAPES may be exempted from the practical part if they wish to teach in private schools, hold a previous PEGC and have taught for at least five years, or have had five years of teaching experience after the *licence*.

The CAPES may be taken in the following disciplines: Art, Classics, Crafts and Home Economics, Economics and Social Sciences, Foreign Languages (German, English, Arabic, Chinese, Spanish, Hebrew, Italian, Portuguese,

Russian), French Language and Literature, History and Geography, Mathematics, Musical Education and Choral Singing, Natural Sciences, Philosophy, and Physical Sciences.

The *Certificat d'Aptitude au Professorat de l'Enseignement Technique*/CAPET (Certificate of Qualification to Teach in Technical Schools) enables its holders to teach technical subjects at *lycées*. The requirements for the CAPET are the same as those of the CAPES. The CAPET is offered in the following disciplines: Biochemistry, Building Technology, Design and Applied Arts, Economic (Business) Science and Techniques, Electrical Technology, Manual and Technical Education, Mechanical Production, and Mechanical Technology.

A *Certificat d'Aptitude au Professorat Technique*/CAPT (Certificate of Qualification of Technical Teacher), not to be confused with the CAPET described above, is required to teach practical subjects at *lycées*. To be admitted to the training program, which is offered at four *Centres de Formation de Professeurs Techniques* (Technical Teacher Training Centers), candidates must hold a DEUG or a higher university degree and pass an entrance *concours*. The certificate is earned following two years of specialized education. The first year of training consists of studies in the chosen field of specialization (allied health, business and commercial subjects, and industrial technology), practical training, and a teaching internship. At the end of the first year, students sit for the first part of the CAPT examination. The second year consists of further education and training in the discipline, supplemented by courses in pedagogy. The final CAPT examination, administered at the end of the second year, consists of teaching a lesson before a panel and an oral examination. Successful candidates become fully qualified and are assigned to a school.

Physical Education Teachers

Physical education teachers are trained at universities. They begin by earning a DEUG in physical education *(sciences et techniques des activités physiques et sportives)* which is followed by a *licence* in the same field. The *licence* calls for 250 hours of theory and 300 hours of physical education practice. With the *licence*, students can either sit for the *concours* for a *Certificat d'Aptitude au Professorat d'Education Physique et Sportive*/CAPEPS (Certificate of Qualification for Teaching Sports and Physical Education) or continue toward a *maîtrise* in order to attempt a recently created *agrégation* in physical education. Upon earning the CAPEPS or the *agrégation*, students are assigned to teach in a *collège* or a *lycée*.

Ecoles Normales Supérieures

The *Écoles Normales Supérieures*/ENS (Higher Normal Schools) were founded early in the nineteenth century to train secondary school teachers. Although their mission has not formally changed, a significant number—close to 50%—of present day graduates end up teaching in institutions of higher education, including universities and *classes préparatoires aux grandes écoles* (preparatory classes for *grandes écoles*). The ENS are *grandes écoles* which offer programs in a variety of literary and scientific disciplines. There are five *écoles normales supérieures*: ENS/Ulm, ENS/Sevres, ENS/Fontenay, ENS/Cachan and the newly established ENS/Lyon.

To enter an ENS, students must complete two years of a *classe préparatoire* and pass a *concours*. Students who wish to study in the literature and humanities section of an ENS complete a special literary *classe préparatoire* while those wishing to study in the science section complete the same *classes préparatoires* as students who are preparing to enter a *grande école* of engineering (see Chapter IV, "Engineering"). The *concours* is administered by each ENS. Since a very limited number of students are admitted each year, competition is very keen. In 1984, ENS/Ulm had spaces for 40 students while 343 sat for the *concours*, and ENS/Sevres, 46 places for 552 candidates. Admission to ENS constitutes completion of a *classe préparatoire* and no diploma or certificate is awarded.

CLASSES PRÉPARATOIRES

Literary *classes préparatoires* offer two-year programs in two main tracks: literature (L) and social sciences (S). The first year is known as *lettres supérieures* and the second, *première supérieure*. The literary track is divided into four sections: Ancient Greek and Latin, Ancient Greek or Latin and Foreign Languages, Literature, and Music. See Table 7.1 for a sample preparatory program in literature.

Table 7.1. Sample *Classe Préparatoire* Program in Literature

First Year *Lettres Superieures* (L)

Subjects	Sections*:	Weekly Hours			
		1	2	3	4
Ancient Greek		4	–	–	–
Foreign Language I		2	4	4	4
Foreign Language II		–	2	2	–
French		5	5	5	5
Geography		2	2	4	–
History		5	5	5	5
Latin		5	5	2	4
Music		–	–	–	6
Philosophy		4	4	4	4
Physical Education		2	2	2	2
	Totals	29	29	28	30

Second Year *Première Supérieure* (L)

Subjects Common to All Students	Hrs.	Electives (one of the following)	Hrs.
Philosophy	6	Ancient Literature	7
French	4	Modern Literature	7
Latin	4	Philosophy (for Ancient Greek Specialists)	7
Contemporary History	4		
Foreign Language I	2	Philosophy (for nonspecialists of Ancient Greek)	5–7
Physical Education	2		
Total	22	History	7
Electives	5–7	Geography	7
Grand Total	27–29	Foreign Languages	6

*1 = Ancient Greek & Latin; 2 = Ancient Greek or Latin & Foreign Languages; 3 = Literature; 4 = Music.

STUDY AT AN ENS

During the first and second year of enrollment at an ENS, students are concurrently enrolled in the second cycle of university studies and earn a *licence* and a *maîtrise,* respectively. In the third year they prepare for the CAPES or the *agrégation* examinations. ENS graduates are exempted from the written part of the CAPES but they must take both the written and oral examinations for the *agrégation* (see below). ENS do not award any diplomas or certificates of their own. Students enrolled at ENS are regarded as civil servants and earn a salary. They are expected to serve for 10 years after completing their studies.

The *Agrégation*

The *agrégation* is the highest national examination *(concours)* for secondary school teachers. *Agrégés* (those who have passed the examination) teach mainly in *lycées* and in *classes préparatoires* but are also eligible to teach at a university. Although the *agrégation* is accessible to holders of the *maîtrise,* a majority of candidates are graduates of an ENS or are teachers who already hold a CAPES or a CAPET. The *agrégation* is also open to graduates of *grandes écoles* of engineering and to holders of a *doctorat* provided that they are not older than 40.

The *agrégation* is offered in the following disciplines: Biochemistry and Biological Engineering, Civil Engineering, Classics, Economics and Business (economics and accounting option, economics and administration option), Electrical Engineering, Foreign Languages (Arabic, English, German, Hebrew, Italian, Polish, Portuguese, Russian, Spanish), French Literature, Geography,

Grammar (French), History, Mathematics, Mechanical Engineering, Mechanics, Music Education and Choral Singing, Natural Sciences (biology option, earth sciences option), Philosophy, Physics (applied physics option, chemistry option, or physics option), Plastic Arts, Social Sciences, and Sports and Physical Education.

The examination consists of two parts: theory and practice. The first part is devoted entirely to the discipline. The practical part takes place after the candidate has spent one year in training at a regional pedagogical center and consists of teaching two classes before a panel of examiners, followed by an interview on pedagogical questions. Candidates who previously held a CAPES are exempted from the practical examination.

As a qualification, the *agrégation* is not easy to categorize. For many candidates, passing the examination is a very difficult undertaking which requires several years of preparation and as many attempts. The *agrégation* is a comprehensive examination designed to demonstrate the candidate's full command of a particular field, including familiarity with the relevant literature. The examination program is published annually by the Ministry of Education and, although special preparatory classes are offered by universities, candidates must study independently. The Ministry of Education determines in advance the number of *agrégé* positions that are available in any given year in each discipline. While the overall rate of success on the *agrégation* has been in the 5% to 8% range, ENS students constitute 50% to 60% of those who pass the examination. *Agrégés* must serve for five years.

Chapter VIII

Health and Social Education

Medical Studies

Programs in medicine, dentistry and pharmacy are offered at major universities. Medicine is offered at 33 universities, dentistry at 15 universities, and pharmacy at 24 universities. Admission to medical programs requires a scientific *baccalauréat*. The *Diplôme d'Etat de Docteur en Médecine* (State Diploma of Doctor of Medicine), *Diplôme d'Etat de Docteur en Chirurgie Dentaire* (State Diploma of Dental Surgery) and the *Diplôme d'Etat de Docteur en Pharmacie* (State Diploma of Doctor of Pharmacy) grant the right to practice the profession in France. Students who are not French citizens follow the same programs as French students but cannot be awarded the *Diplôme d'Etat*. They graduate with university diplomas *(diplômes d'université)* which are academically equivalent but do not permit them to practice in France. In 1982-83, the enrollment in medicine totalled 136,171; in pharmacy, 37,645; and in dentistry, 11,375.

Medicine (8-11 Years)

A *Diplôme d'Etat de Docteur en Médecine* is required to practice medicine in France. Medical education, which lasts eight to eleven years, is divided into three cycles.

FIRST CYCLE—2 YEARS

The first cycle of medicine is known as the *premier cycle des études médicales/* PCEM. The program covers basic and biological sciences including anatomy, biochemistry, biology, biophysics, chemistry, cytology, embryology, histology, mathematics, physics, physiology, psychology, and social sciences. The first year of PCEM (PCEM 1) ends with a *concours* (competitive examination) and may be repeated only once. The number of students who will pass the examination in each medical school is determined in advance by the Ministry of Health. In making the determination, the Ministry takes into consideration such factors as the number of physicians that are required in the nation, and the availability of hospital teaching facilities.

SECOND CYCLE—4 YEARS

The second cycle, *deuxième cycle d'études médicales*/DCEM, is divided into two parts. The first part (DCEM 1) is one year long and is devoted to pre-clinical studies in basic clinical medicine, medical semiology, pathological anatomy, and pharmacology. Students also begin clinical work on a part-time basis. The second part of the cycle corresponds to years 2, 3 and 4 (DCEM 2, DCEM 3, DCEM 4). In this stage, students spend half their time in clinical training and study pathology and therapeutics. The second cycle ends with an examination which leads to an interim qualification, the *Certificat de Synthèse Clinique et Thérapeutique* (Certificate of Clinical and Therapeutic Synthesis).

THIRD CYCLE—2-5 YEARS

The third cycle begins with a common first semester (six months) at the end of which students must declare a medical speciality. Admission to all specialities requires the passing of a national *concours d'internat de spécialité* (speciality internship examination). Those who pass the *concours* may continue their studies in their chosen field. Students who do not pass the *concours* and those who have chosen not to sit for it continue their studies in general medicine. Three major tracks are available: medical specialities and surgery, medical research, and public health. The *concours*, although national, is administered in seven regional examinations. Students may sit for three regional examinations to improve their chances for success. Upon passing the *concours*, students enroll in a program of specialized training which includes classroom instruction and clinical internship except for the medical research track.

General Medicine. This is the only area of medicine that is not regarded as a speciality and does not require the *concours d'internat.* The third cycle program in general medicine lasts two years. The majority of students, including those who were not successful on the *concours d'internat,* enroll in general medicine.

Medical Specialities and Surgery. The training in medical specialities and surgery lasts four to five years. In the course of the program students pass a series of examinations in required areas specific to each speciality and earn *Diplômes d'Etudes Spécialisées*/DES (diplomas of specialized studies). The final *Diplôme d'Etat de Docteur en Médecine* is awarded upon fulfillment of all requirements including all DES, clinical internships and the submission and defense of a thesis. Physicians have the option of earning a *Diplôme d'Enseignement Spécialisé Complémentaire* (Diploma of Complementary Specialized Education) after one further year of specialization.

Medical Research. This program consists of four years of research in a laboratory with no clinical internship. A *diplôme d'études approfondies*/DEA is awarded after the second year and a *Diplôme d'Etat de Docteur en Médecine, Mention Recherche Médicale,* by dissertation, after two further years.

Public Health. The public health track is four years long. Students may opt for community health or occupational medicine as their major field.

Dentistry (5 Years)

The program in dentistry lasts five years and leads to the *Diplôme d'Etat de Docteur en Chirurgie Dentaire* (State Diploma of Doctor of Dental Surgery). The program is divided into three cycles.

FIRST CYCLE—1 YEAR

The first year is common with the first year of medicine (PCEM 1). Students sit for the *concours* at the end of the year and are admitted to dental programs in accordance with their rank on the examination.

SECOND CYCLE—4 YEARS

The second cycle consists of professional education in dentistry and dental surgery, including clinical practice. Promotion from year to year requires the passing of two sets of examinations each year. The *Diplôme d'État de Docteur en Chirurgie Dentaire* is awarded at the end of the program.

THIRD CYCLE—3 YEARS

The third cycle is optional and is reserved for students who wish to specialize in orthodontics. They are awarded a *Certificat d'Etudes Spéciales, Mention Orthodontie* (Certificate of Special Studies, Orthodontics Option) after three years of study.

Pharmacy (5 Years)

The program in pharmacy lasts five years and leads to the *Diplôme d'Etat de Docteur en Pharmacie* (State Diploma of Doctor of Pharmacy). Although the current program is five years long, a reform extending it to six years is being introduced.

Promotion from the first to the second year is by *concours*. *Numerus clausus* limits the number of second year openings that are available. The first three years of study are common for all students. The first year consists of courses in anatomy, biophysics, botany, cell biology, general physical chemistry, genetics, human embryology, introduction to pharmacy, mathematics, organic chemistry, physics, physiology, and statistics. In the second year courses in plant and molecular biology and parasitology are added to the curriculum. In the third year students begin courses in biopharmacy, molecular pharmacy, pharmacology, etc. In the fourth year students declare a major: industrial pharmacy, pharmacy practice, or research. The fifth year is devoted to studies in the major and ends with the award of the *Diplôme d'Etat de Docteur en Pharmacie*.

SPECIALIZATION (RESEARCH)

To be admitted to the research track, candidates must take an admission *concours* in the fourth year as there are very few openings in this area. Programs are available in three tracks: biological sciences, medical research, and specialized pharmacy. Each track leads to a *Diplôme d'Etudes Spécialisées*/DES (diploma of specialized studies). The DES requires a thesis which must be defended before a jury. On graduation, students earn a DES and a *Diplôme d'Etat de Docteur en Pharmacie*.

Paramedical Education

Education in paramedical professions is offered mostly at special schools which are controlled by the Ministry of Health. A limited number of programs are available at medical schools, university institutes of technology and at private institutions authorized by the government to offer programs leading to state diplomas in health sciences. Programs generally last from two to three years and generally lead to a state diploma (*diplôme d'Etat*).

University Paramedical Education

AUDIOPROSTHESIS—2 YEARS

Audioprosthesists are trained in two-year programs offered by schools of medicine or schools of pharmacy. Training leads to a *Diplôme d'Etat d'Audioprothesiste* (State Diploma of Audioprosthesist). Admission requires the *baccalauréat*.

MIDWIFERY—4 YEARS

In France, midwifery is classified as a medical profession and is offered at specialized schools of midwifery which operate under the auspices of the Ministry of Health. Admission to midwifery programs requires the *baccalauréat* and the passing of an entrance *concours*. Training in midwifery has been open to men since 1982. The program, which had been three years long until 1985, has since been extended to four years. Students enrolled before the 1985-86 academic year will graduate from the former three-year program. The first year consists of courses in anatomy, dietetics, legislation, medical and obstetric pathology, pediatrics, and physiology, as well as an internship in a hospital. The second, third and fourth years are devoted to courses specific to midwifery and to clinical practice including child care, gynecology, obstetrics, and pediatrics. A *Diplôme d'Etat de Sage-Femme* (State Diploma of Midwife) is awarded.

SPEECH THERAPY—3 YEARS

Speech therapy is offered at 12 university medical schools. The program is three years long and leads to a *Certificat de Capacité d'Orthophoniste* (Certificate of Qualification of Speech Therapist) which is recognized by the state. Admission requires the *baccalauréat* and an entrance examination. Most candidates, however, are university graduates who hold various qualifications in science or in psychology. See document 8.1 for a Certificate of Qualification of Speech Therapist.

Nonuniversity Paramedical Education

Since 1984-85, admission to programs in medical laboratory technology, nursing, occupational therapy, physical therapy, chiropody, and x-ray technology is by a *baccalauréat*-level common entrance *concours* open to students who have completed the *terminale* (final year of *lycée*) and who are at least 17 years old. Although students may indicate the program they wish to follow, their placement is determined by the results obtained on the *concours*. Those who earn the highest grades are eligible for schools of physical therapy and the lowest, for nursing.

8.1. Certificate of Qualification of Speech Therapist Awarded by the University of Paris VI

MEDICAL LABORATORY TECHNOLOGY—2 YEARS

Medical laboratory technologists are trained through different educational programs:

The *Diplôme d'Etat de Laborantin d'Analyses Médicales* (State Diploma of Medical Laboratory Analyst) is earned in two years, including two months of clinical practice, in hospital schools and in schools recognized by the Ministry of Health. Admission is by the common entrance examination for paramedical professions (see above). The program includes courses in bacteriology, cytology, hematology, hemostasis, histology, human anatomy and physiology, immunology, mathematics, mycology, parasitology, pathology, physics and chemistry, technology, and virology.

A medical laboratory technologist can also qualify through a *Brevet de Technicien Supérieur d'Analyses Biologiques*/BTS (Higher Technician's Certificate of Biological Analysis) two years after the *baccalauréat* or a *Diplôme Universitaire de Technologie de Biologie Appliquée*/DUT (University Diploma in Technology of Applied Biology) two years after the *baccalauréat*. (See Chapter III for more information on the BTS and DUT programs.)

NURSING—3 YEARS

Training in nursing is offered at public and private schools of nursing. The training program is 33 months long and includes approximately 2200 hours of clinical practice (see Table 8.1 for a sample nursing program). It leads to a *Diplôme d'Etat d'Infirmier* (State Diploma of Nurse). The first year is 36 weeks

Table 8.1. Sample Program in Nursing

General Program	Hours	Clinical Practice	Hours
Introduction		Basic Care	128
Health & Hygiene	38	Geriatric	40
Methodology	30	Maternal Care	40
The Profession	48	Medicine/Surgery	1024
Nursing Subjects		Pediatric	240
		Psychiatry/Mental Health	96
Geriatric Nursing	44	Fulltime Practice	584
Medical & Surgical Nursing	543		
Nursing	359	Total:	2152
Obstetric & Pediatric Nursing	169		
Psychiatry & Mental Health	47		
Synthesis	50		
Total:	1328		
Review	106		
Grand Total:	1434		

long and consists of an introduction to the profession and four weeks of fulltime clinical practice. The second and third years are organized in seven segments of 10 weeks each. During the same period, three periods of clinical internship of four weeks each must be completed. The *diplôme* is awarded by external examination. See document 8.2 for a State Diploma of Nurse.

Specialization

After three years of practice with a *diplôme d'Etat*, nurses may undertake programs of specialization in anesthesia (two years), pediatrics (nine months), and surgical nursing (nine months), leading to *certificats d'aptitude* (certificates of qualification) in the respective fields.

Psychiatric Nursing

The training of psychiatric nurses is not part of general nursing. The *Diplôme d'Etat d'Infirmier de Secteur Psychiatrique* (State Diploma of Psychiatric Nurse) is awarded following 33 months of training in centers affiliated with psychiatric hospitals. Admission is by an examination from which holders of the *baccalauréat* and persons who have completed a *terminale* (final year of secondary education) are exempted. The first year of the training program is identical with that of general nursing. The next two years are spent in practical training in mental institutions.

8.2. State Diploma of Nurse

OCCUPATIONAL THERAPY—3 YEARS

The *Diplôme d'Etat d'Ergothérapeute* (State Diploma of Occupational Therapist) is earned after a three-year program offered at special schools of occupational therapy. Admission is by the common entrance examination for paramedical professions. The program has theoretical, practical and clinical components. The courses include anatomy, communication techniques, medical and surgical pathology, physiology, psychology and psychiatry, and practical courses in arts and crafts. A total of 1440 hours of clinical practice (nine months fulltime) is included in the curriculum.

PHYSICAL THERAPY—3 YEARS

Training in physical therapy is offered at private and public schools. Admission is by the common entrance examination for paramedical professions. The program leads to a *Diplôme d'Etat de Masseur Kinésithérapeute* (State Diploma of Masseur and Kinesitherapist). A sample program in physical therapy is presented in Table 8.2. See document 8.3 for a State Diploma of Masseur-Kinesitherapist.

Table 8.2. Sample Physical Therapy Program

First Year	Hours	Third Year	Hours
Active Kinesitherapy	90	Cardiovascular Diseases	25
Anatomy, Morphology		Deontology (Ethics)	5
& Physiology	200	Ergotherapy	5
Biology & Physiology	50	Labor Legislation	10
First Aid	20	Legislation	15
Hygiene	20	Medicine & Surgery	20
Introduction	10	Morphology	10
Introductory Workshop	60	Obstetrics	5
Massage	90	Physical & Mentally Handicapped	15
Medical Pathology	25	Physical Agents	30
Passive Kinesitherapy	60	Physical Education	28
Physical Education	44	Prosthetics/Orthotics	30
Sports Techniques	66	Psychology of Rehabilitation	20
Surgical Pathology	25	Respiratory Diseases	40
Discussions	44	Special Techniques	30
		Discussions & Tests	72
Total:	949		
		Total:	362
Second Year	Hours	**Clinical Education** (5 half-days/week)	
Anatomy & Physiology	60	*First Year*	Months
Neurology & Muscular		Introduction to	
Diseases	100	Physical Therapy	1
Psychology	20		
Rheumatism	80		
Sport	64		

Second Year (continued)	Hours	Clinical Education (continued)	
Trauma & Orthopedics	140	Second Year	Months
Discussion & Tests	64	Adult Surgery	3
		Medicine & Rheumatology	3
		Pediatric Surgery	3
		Third Year	
		Cardiovascular Diseases	2
		Fulltime Training	2
		Neurology	4
		Total:	18

CHIROPODY—2 YEARS

Training in chiropody is offered at institutions recognized by the Ministry of Health. Admission is by the common entrance examination for paramedical professions. The program is two years in length and is largely practical. It leads to a *Diplôme d'Etat de Pédicure* (State Diploma of Chiropodist).

RADIOLOGY—2 YEARS

Training in radiology (x-ray technology) takes place at institutions affiliated with university hospitals. Admission is by the common entrance examination for paramedical professions. The program is two years in length and leads to a *Diplôme d'Etat de Manipulateur d'Electro-Radiologie* (State Diploma of Electro-Radiology Operator). The first year of the program consists of instruction in administration, anatomy, deontology, electricity, law, medicine, physiology, radiation physics, and surgery. The second year is devoted to the study of radiology and to practical training in a hospital. Radiologists can also qualify by way of a *brevet de technicien supérieur*/BTS (higher technician's certificate) in radiology. See Chapter III for more information on the BTS program.

REHABILITATION COUNSELORS

Rehabilitation counselors *(psychomotriciens)* work, under the supervision of a physician, with persons afflicted with psychological problems. They are recruited by the common entrance examination for paramedical professions with the stipulation that the *baccalauréat* is a requirement for this particular program. Their training, which lasts three years, takes place at medical schools and at recognized private institutions and leads to a *Diplôme d'Etat de Psychomotricien*. The program consists of courses in anatomy, child psychology, pedagogy, physiology, psychology, and rehabilitation. Students also undergo clinical education in hospitals and must prepare a thesis for graduation.

8.3. State Diploma of Masseur-Kinesitherapist

Social Professions

The education and training of social and community workers and child care workers takes place at university and nonuniversity institutions in programs lasting two to three years.

Social Work

A *Diplôme d'Etat d'Assistant de Service Social* (State Diploma of Social Service Assistant) is awarded after three years of training offered at schools of social work which operate under the Ministry of Social Affairs. Admission requires the *baccalauréat* although mature adults may be admitted if they have had five years of relevant work experience. All applicants must submit to a two-stage entrance examination designed to determine their maturity and fitness for the profession. The first stage is administered by regional health authorities and the second stage by each institution.

Social work education is also available at the university institutes of technology. In addition to the *baccalauréat*, admission to such programs requires candidates to pass the entrance examination for schools of social work. Students earn a first cycle university degree (DEUG) after two years and a *Diplôme d'État d'Assistant de Service Social* (State Diploma of Social Service Assistant) following one additional year of study. The program includes 1400 hours of instruction distributed into six teaching units including 160 hours each in social action in institutional settings, human relations, social environment and social economics, health and health education, and public health protection; and 400 hours in the theory and practice of social service. An additional 200 hours are devoted to courses specific to each institution.

FURTHER EDUCATION IN SOCIAL WORK

Nine universities (Angers, Caen, Limoges, Paris XII, Pau, Rennes, Saint Etienne, Strasbourg and Toulouse) offer three-year part-time continuing education programs for qualified social workers who have had five years of professional experience. Programs lead to a *Diplôme Supérieur en Travail Social* (Higher Diploma in Social Work) or to a *Maîtrise de Sciences Sociales Appliquées au Travail* (*Maîtrise* of Social Sciences Applied to Labor) after a total of approximately 500 hours of study.

Social and Cultural Organizers

Social and cultural organizers develop and coordinate cultural, educational and social activities in community organizations. They work with senior citizens, immigrants, prisoners, etc. There are various types of training programs offered at university and nonuniversity institutions.

The *Diplôme d'Etat Relatif aux Fonctions d'Animation* (State Diploma of Coordinator of Social Activities) is awarded jointly by the Ministry of Youth and Sports and the Ministry of Health after three years of professional experience to persons who have been working in the field. This is not an academic diploma. Social organizers can also qualify by way of a *Diplôme Universitaire de Technologie, Option Animation Culturelle*/DUT (University Diploma of Technology, Cultural Events Coordination Option) which is earned by two years of study at a university institute of technology or by university degrees including the DEUG, DEUST, *licence* and *maîtrise* in cultural and social disciplines. (See Chapters II and III for further information on these degrees.)

Child Care Workers

A *Diplôme d'Etat d'Educateur Spécialisé* (State Diploma of Special Educator) is required to work with emotionally, mentally and physically handicapped youth. Special educators are trained at special schools under the Ministry of Social Affairs. Although most teachers are trained on a part-time basis while they are employed, some follow fulltime programs. Fulltime programs are three years in length and part-time programs are four years long. Admission to both requires the completion of secondary education even though the *baccalauréat* is not required. All applicants must have had experience in teaching or in a related field. The program is divided evenly between theory and practical training.

A *Diplôme d'Etat d'Educateur de Jeunes Enfants* (State Diploma of Teacher of Young Children) is awarded after two years of training at schools which operate under the Ministry of Social Affairs. Admission to training programs for kindergarten teachers and day care workers requires the completion of secondary education (although the *baccalauréat* is not required) and an entrance examination. The two-year curriculum includes 36 weeks of practical training.

Chapter IX

Architecture, Art, Music, Drama

Architecture

Architectural education is offered at 24 public institutions. The 23 schools of architecture *(écoles d'architecture)* which were formerly known as *unités pédagogiques d'architecture*/UPA (architectural teaching units) operate under the joint control of the Ministry of Housing and Urban Affairs and the Ministry of Education. Two other institutions, one private and one public, also offer recognized programs in architecture: Ecole Spéciale d'Architecture (Paris) (Special School of Architecture) and Ecole Nationale Supérieure des Arts et Industries de Strasbourg (Higher National School of Arts and Crafts of Strasbourg). All diplomas in architecture permit professional practice by registration with the Ordre des Architectes (Order of Architects).

To be admitted to a program in architecture, students must hold a scientific *baccalauréat* except for the Ecole Nationale Supérieure des Arts et Industries de Strasbourg which, in addition, requires the completion of the first year of a *classe préparatoire aux grandes écoles*. (See Chapter IV, "Engineering" for more information on *classes préparatoires*.) Until 1984, architectural programs were six years in length divided into three two-year cycles.

Schools of Architecture *(Ecoles d'Architecture)*

Beginning with the 1984-85 academic year, the program at the 23 public *écoles d'architecture* was restructured and is now five years in length, divided into two cycles. The curriculum is organized in terms of *certificats* (certificates). In this case, a *certificat* is not a credential but identifies a component of the program and represents a given quantity of instruction or practical work.

The first cycle, which is two years in length, is devoted to introductory studies. It leads to a *Diplôme d'Etudes Fondamentales en Architecture*/DEFA (Diploma of Foundation Studies in Architecture), a qualification which has the same academic standing as a first cycle university degree (DEUG) and is awarded jointly by the Ministry of Education and the Ministry of Housing and Urban Affairs. (See Chapter II for more information on university programs.) In the first cycle of architectural programs, students are expected to learn basic natural and social sciences which will serve as the foundation for further study in architecture or in other fields, should they wish to continue their studies at a university. The program consists of eight *certificats* which represent a combined total of 1000 hours of instruction.

The second cycle, which is three years long, culminates in a *Diplôme d'Architecte Diplômé par le Gouvernement*/DPLG (Government Diploma of Architect) awarded by the Ministry of Housing and Urban Affairs. Admission requires a foundation diploma. By law, the program must consist of at least 12 *certificats* covering the subjects listed below in Table 9.1 and includes supervised practical experience. Each *certificat* represents 150-200 hours of instruction. In developing curricula, institutions must adhere to the mandated subjects and hours although individual programs may be structured in terms of semester- or year-long courses. Students cannot take more than five *certificats* in a single 32-week academic year. In addition to courses mandated by law, institutions may offer their own courses.

Table 9.1. Second Cycle Curriculum, *Ecoles d'Architecture*

Subject	Total Hours
Architectural & Urban Law	50
Art History	25
Building & Construction Economics	70
Building Renovation	65
Data Processing	50
Drawing & Modelling	100
Ecology & Landscape	30
Environmental Management	60
Foreign Language	25
History of Architecture	25
History of Cities	40
Knowledge of Production Techniques	60
Orientation to Professional Practice: Regulations, Management, Budget Accounting	30
Structures	60
Supervision & Work Organization	30
Technical Planning & Materials	100
Theory & Practice in Urban Studies	40
Theory of Architecture	40
Urban Economics	50
Urban Sociology	50
Practical Experience & Project	400

See document 9.1 for a provisional certificate of the Diploma of Architect. The public schools of architecture *(ecoles d'architecture)* are as follows:

Ecole d'Architecture de Bordeaux
Ecole d'Architecture de Clermont-Ferrand
Ecole d'Architecture de Grenoble
Ecole d'Architecture de Lille

ARCHITECTURE, ART, MUSIC, DRAMA

Ecole d'Architecture de Lyon
Ecole d'Architecture de Marseille
Ecole d'Architecure de Montpellier
Ecole d'Architecture de Nancy
Ecole d'Architecture de Nantes
Ecole d'Architecture No.1 (Paris-Villemin)
Ecole d'Architecture No.2 (Paris-Nanterre)
Ecole d'Architecture No.3 (Versailles)
Ecole d'Architecture No.4 (Paris-Conflans)
Ecole d'Architecture No.5 (Paris-la Defense)
Ecole d'Architecture No.6 (Paris-La Villette)
Ecole d'Architecture No.7 (Paris-Tolbiac)
Ecole d'Architecture No.8 (Paris-Belleville)
Ecole d'Architecture No.9 (Paris-la Seine)
Ecole d'Architecture de Rennes
Ecole d'Architecture de Rouen
Ecole d'Architecture de Saint-Etienne
Ecole d'Architecture de Strasbourg
Ecole d'Architecture de Toulouse

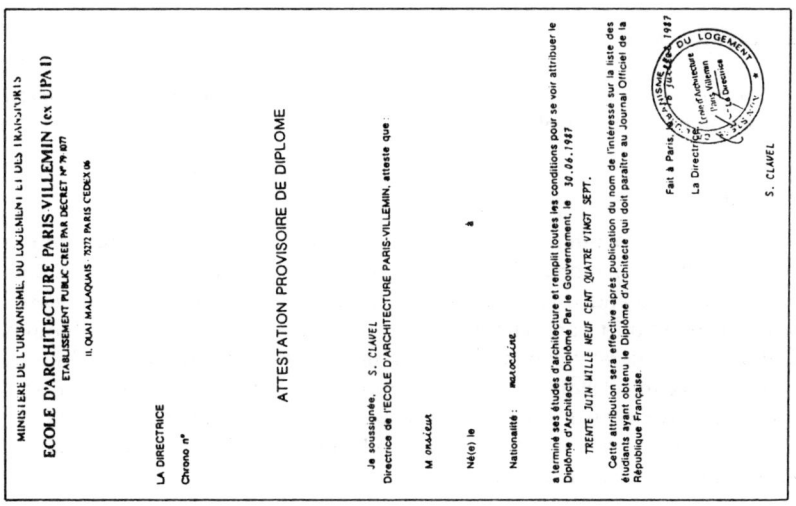

9.1. Provisional Certificate of Diploma of Architect Awarded by the Ecole d'Architecture Paris-Villemin

Other Institutions

The Ecole Spéciale d'Architecture/ESA (Special School of Architecture) (Paris) is a recognized private institution offering a five-year program which leads to the *Diplôme de l'Ecole Spéciale d'Architecture* (Diploma of the Special School of Architecture).

The Ecole Nationale Supérieure des Arts et Industries de Strasbourg/ENSAIS (Higher National School of Art and Crafts of Strasbourg) offers a four-year program which leads to the *Diplôme d'Architecte de l'Ecole Nationale Supérieure des Arts et Industries de Strasbourg* (Diploma of Architect of the Higher National School of Arts and Crafts of Strasbourg). Admission requires the completion of the first year of a *classe préparatoire aux grandes écoles*.

Further Education

Since 1983, architectural schools have instituted post-*diplôme* certificates known as *Certificat d'Etudes Approfondies d'Architecture* (Certificate of Advanced Studies in Architecture). The content and length of each program range from one to two years. Under the 1984 reform, architectural schools may also offer programs in conjunction with universities. Such programs lead to a *diplôme d'études approfondies*/DEA, a *diplôme d'études supérieures spécialisées*/DESS or a *diplôme universitaire*/DU. (See Chapter II for more information on these diplomas.) All university programs are offered in the third cycle.

Art Education

Art education is divided into two broad categories: studio arts *(arts plastiques)* and graphic arts *(arts appliqués)*.

Studio Arts

Schools of art, operated by the Ministry of Culture, are divided into three categories: higher national schools *(écoles nationales supérieures)*, national schools *(écoles nationales)* and regional or municipal schools *(écoles régionales ou municipales)*. Admission to art schools is by examination and portfolio. Although students are generally expected to have reached the level of the *baccalauréat*, talent and technical skill are the most important considerations. Regional and municipal schools award national diplomas endorsed by the Ministry of Culture. The higher national art schools, all located in Paris, award national diplomas specific to each institution.

HIGHER NATIONAL INSTITUTIONS

The Ecole Nationale Supérieure des Beaux Arts/ENSBA (Higher National School of Fine Arts), commonly referred to as Beaux Arts, is the principal school of fine art in France. ENSBA awards a *Diplôme Supérieur d'Arts Plastiques* (Higher Diploma of Studio Arts). Admission is by portfolio and examination for students between 18 and 26 years. Candidates who hold a five-year *diplôme national supérieur d'expression plastique* (higher national diploma of artistic expression) from a regional or municipal school or a final diploma from a four-year graphic art program (see below) are exempted from the entrance examination. The curriculum is organized in studios specific to each discipline (painting, sculpture, etc.) and takes five years or longer to complete. Courses in general education and science are also included in the program. The final diploma, which must be earned before age 31, requires that candidates present a collection of their work to a jury.

The Ecole Nationale Supérieure des Arts Décoratifs/ENSAD (Higher National School of Decorative Arts), also known as Arts Deco, is an institution with multiple programs in art and design. The *Diplôme de l'Ecole Nationale Supérieure des Arts Décoratifs* (Diploma of the Higher National School of Decorative Arts) is the final award. Admission is by a competitive entrance examination for candidates between 17 and 25 years. Although the *baccalauréat* is not required, the majority of the students who are admitted hold the diploma. More than half have either earned a two-year first cycle university degree (DEUG) or have completed a preparatory program in other art schools. Students who hold the *baccalauréat* or a one-year *certificat d'initiation plastique* (elementary certificate in studio art) from a regional or municipal school are admitted into the first year.

Graduates of regional and municipal schools who hold a four-year *diplôme national d'arts et techniques*/DNAT (national diploma of arts and crafts) are admitted into the second year. Students with a five-year *diplôme national supérieur d'expression plastique* (higher national diploma of artistic expression) are admitted into the third year.

The program at Arts Deco is four years in length and is organized in two stages of two years each. The first stage of the program is common for all beginning students. The second stage is divided into several sections: cinema, studio arts, industrial design, interior architecture, photography, stage design, textile design, and visual communication.

The Ecole Nationale Supérieure de Création Industrielle/ENSCI (Higher National School of Industrial Design) was founded in 1982 to train industrial designers. The institution operates under the joint control of the Ministry of Culture and the Ministry of Industry. The *Diplôme de l'Ecole Nationale Supérieure de Création Industrielle* (Diploma of the Higher National School of Industrial Design) is awarded upon the completion of studies in programs lasting from one to five years, depending on entrance qualifications. *Baccalauréat* holders are admitted to the five-year curriculum. Applicants who hold a two-year first cycle university degree (DEUG) or an equivalent are admitted into the third year. Holders of a *maîtrise* or a higher qualification are admitted into the fourth year. All admission is determined by competitive entrance examination.

NATIONAL, REGIONAL AND MUNICIPAL INSTITUTIONS

There are eight national schools and 48 regional and municipal schools located throughout France. Studies completed at these institutions lead in three or five years to national diplomas awarded by the Ministry of Culture.

The *Diplôme National d'Arts et Techniques*/DNAT (National Diploma of Arts and Crafts) is awarded after a three-year program at a regional or municipal art school. The first year is common with that offered in five-year programs and is a probationary year. Upon its completion, students' progress is reviewed by a panel which determines whether they have the talent and skills required to continue in the program. In the second and third years, programs are offered in graphic art and design.

The *Diplôme National Supérieur d'Expression Plastique*/DNSEP (Higher National Diploma of Artistic Expression) is awarded by regional and municipal art schools after five years of study, divided into two stages. The first stage is common for all students and leads in two years to a *Certificat d'Initiation Plastique* (Elementary Certificate in Studio Art). The second stage lasts three years and may be taken in one of three sections: environmental design, studio arts, and visual and audiovisual communications.

OTHER INSTITUTIONS

Many private schools offer postsecondary education in art. Each school sets its own entrance requirements and awards credentials after programs of varying length. Students enroll in private art schools to prepare for the entrance *concours* to higher national art schools.

Some of the major private institutions include the following:

Académie Charpentier (1-2 years)
Ecole Camondo (5 years)
Ecole des Métiers de l'Image (1-2 years)
Ecole Privée de l'Union Centrale des Arts Décoratifs (4 years)
Ecole Supérieure d'Arts Graphiques/ESAG (3 years)
Ecole Supérieure des Arts Modernes (3 years)

Graphic Art

Graphic art is taught at four institutions located in Paris. Admission requires the *baccalauréat* (F-12). Students who hold another *baccalauréat* must complete a one-year preparatory program offered at the art school. Schools of graphic art offer two-year programs leading to the *brevet de technicien supérieur*/BTS (Higher Technician's Certificate) (see Chapter III for a description of the BTS). The *Diplôme Supérieur d'Arts Appliqués* (Higher Diploma of Graphic Art) is awarded following one year of study beyond the BTS. Since 1986, the same diploma requires two years of study after the BTS. Located in Paris, the schools of graphic art are as follows:

Ecole Supérieure d'Arts Appliqués aux Industries de l'Ameublement et de l'Architecture Interieure (Higher School of Art Applied to Furniture and Interior Architecture)

Ecole Supérieure d'Arts Appliqués Duperré (Duperré Higher School of Graphic Art)
Ecole Supérieure d'Arts et Industries Graphiques Estienne (Estienne Higher School of Graphic Arts and Crafts)
Ecole Municipale Supérieure des Arts Appliqués et des Métiers d'Arts (Higher Municipal School of Graphic Arts and Crafts)

Cinema and Photography

Cinema and photography are taught at three major institutions. Admission requires the *baccalauréat* and the passing of an entrance *concours*.

The Ecole Nationale de la Photographie (Arles) (National School of Photography) offers a three-year program leading to the *Diplôme National d'Etudes Photographiques* (National Diploma of Studies in Photography). The Institut Supérieur du Cinéma et de l'Audiovisuel (Bry-sur-Marne) (Higher Institute of Cinema and Audiovisual Techniques), known until 1986 as Ecole des Hautes Etudes Cinématographiques, offers a three-year program in film leading to a *diplôme*. The Ecole Nationale Louis Lumiere (Louis Lumiere National School) offers two-year programs in photography and cinematography which lead to a specific *brevet de technicien supérieur*/BTS.

Art History, Restoration and Conservation

The Institut Français de Restauration des Oeuvres d'Art (French Institute of Restoration of Art Objects) is a public institution which offers a four-year program for holders of previous diplomas in art. Admission is by competitive entrance examination and enrollment is limited to 20 students. The institute awards its own *Diplôme de l'Institut Français de Restauration des Oeuvres d'Art* (Diploma of the French Institute of Restoration of Art Objects).

The Ecole du Louvre (School of the Louvre Museum) offers programs in art history, archeology and museology. The *baccalauréat* is required for admission to the three-year program leading to the *Diplôme de Premier Cycle de l'Ecole du Louvre* (First Cycle Diploma of the School of the Louvre Museum), which was formerly known as *Ancien Elève de l'Ecole du Louvre* (Former Student of the School of the Louvre Museum). A *Diplômé de Muséologie de l'Ecole du Louvre* (Diploma of Museology of the School of the Louvre Museum) is awarded after one additional year of study and the submission of a thesis. Prior to 1985, this credential was known as *Eléve Diplôme de l'Ecole du Louvre* (Student with a Diploma from the School of the Louvre Museum). See document 9.2 for a First Cycle Diploma of the School of the Louvre Museum.

The Ecole des Chartes is classified as a *Grand Etablissement* (Major Institution) and offers programs in the conservation of historical and artistic documents. Admission is by *concours* (competitive examination) following the completion of two years of a special *classe préparatoire* which is offered in two *lycées* located

9.2. First Cycle Diploma of the Ecole du Louvre

in Paris and Toulouse. The program offered at the Ecole des Chartes is four years in length, including an internship in the final year. On completion of studies, including the submission and defense of an extensive thesis, a *Diplôme d'Archiviste Paléographe* (Diploma of Archivist Paleographer) is awarded.

Music

General Music Education

Public education in music is offered throughout France at national and regional music conservatories and schools. These institutions operate under the joint auspices of local governments and the Ministry of Culture. Instruction is available at various levels beginning with classes for children. Performance programs are organized in four cycles. Promotion from one cycle to the next is based on examinations and performance skills. At the end of the program, which may take several years, regional schools award medals *(médailles)* which indicate levels of skill in performance. The gold medal *(Médaille d'Or)* indicates the highest level of virtuosity. See document 9.3 for a *Médaille d'Or* certificate.

RÉPVBLIQVE FRANÇAISE

VILLE DE GRENOBLE

CONSERVATOIRE NATIONAL DE REGION

MEDAILLE D'OR

Décerné à M ⟨ ⟩

Discipline _orgue_

Elève de M ⟨ Perdigon ⟩

Décision du Jury en date du _20 juin 1983_

9.3. *Médaille d'Or* (Gold Medal) Awarded by the National Regional Conservatory of Grenoble

Professional Music Education

THE NATIONAL CONSERVATORIES OF MUSIC

Two national conservatories of music, located in Lyon and Paris, offer advanced professional training. Admission is by audition and requires a strong musical background and the completion of secondary studies (though not necessarily the *baccalauréat*). Applicants are usually medal winners from regional schools. The program offered at national conservatories is four to five years long and consists of a major, complementary studies, and electives. Conservatories have several departments including ancient music, choir conducting, composition, dance, ethnomusicology, instrumental music, musical research, orchestral conducting, organ, voice and singing.

In addition to awarding medals and diplomas, national conservatories prepare students for national and international musical competitions. The Conservatoire National Supérieur de Musique de Lyon awards a *Diplôme National d'Etudes Supérieures de la Musique* (National Diploma of Higher Musical Education) in three or four years. The Conservatoire National Supérieur de Musique de Paris (Higher National Conservatory of Music of Paris) awards various diplomas and prizes *(prix)* following programs lasting two to five years.

PRIVATE INSTITUTIONS

Private institutions offer programs ranging from elementary instruction in music to advanced classes for music teachers and concert artists as well as complementary musical instruction for students enrolled in university programs in music. The following are some of the private schools of music.

Chants et Danse de France
Conservatoire International de Musique
Ecole César Franck
Ecole Normale de Musique de l'Institut Catholique de Paris
The Schola Cantorum
Université Internationale Musicale de Paris

Music Therapy

A *Certificat d'Université de Musicothérapie* (University Certificate in Music Therapy) is awarded by the University of Montpellier III after a three-year program following the *baccalauréat*. One further year of study and a thesis lead to a *Diplôme d'Université de Musicothérapie* (University Diploma in Music Therapy) which represents four years of university study.

A *Certificat d'Aptitude à la Pratique Psychomusicale* (Certificate of Qualification for the Practice of Musical Rehabilitation) is awarded by the University of Bordeaux following a two-year program designed for qualified rehabilitation specialists.

Music Education

The *Diplôme d'Etat de Professeur de Musique* (State Diploma of Music Teacher) was created in 1983 as a qualification for practicing conservatory and private music teachers who are graduates of national music conservatories or gold medalists from regional conservatories. It is earned by an examination which has two components: performance and pedagogical skills.

Dance

The dance school of the Paris Opera (Ecole de Danse de l'Opéra de Paris) trains ballet dancers for the company. Students are enrolled from the *sixième* (first year of *collège*) and continue in the school through the *terminale*. They may take the *baccalauréat* at the Lycée Racine in Paris. In addition to academic studies, students follow instruction in anatomy, art, foreign languages, and history of dance. A final examination determines whether a dancer joins the company.

Drama

Dramatic arts are offered at three national institutions.

A three-year program offered at the Conservatoire National Supérieur d'Art Dramatique (Higher National Conservatory of Dramatic Arts) leads to a *Diplôme d'Art Dramatique du Conservatoire National Supérieur* (Diploma of Dramatic Art of the Higher National Conservatory). Admission is by *concours* and requires special preparation usually done in a conservatory or through private instruction.

The Ecole Supérieure d'Art Dramatique du Théâtre National de Strasbourg (Higher National School of Dramatic Arts of the National Theatre of Strasbourg) offers programs in three sections: acting (three years), direction (two years), and stage design (three years). Admission is by *concours* for all sections. In addition, candidates for the acting program must undergo an audition while candidates for the other sections present a portfolio.

The Ecole Nationale Supérieure des Arts et Techniques du Théâtre (Higher National School of Theatre Arts and Crafts) offers two-year programs in acting and stage design. Both lead to a *Diplôme de l'Ecole Nationale Supérieure des Arts et Techniques du Théâtre* (Diploma of the Higher National School of Theatre Arts and Crafts) which is equivalent to a *brevet de technicien supérieur*/BTS (higher technician's certificate). Admission is by *concours*.

Chapter X

Suggestions for U.S. Admissions Officers

Credentials and Documentation

National diplomas of higher education awarded by universities and university institutes of technology and state diplomas awarded by the Ministry of Education or by other ministries represent the same quantity and quality of education regardless of the institution attended. The same applies to diplomas from *grandes écoles* of engineering and business since awards are strictly regulated by the Ministry of Education. Thus, for instance, whether an applicant submits a *brevet de technicien supérieur*/BTS (higher technician's certificate) in engineering, secretarial science or medical laboratory technology, the key is the name of the certificate. Identifying each credential by its name in French and thus becoming familiar with the conditions for the award of academic credentials is the most reliable way of understanding French higher education and the relationship of one institution or credential to another.

French institutions issue annual records *(relevé de notes)* bearing all courses studied and grades earned. Records in French should be requested. However, some *grandes écoles* of engineering and business will issue records in English. French institutions usually issue an academic record only once. It is the responsibility of each student to make duplicates which are then authenticated by a municipality, the police or French diplomatic services abroad.

Examinations and Grades

Examinations are administered internally unless they lead to a state diploma *(diplôme d'Etat)* in which case they are administered by the Ministry of Education. Examinations are generally graded on a scale of 0 to 20, and 10 is the passing grade. It is common, however, for students to pass an annual examination or earn a degree or diploma even with grades below 10 in individual subjects. Success is determined by the cumulative average of grades earned on all subjects. Conversely, students who fail to earn a cumulative average of 10 must repeat the entire year since grades are not carried over from one year to the next.

The minimum passing grade in France, 10/20, indicates a satisfactory performance and does not correspond to the U.S. grade of "D." By tradition, the highest grades awarded by French teachers seldom exceed 14 or 15/20 and grades of 8 and 9 reflect satisfactory performance.

Concours Grades

The essence of a *concours* (competitive examination) is that the number of candidates who are allowed to pass is determined in advance. Thus, even if a given *concours* leads to 27 openings and 350 candidates earn passing grades, only the top twenty-seven candidates are deemed to have passed and are entitled to enter the program or receive the award for which they were competing. The remaining candidates are turned away whether or not they earned passing grades. Passing a *concours*, therefore, is not only a matter of grades, but depends primarily on the number of available openings.

Accordingly, it is not reasonable to make judgments about the admissibility to U.S. institutions of French students who had attempted a *concours* but could not secure a position as it does not necessarily denote failure but lack of space. U.S. admissions officers are advised to request transcripts for the coursework leading to the *concours* and to base their decisions on grades earned in the classroom.

Additional Resources

This volume is designed to explain the organization of French education and the structure of programs leading to the most common academic credentials. It is far from being an exhaustive account of all the credentials that may be earned in France and, except for the major universities and university-level institutions, it does not list institutions. The *Annuaire National de l'Enseignement Supérieur*, a directory of all institutions of higher education, can be obtained from *L'Etudiant*, 27, rue du Chemin Vert, 75011 Paris, France. Universities and university-level institutions are also described in the *International Handbook of Universities* (10th edition), which is available from Walter de Gruyter, Inc., 200 Sawmill River Road, Hawthorne, New York 10532. Additional resources are listed in the Useful References.

Placement Recommendations

The Role of the National Council on the Evaluation of Foreign Educational Credentials

The placement recommendations that follow have been approved by the National Council on the Evaluation of Foreign Educational Credentials. In order that these recommendations may be of maximum use to admissions officers, the following information on the development of the terminology used in stating the recommendations, along with instructions for their use, is offered by the Council and the World Education Series Committee.

The recommendations deal with all levels of formal education in roughly chronological order up through the highest degree conferred. Recommendations, as developed through discussion and consensus in the Council, are not directives. Rather, they are general guidelines to help admissions officers determine the admissibility and appropriate level of placement of students from the country under study.

The recommendations should be applied flexibly rather than literally. Before applying the recommendations, admissions officers should read the supporting pages in the text and take into account their own institutional policies and practices. For example, a recommendation may be stated as follows: ". . . may be considered for up to 30 semester hours of transfer credit. . ." The implication is that the U.S. institution may consider giving less than or as much as one year of transfer credit, the decision to be based on various factors—the currentness of the applicant's transfer study, applicability of the study to the U.S. curriculum, quality of grades, and the receiving institution's own policies regarding transfer credit. Similarly, the recommendation ". . . may be considered for freshman admission" indicates possible eligibility only; it is not a recommendation that the candidate be admitted. Although consideration for admission at the same level may be recommended for holders of two different kinds of diplomas, use of identical phrasing in the recommendations does not mean that the two diplomas are identical in nature, quality, or in the quantity of education they represent.

In most cases, the Council will not have attempted to make judgments about the quality of individual schools or types of educational programs within the system under study. Quality clues are provided by the author and must be inferred from a careful reading of the text.

Certain phrases used repeatedly in the recommendations have acquired, within Council usage, specific meanings. For example, "through a course-by-course analysis" means that in dealing with transfer credit, each course taken at the foreign institution is to be judged on an individual basis for its transferability to the receiving institution. When the phrase "may be considered for undergraduate admission based upon a careful review of the syllabus" is used, it implies that many of the courses in the program may not be appropriate for transfer credit in a U.S. bachelor's degree program. Another phrase "where technical training is considered appropriate preparation" suggests that the curriculum followed by the candidate is specialized, and this wording is often a hint that within the foreign system the candidate's educational placement options are limited to certain curriculums. However, while the Council is aware of the educational policies of the country under study, the Council's policies are not necessarily set in conformity with that country's policies. Rather, the recommendations reflect U.S. philosophy and structure of education.

In voting on individual recommendations, Council decisions are made by simple majority. Although consistency among volumes is sought, some differences in philosophy and practice may occur from volume to volume.

Placement Recommendations

Credential	Minimum Entrance Requirement	Length of Study	Gives Access in Country to	Placement Recommendations
Secondary Credentials				
1. *Brevet des Collèges* (Certificate of Lower Secondary Education) (p. 3)	completion of primary education (5th year)	4 years	*Lycée* (not required, however)	May be placed in grade 10.
2. *Certificat d'Aptitude Professionnelle/CAP* (Certificate of Vocational Qualification) (p. 29)	a. completion of 5° (7th year) b. completion of 3° (9th year)	2–3 years	employment or *Baccalauréat Professionnel* program	Primarily a vocational credential; may be placed in grade 10.
3. *Brevet d'Enseignement Professionnel/BEP* (Certificate of Vocational Education) (p. 29)	completion of *collège* (9th year)	2 years	employment or *Baccalauréat Professionnel* program	Primarily a vocational credential; may be placed in grade 10.
4. *Diplôme de Bachelier de l'Enseignement du Second Degré* (*Baccalauréat* of Secondary Education) (pp. 14–27)	completion of *collège* (9th year)	3 years	higher education	May be considered for freshman admission with possible advanced standing based on a careful review of examination results. (See credit for *baccalauréat*, p. 28.)
5. *Diplôme de Baccalauréat de Technicien* (*Baccalauréat* of Technician) (pp. 14–27)	completion of *collège* (9th year)	3 years	higher education	See placement recommendation #4.
6. *Brevet de Technicien* (Certificate of Technician) (p. 30)	completion of *collège* (9th year)	3 years	nonuniversity higher technical education	May be considered for freshman admission where vocational preparation is appropriate.
7. *Baccalauréat Professionnel* (Vocational *Baccalauréat*) (p. 30)	a. CAP b. BEP	3 years 2 years	higher education	Because this credential had not been awarded, no placement recommendation was made.

continued

8. *Certificat de Fin d'Etudes Secondaires*/CFES (Certificate of Completion of Secondary Studies) (p. 26)	completion of *collège* (9th year)	3 years	some postsecondary programs which do not require the *baccalauréat*	May be considered for freshman admission.
9. *Examen Spécial d'Entrée à l'Université* (Special University Entrance Examination) (p. 39)	20+ years of age + 2 years of work experience	—	first year of university study	May be considered for freshman admission.

University Credentials

Note: Students who have completed some coursework for any of the programs listed below may be considered for undergraduate or graduate admission with up to 30 semester hours of transfer credit for each year, determined through a course-by-course analysis. When the length of a program is cited, it refers to the standard length of the program when pursued fulltime. The actual period of attendance may vary.

10. *Certificat de Capacité en Droit* (Certificate of Qualification in Law) (p. 39)	17 years of age	2 years part-time	employment	Primarily a vocational qualification; admission should be based on other credentials.
11. *Diplôme d'Etudes Universitaires Générales*/DEUG (Diploma of General University Studies) (pp. 43–60)	*Baccalauréat*	2 years	second cycle university study	May be considered for undergraduate admission with up to 60 semester hours of transfer credit determined through a course-by-course analysis.
12. *Diplôme d'Etudes Universitaires Scientifiques et Techniques*/DEUST (Diploma of University Scientific and Technical Studies) (p. 46)	*Baccalauréat*	2 years	employment or second cycle university study	See placement recommendation #11.
13. *Licence* (p. 60)	DEUG	1 year	second year of second cycle university study	May be considered for undergraduate admission with up to 30 semester hours of

14. *Maîtrise* (p. 60)	*Licence*	1 year	third cycle university study	May be considered for graduate admission. transfer credit (in addition to credits awarded for previous credentials), determined through a course-by-course analysis.
15. *Maîtrise des Sciences et Techniques*/MST, *Maîtrise des Sciences de Gestion*/MSG, *Maîtrise d'Informatique Appliquée à la Gestion*/MIAG (Master of Science and Technology, Master of Business Science, Master of Computer Science Applied to Business, respectively) (pp. 62–67)	DEUG + preparatory program	2 years	third cycle university study	May be considered for graduate admission.
16. *Magistère* (p. 67)	DEUG	3 years	employment	Because this credential had not been awarded, no placement recommendation was made.
17. *Diplôme d'Etudes Politiques* (Diploma of Political Studies) (p. 69)	a. *Bacc.* + 1 year preparatory program b. *Licence*	3 years 2 years	third cycle university study	May be considered for graduate admission.
18. *Diplôme d'Etudes Supérieures Spécialisées*/DESS (Diploma of Higher Specialized Studies) (p. 71)	*Maîtrise*	1 year	employment	May be considered for graduate admission with graduate transfer credit determined through a course-by-course analysis.

continued

19. *Diplôme d'Etudes Approfondies/DEA* (Diploma of Advanced Studies) (p. 72)	*Maîtrise, Diplôme d'Etudes Politiques, Diplôme d'Ingénieur, Diplôme* from a *grande école* of business	1 year	*Doctorat*	May be considered comparable to a U.S. master's degree.
20a. *Doctorat* (introduced in 1984) (pp. 73–74)	DEA	2–4 years	employment	May be considered comparable to a U.S. earned doctorate.
b. *Doctorat de Troisième Cycle* (Doctorate of the Third Cycle); *Doctorat d'Etat* (State Doctorate) abolished in 1984 (pp. 75–78)	See Chapter II, "Universities," for more information on these earlier doctorates taken from *France* (1975) by Raymond E. Wanner and for the placement recommendations passed in 1975 by the Council on Evaluation of Foreign Student Credentials.			
21. *Habilitation à Diriger des Recherches* (Entitlement to Direct Research) (p. 74)	*Doctorat*	variable	right to direct doctoral research	Represents recognition of published scholarly research.
22. *Diplôme Universitaire/DU* (University Diploma) (p. 40)				
a. First Cycle	*Baccalauréat*	variable	employment, further study	Undergraduate admission should be based on other credentials; may be considered for undergraduate transfer credit determined through a course-by-course analysis.
b. Second Cycle	DEUG, DUT	variable	—	Undergraduate admission should be based on other credentials; may be considered for undergraduate transfer credit determined through a course-by-course analysis.

SUGGESTIONS FOR U.S. ADMISSIONS OFFICERS

c. Third Cycle	*Maîtrise*	variable	—	Graduate admission should be based on other credentials; may be considered for graduate transfer credit determined through a course-by-course analysis.
French As A Foreign Language				
23. *Diplôme Elémentaire de Langue Française*/DELF (Elementary Diploma in French Language)* (p. 79)	—	by examination, following approximately 1 year of study	—	Represents a level of achievement in French.
24. *Diplôme Approfondi de Langue Française*/DALF (Advanced Diploma in French Language) (p. 79)	—	see #23	—	Represents an advanced level of achievement in French.*
25. *Certificat Pratique de Langue Française* (Practical Certificate in French Language) (p. 79)	—	1 year	—	Represents a level of achievement in French.
26. *Diplôme d'Etudes Françaises* (Diploma of French Studies) (p. 79)	*Certificat Pratique de Langue Française*	1 year	—	Represents an advanced level of achievement in French; may be considered for up to 30 semester hours of upper-division undergraduate transfer credit in French determined through a course-by-course analysis.
27. *Diplôme Supérieur d'Etudes Françaises* (Higher Diploma of French Studies) (p. 79)	*Diplôme d'Etudes Françaises*	1 year	—	Represents an advanced level of achievement in French; may be considered for up to 30 semester

*It is suggested that credit by examination may be appropriate for these credentials.

continued

170 SUGGESTIONS FOR U.S. ADMISSIONS OFFICERS

			hours of upper-division undergraduate transfer credit in French determined through a course-by-course analysis.

Short Higher Technical Credentials

28. *Brevet de Technicien Supérieur*/BTS (Higher Technician's Certificate) (pp. 83–85)	*Brevet de Technicien* or *Baccalauréat*	2 years	employment or further education	May be considered for undergraduate admission with up to 60 semester hours of transfer credit based on a careful review of the program.
29. *Diplôme Universitaire de Technologie*/DUT (University Diploma of Technology) (pp. 81–83)	*Baccalauréat*	2 years	employment or further education	May be considered for undergraduate admission with up to 60 semester hours of transfer credit determined through a course-by-course analysis.

Engineering Credentials

30. Record of completion of 2 years of *classes préparatoires* (pp. 88–90)	*Baccalauréat*	2 years	*grande école*	May be considered for undergraduate admission with up to 60 semester hours of transfer credit determined through a course-by-course analysis.
31. *Diplôme d'Ingénieur* (Diploma of Engineer)				
a. (pp. 87–92)	2 years of *classes préparatoires* + *concours*	3 years	third cycle university study, *Mastère*, or employment	May be considered for graduate admission with graduate transfer credit determined through a course-by-course analysis of the last year of study. See placement recommendation #31a.
b. (pp. 92–100)	*Baccalauréat* + *concours*	5 years	See #31a	

SUGGESTIONS FOR U.S. ADMISSIONS OFFICERS 171

c. (pp. 92–100)	DEUG or DUT + concours	3 years	See #31a	See placement recommendation #31a.
d. (pp. 92–100)	Maîtrise + examination	1 year	See #31a	See placement recommendation #31a.
32. *Diplôme d'Ingénieur* a. (p. 101)	1 year of *classe préparatoire* + *concours*	3 years	third cycle university study or employment	May be considered for graduate admission.
b. (p. 101)	*Baccalauréat* + *concours*	4 years	See #32a	May be considered for graduate admission.
33. *Diplôme d'Ingénieur* (p. 103)	*Diplôme d'Ingénieur*	1 or 2 years	employment	May yield graduate transfer credit determined through a course-by-course analysis.
34. *Doctorat* introduced in 1984 (p. 103)	DEA	2–4 years	employment	May be considered comparable to a U.S. earned doctorate.
35. *Diplôme d'Etudes Approfondies*/DEA (Diploma of Advanced Studies) (p. 103)	*Diplôme d'Ingénieur* or completion of second year of engineering curriculum at a *grande école*	1 year	*Doctorat*	May be considered comparable to a U.S. master's degree.
36. *Diplôme de Docteur-Ingénieur* (Diploma of Doctor in Engineering) abolished in 1984 (pp. 75–78)	See Chapter II, "Universities," for more information on this credential taken from *France* (1975) by Raymond E. Wanner and for the placement recommendation passed in 1975 by the Council on Evaluation of Foreign Student Credentials.			
37. *Mastère*/MS (pp. 103–108)	*Diplôme d'Ingénieur, Diplôme d'Etudes Approfondies*/DEA	1 year	employment	May be considered comparable to a U.S. master's degree.
38. *Diplôme de Premier Cycle Technique*/DPCT (Diploma of First Technical Cycle) (p. 101)	*Baccalauréat* level entrance examination	approximately 500 contact hours of part-time study	DEST	May be considered for undergraduate admission with up to 30 semester hours of transfer

continued

Credential	Prerequisite	Length	Gives Access to	Placement Recommendation
39. *Diplôme d'Etudes Supérieures Techniques*/DEST (Diploma of Higher Technical Studies) (p. 101)	DPCT	approximately 450 contact hours of part-time study	admission to the first year of a *diplôme d'ingénieur* program	credit determined through a course-by-course analysis. May be considered for undergraduate admission with up to 30 semester hours of transfer credit determined through a course-by-course analysis.
Agricultural Credentials				
40. *Brevet de Technicien Supérieur Agricole*/BTSA (Higher Technician's Certificate in Agriculture) (p. 109)	*Baccalauréat*	2 years	employment or further study	May be considered for undergraduate admission with up to 60 semester hours of transfer credit determined through a course-by-course analysis.
41. *Diplôme National d'Oenologie* (National Diploma of Oenology) (p. 110)	BTSA, DUT or DEUG in science	2 years	employment	May yield up to 60 semester hours of undergraduate transfer credit determined through a course-by-course analysis.
42. *Diplôme d'Agronomie Générale* (Diploma in General Agriculture) (pp. 110–111)	2 years of *classe préparatoire* + *concours*	2 years	final year of *Diplôme d'Ingénieur Agronome*	May be considered for graduate admission.
43. *Diplôme d'Ingénieur Agronome* (Diploma of Agricultural Engineer)				
a. (p. 111)	*Diplôme d'Agronomie Générale*	1 year	third cycle university study, employment	May be considered for graduate admission with graduate transfer credit determined through a course-by-course analysis of the last year of study.
b. (pp. 112–115)	*Baccalauréat* + *concours*	5 years	See #43a	See placement recommendation #43a.
c. (pp. 112–115)	DEUG + *concours*	3 years	See #43a	See placement recommendation #43a.

SUGGESTIONS FOR U.S. ADMISSIONS OFFICERS 173

44.	Diplôme d'Ingénieur des Techniques Agricoles (Diploma of Engineer of Agricultural Technology) (pp. 112–116)	1 year of classe préparatoire + concours	3 years	third cycle university study, employment	May be considered for graduate admission.
45.	Diplôme d'Ingénieur (Diploma of Engineer) (p. 116)	Diplôme d'Agronomie Générale, Diplôme d'Ingénieur Agronome	2 years	third cycle university study, employment	May yield graduate transfer credit determined through a course-by-course analysis.
46.	Diplôme d'Etat de Docteur Vétérinaire (State Diploma of Veterinary Doctor) (pp. 116–117)	1 year of classe préparatoire + concours	4 years	employment or specialization	A first professional degree in veterinary medicine; may be considered for graduate admission.

Business Credentials

47.	Records of completion of classe préparatoire (for grande école of business) (pp. 121–123)	Baccalauréat	1 year	grande école of business	May be considered for undergraduate admission with up to 30 semester hours of transfer credit determined through a course-by-course analysis.
48.	Diplôme visé (sealed diploma) from a traditional grande école of business (pp. 121–125)	1 year of classe préparatoire + concours	3 years	third cycle university study, Mastère	May be considered for graduate admission.
49.	Diplôme d'Etudes Supérieures Commerciales, Administratives et Financières/DESCAF (Diploma of Higher Studies in Commerce, Administration and Finance) (pp. 121–125)	1 year of classe préparatoire + concours	3 years	third cycle university study, Mastère	May be considered for graduate admission.
50.	Diplôme or Certificat de Fin d'Etudes (Certificate of	Baccalauréat	3 or 4 years	employment	May be considered for undergraduate admission with up to *continued*

	Credential	Given to holders of	Length of program	Leads to	Suggestions
					Completion) from a recognized institution (*établissement reconnu par l'Etat*) (p. 125)			90 semester hours of transfer credit determined through a course-by-course analysis.
51.	*Diplôme* or *Certificat de Fin d'Etudes* (Diploma or Certificate of Completion) from a nonrecognized institution (*établissement non reconnu par l'Etat*) (p. 125)	*Baccalauréat*	3 or 4 years	employment	May be considered for admission and placement in accordance with institutional policy regarding students from U.S. institutions that do not have regional accreditation.
52.	*Mastère*/MS (p. 125)	*Diplôme* from *grande école* of business, DESCAF, DEA, *Diplôme d'Ingénieur*	1 year	employment	May be considered comparable to a U.S. master's degree.
53.	*Certificat d'Aptitude à l'Administration des Entreprises*/CAAE (Certificate of Qualification in Business Administration) (p. 127)	*Maîtrise, Diplôme d'Ingénieur*	1 year	employment	May yield graduate transfer credit determined through a course-by-course analysis.
54.	Complementary Study Certificates (e.g., *Certificat, Diplôme*, etc.) awarded by a *grande école* of business (pp. 125–126)	*Diplôme d'Ingénieur, Maîtrise* or DEA awarded by universities + professional experience	1 year	employment	May yield graduate transfer credit determined through a course-by-course analysis.
55.	*Certificat Préparatoire aux Etudes Comptables et Financières*/CPECF (Preparatory Certificate for Studies in Accounting and Finance) (p. 128)	*Baccalauréat*	variable	further studies toward professional qualification in accounting	May be considered for undergraduate admission with up to 30 semester hours of transfer credit determined through a course-by-course analysis.
56.	*Diplôme d'Etudes Comptables Supérieures*/DECS (Diploma of Higher Studies in Accounting) (pp. 128–129)	CPECF; BTS, DUT in business; or *Diplôme* from a *grande école* of business	variable	*Diplôme d'Expert Comptable*	Primarily a professional qualification; may be considered for graduate admission.

57. *Diplôme d'Expert Comptable* (Diploma of Accounting Expert) (p. 129)	DECS	3 years of supervised professional practice + 2400 hours of seminars	professional practice as an accountant	A professional qualification in accounting; may be considered for graduate admission.
Teaching Credentials				
58. *Certificat de Fin d'Etudes Normales*/CFEN (Certificate of Completion of Normal School Studies) prior to 1986 (p. 131)	*Baccalauréat*	2 years	employment and further study	May be considered for undergraduate admission with up to 60 semester hours of transfer credit determined through a course-by-course analysis.
59. *Diplôme d'Etudes Supérieures d'Instituteur* (Elementary School Teacher Education Diploma) introduced in 1986 (pp. 131–132)	DEUG	2 years	employment	Because the credential had not been awarded, no placement recommendation was made.
60. *Certificat d'Aptitude à l'Education des Enfants et Adolescents Déficients ou Inadaptés* (Certificate of Qualification to Teach Deficient or Maladjusted Children and Adolescents) (p. 132)	CFEN + 2 years of teaching experience	1 year	employment	May yield up to 30 semester hours of undergraduate transfer credit determined through a course-by-course analysis.
61. *Diplôme de Psychologue Scolaire* (Diploma of School Psychologist) (p. 133)	CFEN + 5 years of teaching experience	2 years	employment	May yield up to 60 semester hours of undergraduate transfer credit determined through a course-by-course analysis.
62. *Certificat d'Aptitude à l'Enseignement dans les Lycées Professionnels*/CAELP (Certificate of Qualification to Teach in Vocational Secondary Schools) (p. 133)	BTS, DUT or DEUG + 2 years of work experience	2 years	employment	May yield up to 60 semester hours of undergraduate transfer credit determined through a course-by-course analysis.

continued

63. *Certificat d'Aptitude au Professorat Technique*/CAPT (Certificate of Qualification of Technical Teacher) (p. 135)	DEUG	2 years	employment	May be considered for graduate admission.
64. *Certificat d'Aptitude au Professorat de l'Enseignement Secondaire*/CAPES; *Certificat d'Aptitude au Professorat de l'Enseignement Technique*/ CAPET; *Certificat d'Aptitude au Professorat d'Education Physique et Sportive*/CAPEPS (Certificate of Qualification to Teach Secondary Education, to Teach in Technical Schools, for Teaching Sports and Physical Education, respectively) (pp. 134–135)	*Licence*	by examination, following at least 1 year of study in the field of specialty + 1 year of practice teaching	employment and further study	May be considered for graduate admission with possible graduate transfer credit in the field of teaching specialization.
65. Record of completion of *classes préparatoires littéraires* (pp. 136–137)	*Baccalauréat*	2 years	*Ecole Normale Supérieure*	See Placement Recommendation #58.
66. *Agrégation* (pp. 137–138)	completion of *école normale supérieure*; CAPES; CAPET; *Maîtrise*	by examination; in addition at least 1–2 years of preparatory study for holders of the *Maîtrise*	employment as teacher in secondary schools as well as in higher education	Represents advanced graduate achievement in the field of specialization.

Health and Social Education Credentials

A. Medical Fields

67. *Certificat de Synthèse Clinique et Thérapeutique* (Certificate of Clinical and Therapeutic Synthesis) (p. 140)	*Baccalauréat*	6 years	third cycle medical study	May be considered for graduate admission.

SUGGESTIONS FOR U.S. ADMISSIONS OFFICERS 177

68.	*Diplôme d'Etat de Docteur en Médecine* (State Diploma of Doctor of Medicine) (p. 140)	*Certificat de Synthèse Clinique et Thérapeutique*	2–5 years depending on speciality	professional practice	A first professional degree in medicine; may be considered for graduate admission.
69.	*Diplôme d'Etat de Docteur en Médecine, Mention Recherche Médicale* (State Diploma of Doctor of Medicine, Medical Research Option) (p. 140)	*Certificat de Synthèse Clinique et Thérapeutique*	4 years	medical research and teaching	May be considered comparable to a U.S. earned doctorate.
70.	*Diplôme d'Etat de Docteur en Chirurgie Dentaire* (State Diploma of Doctor of Dental Surgery) (p. 141)	*Baccalauréat*	5 years	professional practice or further study	A first professional degree in dentistry; may be considered for graduate admission.
71.	*Certificat d'Etudes Spéciales—Mention Orthodontie* (Certificate of Special Studies—Orthodontics Option) (p. 141)	*Diplôme d'Etat de Docteur en Chirurgie Dentaire*	3 years	professional practice	A professional specialization.
72.	*Diplôme d'Etat de Docteur en Pharmacie* (State Diploma of Doctor of Pharmacy) (p. 141)	*Baccalauréat*	5 years	professional practice	A first professional degree in pharmacy; may be considered for graduate admission.

B. Paramedical Education

73.	*Diplôme d'Etat d'Audioprothésiste* (State Diploma of Audioprosthesist) (p. 142)	*Baccalauréat*	2 years	professional practice	May be considered for undergraduate admission with up to 60 semester hours of transfer credit determined through a course-by-course analysis.
74.	*Diplôme d'Etat de Sage-Femme* (State Diploma of Midwife) (p. 142)	*Baccalauréat*	a. 3 years (until 1986)	professional practice	May be considered for undergraduate admission with up to 90 semester hours of transfer credit determined through a course-by-course analysis.

continued

		b. 4 years (after 1986)	professional practice	Because the credential had not been awarded, no placement recommendation was made.
75.	*Certificat de Capacité d'Orthophoniste* (Certificate of Qualification of Speech Therapist) (p. 143)	*Baccalauréat + concours*	3 years	professional practice	May be considered for undergraduate admission with up to 90 semester hours of transfer credit determined through a course-by-course analysis.
76.	*Diplôme d'Etat de Laborantin d'Analyses Médicales* (State Diploma of Medical Laboratory Analyst) (p. 144)	completion of secondary education + *concours*	2 years	professional practice	May be considered for undergraduate admission with up to 60 semester hours of transfer credit based on a careful review of the program.
77.	*Diplôme d'Etat d'Infirmier* (State Diploma of Nurse) (pp. 144–145)	completion of secondary education + *concours*	3 years	professional practice	May be considered for undergraduate admission with transfer credit determined as for graduates of U.S. hospital schools of nursing.
78.	*Diplôme d'Etat d'Infirmier de Secteur Psychiatrique* (State Diploma of Psychiatric Nurse) (p. 145)	by examination	3 years	professional practice	A vocational qualification.
79.	*Diplôme d'Etat d'Ergothérapeute* (State Diploma of Occupational Therapist) (p. 146)	completion of secondary education + *concours*	3 years	professional practice	May be considered for undergraduate admission with up to 90 semester hours of transfer credit determined through a course-by-course analysis.
80.	*Diplôme d'Etat de Masseur Kinésithérapeute* (State	completion of secondary education +	3 years	professional practice	May be considered for undergraduate admission with up to

Diploma of Masseur and Kinesitherapist (p. 146)	concours	professional practice	90 semester hours of transfer credit determined through a course-by-course analysis.
81. Diplôme d'Etat de Pédicure (State Diploma of Chiropodist) (p. 147)	completion of secondary education + concours	professional practice	A vocational qualification.
82. Diplôme d'Etat de Manipulateur d'Electro-Radiologie (State Diploma of Electro-Radiology Operator) (p. 147)	completion of secondary education + concours	professional practice	May be considered for undergraduate admission with up to 60 semester hours of transfer credit determined through a course-by-course analysis.
83. Diplôme d'Etat de Psychomotricien (State Diploma of Rehabilitation Counselor) (p. 147)	Baccalauréat + concours	professional practice	May be considered for undergraduate admission with up to 90 semester hours of transfer credit determined through a course-by-course analysis.
84. Diplôme d'Etat d'Assistant de Service Social (State Diploma of Social Service Assistant) (p. 149)	Baccalauréat or 5 years of relevant experience + entrance examination	professional practice and further education	May be considered for undergraduate admission with up to 90 semester hours of transfer credit determined through a course-by-course analysis.
85. Diplôme Supérieur en Travail Social (Higher Diploma in Social Work) (p. 149)	Diplôme d'Etat d'Assistant de Service Social	professional practice	May be considered for graduate admission.
86. Maîtrise de Sciences Sociales Appliquées au Travail (Maîtrise of Social Sciences Applied to Labor) (p. 149)	Diplôme d'Etat d'Assistant de Service Social	professional practice	May be considered for graduate admission.

continued

SUGGESTIONS FOR U.S. ADMISSIONS OFFICERS

87. *Diplôme d'Etat Relatif aux Fonctions d'Animation* (State Diploma of Coordinator of Social Activities) (pp. 149–150)	relevant professional experience	3 years	employment	A vocational qualification.
88. *Diplôme d'Etat d'Educateur Spécialisé* (State Diploma of Special Educator) (p. 150)	completion of secondary education + work experience	3 years fulltime or 4 years part-time	employment	May be considered for undergraduate admission with up to 90 semester hours of transfer credit based on a careful review of the syllabus.
89. *Diplôme d'Etat d'Educateur de Jeunes Enfants* (State Diploma of Teacher of Young Children) (p. 150)	completion of secondary education + entrance examination	2 years including 36 weeks of practical training	employment	May be considered for undergraduate admission with up to 30 semester hours of transfer credit based on a careful review of the syllabus.

Architecture, Art, Music and Drama Credentials

A. Architecture

90. *Diplôme d'Etudes Fondamentales en Architecture*/DEFA (Diploma of Foundation Studies in Architecture) (p. 151)	*Baccalauréat*	2 years	second cycle architectural study	May be considered for undergraduate admission with up to 60 semester hours of transfer credit determined through a course-by-course analysis.
91. *Diplôme d'Architecte Diplômé par le Gouvernement*/DPLG (Government Diploma of Architect)				
a. before 1986 (p. 152)	*Baccalauréat*	6 years	professional practice or third cycle university study See #91a	A first professional degree in architecture; may be considered for graduate admission. See placement recommendation #91a.
b. after 1986 (p. 152)	DEFA	3 years		

92. *Diplôme de l'Ecole Spéciale d'Architecture* (Diploma of Special School of Architecture) (p. 154)	*Baccalauréat*	5 years	professional practice or third cycle university study	A first professional degree in architecture; may be considered for graduate admission.
93. *Diplôme d'Architecte de l'Ecole Nationale Supérieure des Arts et Industries de Strasbourg* (Diploma of Architect of the Higher National School of Arts and Crafts of Strasbourg) (p. 154)	*Baccalauréat* + 1 year of *classe préparatoire*	4 years	professional practice or third cycle university study	A first professional degree in architecture; may be considered for graduate admission.
94. *Certificat d'Etudes Approfondies d'Architecture* (Certificate of Advanced Studies in Architecture) (p. 156)	*Diplôme d'Architecte*	1–2 years	employment	May be considered comparable to a U.S. master's degree.
B. Art				
95. *Certificat d'Initiation Plastique* (Elementary Certificate in Studio Art) (p. 156)	completion of secondary education + portfolio	2 years	further study in art	May be considered for undergraduate admission with up to 60 semester hours of transfer credit determined through a course-by-course analysis in accordance with policies for students from U.S. schools of art.
96. *Diplôme National d'Arts et Techniques*/DNAT (National Diploma of Arts and Crafts) (p. 156)	completion of secondary education + portfolio and examination	3 years	further study in art or employment	May be considered for undergraduate admission and placement with up to 90 semester hours of transfer credit determined through a course-by-course analysis in accordance with policies for students from U.S. schools of art.

continued

97. *Brevet de Technicien Supérieur*/BTS (Higher Technician's Certificate) (p. 156)	*Baccalauréat* F-12	2 years	employment or further study in art	May be considered for undergraduate admission with up to 60 semester hours of transfer credit based on a careful review of the program.
98. *Diplôme Supérieur d'Arts Appliqués* (Higher Diploma of Graphic Arts) (p. 156)	*Brevet de Technicien Supérieur*	a. 1 year (until 1986)	employment or further study in art	May be considered for undergraduate admission with up to 30 semester hours of transfer credit determined through a course-by-course analysis. Because the credential had not been awarded, no placement recommendation was made.
		b. 2 years (after 1986)	employment or further study in art	
99. *Diplôme National Supérieur d'Expression Plastique* DNSEP (Higher National Diploma of Artistic Expression) (p. 154)	*Certificat d'Initiation Plastique*	3 years	employment or further study in art	May be considered for graduate admission as are graduates of U.S. schools of art.
100. *Diplôme de l'Ecole Nationale Supérieure de Création Industrielle* (Diploma of the Higher National School of Industrial Design) (p. 155)	*concours*	1–5 years depending on entrance qualification	employment	May be considered for graduate admission as are graduates of U.S. schools of art.
101. *Diplôme de l'Ecole Nationale Supérieure des Arts Décoratifs* (Diploma of the Higher National School of Decorative Arts) (p. 155)	*concours*	2–4 years depending on entrance qualification	employment	May be considered for graduate admission as are graduates of U.S. schools of art.

102. *Diplôme Supérieur d'Arts Plastiques* (Higher Diploma of Studio Art) awarded by the Ecole Nationale Supérieure des Beaux Arts (p. 155)	portfolio and *concours*	5 years minimum	—	May be considered comparable to a U.S. master of fine arts degree.
103. Diplomas or certificates from private art schools (p. 156)	generally completion of secondary education	1–5 years depending on entrance qualification	employment or further study in art	May be considered for undergraduate admission and placement after a careful review of the program and previous qualifications in accordance with policies for students from U.S. schools of art.
104. *Diplôme National d'Etudes Photographiques* (Arles) (National Diploma of Studies in Photography) (p. 157)	*Baccalauréat + concours*	3 years	employment	May be considered for undergraduate admission and placement with up to 90 semester hours of transfer credit determined through a course-by-course analysis in accordance with policies for students from U.S. schools of art.
105. *Diplôme de l'Institut Supérieur du Cinéma et de l'Audiovisuèl* (Diploma of the Higher Institute for Cinema and Audiovisual Techniques) (formerly Ecole des Hautes Etudes Cinématographiques) (p. 157)	*Baccalauréat + concours*	3 years	employment	May be considered for undergraduate admission and placement with up to 90 semester hours of transfer credit determined through a course-by-course analysis in accordance with policies for students from U.S. schools of art.

continued

184 SUGGESTIONS FOR U.S. ADMISSIONS OFFICERS

106.	*Diplôme de l'Institut Français de Restauration des Oeuvres d'Art* (Diploma of the French Institute of Restoration of Art Objects) (p. 157)	graduation from a postsecondary art school + *concours*	4 years	employment	May be considered for graduate admission.
107.	*Diplôme de Premier Cycle de l'Ecole du Louvre* (First Cycle Diploma of the School of the Louvre Museum) formerly known as *Ancien Elève de l'Ecole du Louvre* (p. 157)	*Baccalauréat*	3 years	further study or employment	May be considered for undergraduate admission with up to 90 semester hours of transfer credit determined through a course-by-course analysis.
108.	*Diplôme de Muséologie de l'Ecole du Louvre* (Diploma of Museology of the School of the Louvre Museum), formerly known as *Elève Diplômé de l'Ecole du Louvre* (p. 157)	*Diplôme de Premier Cycle de l'Ecole du Louvre*	1 year + thesis	employment	May be considered for graduate admission.
109.	*Diplôme d'Archiviste Paléographe* (Diploma of Archivist Paleographer) (pp. 157–158)	*Baccalauréat* + 2 years *classe préparatoire aux grandes écoles* + *concours*	4 years	employment	May be considered comparable to a U.S. master's degree.

C. **Music**

110.	*Médaille* (Medal) from a music conservatory (p. 158)	audition	variable	—	Represents a level of skill in music performance.
111.	*Diplôme National d'Etudes Supérieures de la Musique* (National Diploma of High-	audition	3–4 years	employment	Represents a high level of skill in music performance. Admission and placement should be deter-

er Musical Education) awarded by the Conservatoire National Supérieur de Musique de Lyon (p. 160)			mined in accordance with institutional policy for students of U.S. schools of music.
112. *Diplôme* (Diploma) or *Prix* (Prize) awarded by the Conservatoire National Supérieur de Musique de Paris (p. 160)	audition	2–5 years	employment	See placement recommendation #111.
113. *Certificat d'Université de Musicothérapie* (University Certificate in Music Therapy) awarded by the University of Montpellier III (p. 160)	*Baccalauréat*	3 years	employment or further study	May be considered for undergraduate admission with up to 90 semester hours of transfer credit determined through a course-by-course analysis.
114. *Diplôme d'Université de Musicothérapie* (University Diploma in Music Therapy) awarded by the University of Montpellier III (p. 160)	*Certificat d'Université de Musicothérapie*	1 year + thesis	employment	May be considered for graduate admission.
115. *Certificat d'Aptitude à la Pratique Psychomusicale* (Certificate of Qualification for the Practice of Rehabilitation through Music) awarded by the University of Bordeaux (p. 160)	qualified therapist	2 years	employment	May be considered for graduate admission.

continued

116. *Diplôme d'Etat de Professeur de Musique* (State Diploma of Music Teacher) (p. 161)	by examination after graduation from a music conservatory and professional music teaching experience	—	employment	Primarily a teaching qualification; admission and placement should be based on other credentials.

D. Drama

117. *Diplôme d'Art Dramatique du Conservatoire National Supérieur* (Diploma of Dramatic Art of the Higher National Conservatory) (p. 161)	audition and *concours*	3 years	employment	May be considered for undergraduate admission with up to 90 semester hours of transfer credit determined through a course-by-course analysis.
118. *Diplôme de l'Ecole Supérieure d'Art Dramatique du Théâtre National de Strasbourg* (Diploma of the Higher School of Dramatic Art of the National Theatre of Strasbourg) (p. 161)	audition or portfolio and *concours*	acting—3 years direction—2 years stage design—3 years	employment	May be considered for undergraduate admission with up to 30 semester hours of transfer credit for each year of study, determined through a course-by-course analysis.
119. *Diplôme de l'Ecole Nationale Supérieure des Arts de Techniques du Théâtre* (Diploma of the Higher National School of Theatre Arts and Crafts) (p. 161)	audition and *concours*	2 years	employment	May be considered for undergraduate admission with up to 60 semester hours of transfer credit determined through a course-by-course analysis.

Appendix A

Universities and Institutions Deemed to be Universities

Universities are generally named after the city in which they are located. When a university bears another name, it has been indicated in parentheses. A roman numeral after the name of a university indicates that there is more than one university in a particular city. The addresses which appear below are for the central administrative offices. As it is common for individual departments and faculties to be housed in different buildings located throughout a city, student credentials may bear different addresses. Correspondence regarding student transcripts should be addressed to the secretary general of the university or to the director of specific UFRs as indicated on student records. General information on academic programs is available from the university information and orientation center *(Cellule Universitaire d'Information et d'Orientation*/CUIO) located on each campus.

The following abbreviations have been used to indicate the diplomas awarded by each French university: **DEA** = *Diplôme d'Etudes Approfondies* (Diploma of Advanced Studies); **DESS** = *Diplôme d'Etudes Supérieures Spécialisées* (Diploma of Higher Specialized Studies); **DEUG** = *Diplôme d'Etudes Universitaires Générales* (Diploma of General University Studies); **DEUST** = *Diplôme d'Etudes Universitaires Scientifiques et Techniques* (Diploma of University Scientific and Technical Studies); **Doct.** = *Doctorat*; **DU** = *Diplôme Universitaire* (University Diploma); **Ing.** = *Diplôme d'Ingénieur* (Diploma of Engineer); **L** = *Licence*; **M** = *Maîtrise*; **MIAG** = *Maîtrise d'Informatique Appliquée à la Gestion* (*Maîtrise* of Computer Science Applied to Business); **MSG** = *Maîtrise des Sciences de Gestion* (*Maîtrise* of Business Science); **MST** = *Maîtrise des Sciences et Techniques* (*Maîtrise* of Science and Technology).

In addition, the following university-affiliated institutions are listed by their initialisms as follows: CPAG = Centre de Préparation à l'Administration Générale (Center for Preparation in General Administration); INALCO = Institut National des Langues et Civilisations Orientales (National Institute of Oriental Languages and Civilizations); IREM = Institut de Recherche sur l'Enseignement des Mathématiques (Institute of Research for Mathematics Education).

Centre Universitaire d'Avignon (2,250 students)
35, avenue Joseph Vernet, 84000 Avignon
Major Programs: Arts & Letters; Social Sciences; Science
Diplomas: DEUG, DEUST, L, M

Institut National Polytechnique de Grenoble (2,749 students)
46, avenue Felix Viallet, 38031 Grenoble Cedex
Major Programs: Electrochemistry & Electrometallurgy; Electronics & Radioelectricity; Hydraulics; Electricity; Paper-Making; Computer Science; Applied Mathematics
Diploma: Ing.

Institut National Polytechnique de Lorraine—Nancy (1,168 students)
Porte de la Craffe, B.P. 3308, 54014 Nancy Cedex
Major Programs: Agronomy; Food Chemistry; Electricity; Mechanics; Applied Geology; Mining; Industrial Chemistry; Metallurgy
Diploma: Ing.

Institut National Polytechnique—Toulouse (2,229 students)
Place des Hauts Murats, 31006 Toulouse Cedex
Major Programs: Astronomy; Chemistry; Chemical Engineering; Electrical Engineering, Electricity, Electronics, Computer Science & Hydraulics
Diploma: Ing.

Université d'Aix-Marseille I (Université de Provence) (16,020 students)
1, place Victor Hugo, 13331 Marseille Cedex 3
Major Programs: Arts & Letters; Social Sciences; Mathematics, Natural Science; Engineering
Diplomas: DEUG, DEUST, L, M, MST, *Magistère, Ing.*, DESS, DEA, *Doct.*

Université d'Aix-Marseille II (20,294 students)
Jardin Emile Duclaux, 58 boulevard Charles Livon, 13007 Marseille
Major Programs: Economics; Geography; Physical Education; Health Sciences; Natural Science
Diplomas: DEUG, DEUST, L, M, MST, MIAG, *Magistère*, DESS, DEA, *Doct.*
Affiliated Institution: IREM

Université d'Aix-Marseille III (Université de Droit, d'Economie et des Sciences) (14,500 students)
3, avenue Robert Schuman, 13621 Aix-en-Provence
Major Programs: Law & Political Science; Economics; Science; Engineering
Diplomas: DEUG, DEUST, L, M, MST, MIAG, *Magistère, Ing.*, DESS, DEA, *Doct.*
Affiliated Institution: CPAG

Université d'Amiens (Université de Picardie) (10,700 students)
Rue Salomon Malhangu, 80025 Amiens Cedex
Major Programs: Law; Economics & Business; Foreign Languages; Arts & Letters; Social Sciences; Medicine; Pharmacy; Mathematics & Science
Diplomas: DEUG, DU, L, M, MST
Affiliated Institution: IREM

Université d'Angers (8,465 students)
30, rue des Arènes, B.P. 532, 49035 Angers Cedex
Major Programs: Medicine; Pharmacy; Science; Applied Sciences; Law, Economics; Arts & Letters, Social Sciences
Diplomas: DEUG, L, M, MST, MIAG, *Magistère*, DESS, DEA, *Doct.*

Université des Antilles-Guyane (4,650 students)
Boulevard Legitimus B.P. 771, 97173 Pointe-à-Pitre Cedex, Guadeloupe
Major Programs: Law; Economics; Arts & Letters; Social Sciences; Medicine; Science
Diplomas: DEUG, DEUST, L, M

Université de Besançon (Université de Franche-Comté) (13,690 students)
30, avenue de l'Observatoire, 25030 Besançon Cedex
Major Programs: Law; Economics; Arts & Letters; Social Sciences; Science
Diplomas: DEUG, DEUST, L, M, MST, DESS, DEA
Affiliated Institution: IREM

Université de Bordeaux I (15,430 students)
351, cours de la Liberation, 33405 Talence Cedex
Major Programs: Law & Political Science (IEP); Economics; Science; Engineering
Diplomas: DEUG, DEUST, L, M, MST, MSG, MIAG, *Ing.*, DESS, DEA, *Doct.*
Affiliated Institutions: CPAG, IREM

Université de Bordeaux II (14,350 students)
146, rue Leo Saignat, 33076 Bordeaux Cedex
Major Programs: Medicine; Pharmacy; Dentistry; Oenology (Wine Study); Social Sciences; Applied Languages; Applied Computer; Audiovisual Communications; Physical Education
Diplomas: DEUG, L, M, DESS, DEA, *Doct.*

Université de Bordeaux III (10,780 students)
Domaine Universitaire, Esplanade Michel de Montaigne, 33405 Talence Cedex
Major Programs: Arts & Letters; Social Sciences; Language & Literature; Communications; Geology; Environmental Science
Diplomas: DEUG, L, M, MST, DESS, DEA, *Doct.*

Université de Brest (Université de Bretagne Occidentale) (9,951 students)
Rue des Archives, B.P. 137, 29269 Brest Cedex
Major Programs: Arts & Letters, Humanities; Law, Economics; Medicine; Dentistry; Science
Diplomas: DEUG, DEUST, L, M, MST, DESS, DEA, *Doct.*
Affiliated Institution: IREM

Université de Caen (15,600 students)
Esplanade de la Paix, 14032 Caen Cedex
Major Programs: Law; Political Science; Economics; Business; Foreign Language; History; Physical Education; Medicine & Pharmacy; Behavioral Science; Science; Geology & Regional Planning; Engineering
Diplomas: DEUG, DEUST, L, M, MST, DESS, DEA, *Doct.*
Affiliated Institutions: CPAG, IREM

Université de Chambery (Université de Savoie Chambery) (3,336 students)
Domaine Universitaire de Jacob Bellecombette, B.P. 1104, 73011 Chambery Cedex
Major Programs: Law; Social & Economics Administration; Languages; Social Sciences; Science
Diplomas: DEUG, DEUST, L, M, MST, DESS, DEA

Université de Clermont-Ferrand I (7,840 students)
49 Boulevard Gergovia, B.P. 32, 63001 Clermont-Ferrand
Major Programs: Law & Political Science; Economics; Social Sciences; Medicine; Pharmacy; Dentistry
Diplomas: DEUG, DEUST, L, M, MST, *Magistère*, DESS, DEA, *Doct.*
Affiliated Institution: CPAG

Université de Clermont-Ferrand II (7,424 students)
34, avenue Carnot, B.P. 185, 63006 Clermont-Ferrand Cedex
Major Programs: Arts & Letters; Social Sciences; Physical Education; Engineering
Diplomas: DEUG, DEUST, L, M, MST, MIAG, *Ing.*, DESS, DEA, *Doct.*
Affiliated Institution: IREM

Université de Compiègne (Université de Technologie de Compiègne) (1,500)
Centre Benjamin Franklin, Rue Roger Couttolenc, B.P. 223, 60206 Compiègne Cedex

Major Programs: Applied Mathematics & Computer Science; Bioengineering; Chemical Engineering; Electrical Engineering, Electronics, Physical & Chemical Analysis; Management & Information Science; Mechanical Engineering
Diplomas: DEUTEC, *Ing.*, DEA, *Doct.*
Instead of the traditional DEUG, the University of Compiègne, a special *university* dedicated to engineering, awards a *diplôme d'études universitaires de technologie/ DEUTEC* (diploma of university studies in technology) at the end of the first cycle of study.

Université de Corte (Université de Corse) (1,298 students)
7, avenue Jean Nicoli, B.P. 24, 20250 Corte
Major Programs: Arts & Letters; Law; Economics; Science
Diplomas: DEUG, L, M, MST

Université de Dijon (13,368 students)
Campus Universitaire de Montmuzard, B.P. 138, 21104 Dijon Cedex
Major Programs: Law & Political Science; Economics & Business; Arts & Letters; Social Sciences; Physical Education; Science; Medicine & Pharmacy; Engineering
Diplomas: DEUG, L, M, MST, DESS, DEA, *Doct.*
Affiliated Institutions: CPAG, IREM

Université de Grenoble I (Université Scientifique et Médicale) (11,726 students)
Domaine Universitaire Saint-Martin-d'Hères, B.P. 53, Centre de Tri, 38041 Grenoble Cedex
Major Programs: Science; Medicine & Pharmacy; Geography; Physical Education; Engineering
Diplomas: DEUG, DEUST, L, M, MST, MSG, MIAG, *Magistère, Ing.*, DESS, DEA, *Doct.*
Affiliated Institution: IREM

Université de Grenoble II (12,262 students)
Domaine Universitaire Saint-Martin-d'Hères, 47 X, 38040 Grenoble Cedex
Major Programs: Law & Political Science; Economics & Business; Social Sciences
Diplomas: DEUG, L, M, MST, MSG, *Magistère*, DESS, DEA, *Doct.*
Affiliated Institution: CPAG

Université de Grenoble III (Université des Langues et Lettres) (4,438 students)
Domaine Universitaire Saint-Martin-d'Hères, 25 X; 38040 Grenoble Cedex
Major Programs: Arts & Letters; Foreign Languages; Linguistics; Language Education
Diplomas: DEUG, DEUST, L, M, MST, DESS, DEA, *Doct.*

Université du Havre (1,200 students)
97, rue Jules-Siegfried, 76600 Le Havre
Major Programs: Economics; Science; Technology
Diplomas: DEUG, L, M, MST

Université de Lille I (Université des Sciences et Techniques) (13,178 students)
Cite Scientifique, 59655 Villeneuve d'Avcq Cedex
Major Programs: Economics & Business; Sociology; Geography & Regional Planning; Mathematics; Science & Applied Science; Engineering
Diplomas: DEUG, DEUST, L, M, MST, MSG, MIAG, *Magistère, Ing.*, DESS, DEA, *Doct.*
Affiliated Institution: IREM

Université de Lille II (Université du Droit et de la Santé) (16,595 students)
42, rue Paul Duez, 59000 Lille
Major Programs: Medicine; Pharmacy; Dentistry; Physical Education; Law & Political Science; Social Sciences

APPENDIX A

Diplomas: DEUG, L, M, MST, DESS, DEA, *Doct.*
Affiliated Institution: CPAG

Université de Lille III (Université des Sciences Humaines, des Lettres et des Arts) (13,360 students)
Domaine Universitaire Litteraire et Juridique, 'Pont-de-Bois' B.P. 149, 59653 Villeneuve d'Ascq Cedex
Major Programs: Arts & Letters; Foreign Languages; Classics; Social Sciences; Mathematics; Economics
Diplomas: DEUG, L, M, DESS, DEA, *Doct.*

Université de Limoges (9,317 students)
Allée Andre Maurois, 87065 Limoges Cedex
Major Programs: Law & Economics; Arts & Letters; Social Sciences; Medicine; Pharmacy; Science
Diplomas: DEUG, DEUST, L, M, MST, DESS, DEA
Affiliated Institution: IREM

Université de Lyon I (Université Claude Bernard) (22,800 students)
86, rue Pasteur, 69365 Lyon Cedex 02
Major Programs: Medicine; Pharmacy; Dentistry; Physical Education; Mathematics; Physics & Astronomy; Nuclear Physics; Mechanics; Chemistry & Biochemistry; Natural Sciences; Biological Sciences
Diplomas: DEUG, DEUST, L, M, MST, MIAG, *Magistère,* DESS, DEA, *Doct.*
Affiliated Institution: IREM

Université de Lyon II (Université Lumiere) (18,000 students)
86, rue Pasteur, 69365 Lyon Cedex 2
Major Programs: Political Sciences; Law; Economics; Arts & Letters; Social Sciences
Diplomas: DEUG, DEUST, L, M, MST, DESS, DEA, *Doct.*
Affiliated Institution: CPAG

Université de Lyon III (Université Jean Moulin) (12,986 students)
1, rue de l'Université, B.P. 155, 69224 Lyon Cedex
Major Programs: Law, Business; Foreign Languages; Philosophy
Diplomas: DEUG, L, M, MST, MSG, DESS, DEA, *Doct.*

Université du Maine, Le Mans (4,719 students)
Route de Laval, B.P. 535, 72017 Le Mans Cedex
Major Programs: Literature & Applied Languages; Law & Economics; Social Sciences; Science
Diplomas: DEUG, L, M, MST, DESS, DEA, *Doct.*

Université de Metz (7,625 students)
Ile du Saulcy, B.P. 794, 57012 Metz Cedex
Major Programs: Arts & Letters, Social Sciences; Law & Economics; Science; Environmental Science
Diplomas: DEUG, L, M, MST, MSG, DESS, DEA

Université de Montpellier I (19,000 students)
5, boulevard Henri IV, B.P. 1017, 34006 Montpellier Cedex
Major Programs: Law; Social Sciences; Economics; Physical Education; Pharmacy; Medicine; Dentistry
Diplomas: DEUG, DEUST, L, M, MST, MSG, *Magistère,* DESS, DEA, *Doct.*
Affiliated Institution: CPAG

Université de Montpellier II (Université des Sciences et Techniques du Languedoc) (6,500 students)
Place Eugene Bataillon, 34060 Montpellier Cedex
Major Programs: Engineering; Science; Business
Diplomas: DEUG, DEUST, L, M, MST, MIAG, *Ing.*, DESS, DEA, *Doct.*
Affiliated Institution: IREM

Université de Montpellier III (Université Paul Valéry) (10,500 students)
Route de Mende, B.P. 5043, 34032 Montpellier Cedex
Major Programs: Arts & Letters, Classics; Social Sciences
Diplomas: DEUG, DU, L, M, MST, DESS, DEA, *Doct.*

Université de Mulhouse (Université de Haute Alsace) (3,393 students)
61, rue Albert Camus, 68093 Mulhouse Cedex
Major Programs: Pure & Applied Science; Arts & Letters, Social Sciences; Engineering
Diplomas: DEUG, DEUST, DU, L, M, MST, MIAG, DESS, DEA, *Doct.*

Université de Nancy I (13,947 students)
24, rue Lionnois, B.P. 3137, 54013 Nancy Cedex
Major Programs: Medicine; Pharmacy; Dentistry; Science; Engineering; Physical Education
Diplomas: DEUG, L, M, MST, *Magistère, Ing.*, DESS, DEA, *Doct.*
Affiliated Institution: IREM

Université de Nancy II (10,630 students)
25, rue Baron-Louis, B.P. 454, 54001 Nancy Cedex
Major Programs: Art & Letters; Social Sciences; Applied Linguistics; Mathematics; Computer Science
Diplomas: DEUG, L, M, MST, MSG, MIAG, DESS, DEA, *Doct.*
Affiliated Institution: CPAG

Université de Nantes (19,077 students)
1, quai de Tourville, B.P. 1026, 44035 Nantes Cedex
Major Programs: Law; Economics, Business; Arts & Letters, Foreign Languages—Classics; Social Sciences; Medicine; Pharmacy; Dentistry; Engineering
Diplomas: DEUG, DEUST, L, M, MST, *Ing.*, DESS, DEA, *Doct.*
Affiliated Institution: IREM

Université de Nice (18,929 students)
Parc Valrose, 06034 Nice Cedex
Major Programs: Law; Economics; Arts & Letters; Social Sciences; Medicine; Dentistry; Mathematics & Science
Diplomas: DEUG, DEUST, L, M, MST, MIAG, *Magistère*, DESS, DEA, *Doct.*
Affiliated Institution: IREM

Université d'Orléans (7,637 students)
Château de la Source, Orléans 2, 45046 Orléans Cedex
Major Programs: Law, Economics; Arts & Letters; Foreign Languages; Social Sciences; Applied Sciences; Engineering
Diplomas: DEUG, DEUST, L, M, MST, MIAG, *Magistère, Ing.*, DESS, DEA, *Doct.*
Affiliated Institution: IREM

Université de Paris I (Université Panthéon-Sorbonne) (33,047 students)
12, place du Panthéon, 75231 Paris Cedex 05
Major Programs: Law, Political Science; Economics; Arts & Letters; Social Sciences
Diplomas: DEUG, DEUST, L, M, MST, MSG, *Magistère*, DESS, DEA, *Doct.*

APPENDIX A

Université de Paris II (Université de Droit, d'Economie et des Sciences Sociales) (17,342 students)
12, place du Panthéon, 75231 Paris Cedex 05
Major Programs: Law & Political Science; Economics; Journalism; Social Sciences
Diplomas: DEUG, L, M, *Magistère*, DESS, DEA, *Doct.*
Affiliated Institution: CPAG

Université de Paris III (Université de la Sorbonne-Nouvelle) (15,413 students)
17, place de la Sorbonne, 75230 Paris Cedex 05
Major Programs: Art & Letters; Foreign Language & Literature
Diplomas: DEUG, L, M, MST, *Magistère*, DESS, DEA, *Doct.*
Affiliated Institution: INALCO

Université de Paris IV (Université de Paris-Sorbonne) (21,148 students)
1, rue Victor Cousin, 75230 Paris Cedex 05
Major Programs: Arts & Letters; Social Sciences
Diplomas: DEUG, L, M, *Magistère*, DESS, DEA, *Doct.*

Université de Paris V (Université René Descartes) (37,136 students)
12, rue de l'Ecole de Médecine, 75270 Paris Cedex 06
Major Programs: Social Sciences; Law; Medical Ethics; Linguistics; Medicine; Pharmacy; Dentistry; Physical Education
Diplomas: DEUG, L, M, MST, *Magistère*, DESS, DEA, *Doct.*

Université de Paris VI (Université Pierre et Marie Curie) (31,416 students)
4, place Jussieu, 75230 Paris Cedex 05
Major Programs: Mathematics; Computer Science; Science; Medicine; Engineering
Diplomas: DEUG, DEUST, L, M, MST, MSG, MIAG, *Magistère, Ing.*, DESS, DEA, *Doct.*

Université de Paris VII (35,000 students)
2, place Jussieu, 75521 Paris Cedex 05
Major Programs: Science; Mathematics; Medicine; Dentistry; Arts, Letters, Social Science, Foreign Languages
Diplomas: DEUG, L, M, *Magistère*, DESS, DEA, *Doct.*
Affiliated Institution: IREM

Université de Paris VIII (Université de Vincennes-Saint-Denis) (24,500 students)
2, rue de la Liberté, 93526 Saint-Denis Cedex
Major Programs: Arts & Letters; Foreign Languages; Computer Science; Social Sciences
Diplomas: DEUG, L, M, *Magistère*, DESS, DEA, *Doct.*

Université de Paris IX (Université de Paris-Dauphine) (5,800 students)
Place du Maréchal de-Lattre-de-Tassigny, 75775 Paris Cedex 16
Major Programs: Business & Applied Economics; Organizational Science; Computers; Mathematics for Business
Diplomas: DEUG, L, M, MST, MSG, MIAG, *Magistère*, DESS, DEA, *Doct.*

Université de Paris X (Université de Paris-Nanterre) (25,148 students)
200, avenue de la République, 92001 Nanterre Cedex
Major Programs: Arts & Letters, Classics, Linguistics; Social Sciences; Law; Economics; Physical Education
Diplomas: DEUG, L, M, *Magistère*, DESS, DEA, *Doct.*
Affiliated Institution: CPAG

Université de Paris XI (Université de Paris-Sud) (23,815 students)
15, rue Georges Clemenceau, 91405 Orsay Cedex
Major Programs: Sciences; Law, Economics; Pharmacy; Medicine; Engineering
Diplomas: DEUG, DEUST, L, M, MST, MIAG, *Magistère, Ing.*, DESS, DEA, *Doct.*

Université de Paris XII (Université Paris-Val-de-Marne) (14,000 students)
Avenue du Général de Gaulle, 94010 Créteil Cedex
Major Programs: Law & Political Science; Economics; Arts & Letters; Social Sciences; Urban Studies
Diplomas: DEUG, DEUST, L, M, MST, MSG, MIAG, DESS, DEA, *Doct.*
Affiliated Institution: CPAG

Université de Paris XIII (Université Paris-Nord) (12,000 students)
Avenue Jean-Baptiste Clement, 93430 Villentaneuse
Major Programs: Law & Political Science; Economics; Arts & Letters, Social Sciences, Science; Engineering
Diplomas: DEUG, L, M, MST, MSG, *Magistère, Ing.*, DESS, DEA, *Doct.*
Affiliated Institution: IREM

Université de Pau et des Pays de l'Adour (7,255 students)
Villa Lawrence, 68, rue Montpensier, B.P. 576, 64010 Pau Cedex
Major Programs: Law; Economics; Arts & Letters; Social Sciences; Science
Diplomas: DEUG, DEUST, L, M, MST, DESS, DEA, *Doct.*

Université de Perpignan (3,637 students)
Avenue de Villeneuve, 66025 Perpignan Cedex
Major Programs: Law; Economics; Applied Languages & Literatures; Science; History, Geography
Diplomas: DEUG, DU, L, M, DESS, DEA.

Université de Poitiers (15,575 students)
15, rue de Blossac, 86034 Poitiers Cedex
Major Programs: Law, Business & Economics; Science; Engineering; Language & Literature; Social Sciences; Medicine; Pharmacy
Diplomas: DEUG, DEUST, L, M, MST, MSG, *Magistère, Ing.*, DESS, DEA, *Doct.*
Affiliated Institutions: CPAG, IREM

Université de Reims Champagne-Ardennes (14,400 students)
23 rue Boulard, 51100 Reims
Major Programs: Law, Economics; Arts & Letters, Social Science; Science; Medicine; Dentistry; Pharmacy
Diplomas: DEUG, DEUST, L, M, MST, DESS, DEA, *Doct.*
Affiliated Institution: IREM

Université de Rennes I (18,600 students)
2, rue du Thabor, 35000 Rennes
Major Programs: Law; Business Economics; Philosophy; Science, Mathematics, Computer Science; Medicine; Dentistry; Pharmacy; Engineering
Diplomas: DEUG, L, M, MST, MSG, MIAG, *Magistère, Ing.*, DESS, DEA, *Doct.*
Affiliated Institutions: CPAG, IREM

Université de Rennes II (Université de Haute-Bretagne) (12,971 students)
6, avenue Gaston-Berger, 35043 Rennes Cedex
Major Programs: Arts & Letters; Foreign Languages; Social Sciences; Applied Sciences; Physical Education
Diplomas: DEUG, L, M, DESS, DEA, *Doct.*

Université de la Réunion (2,928 students)
  12, avenue de la Victoire, B.P. 847, 97489 Saint-Denis, La Réunion
  Major Programs: Law, Political Science; Economics; Arts & Letters; Social Sciences; Science
  Diplomas: DEUG, DEUST, L, M

Université de Rouen (Université de Rouen-Haute Normandie) (14,492 students)
  Rue Thomas Beckett, 76130 Mont-Saint-Aignan
  Major Programs: Law, Economics; Arts & Letters, Humanities; Medicine; Pharmacy; Sciences
  Diplomas: DEUG, DEUST, L, M, MST, DESS, DEA, *Doct.*
  Affiliated Institution: IREM

Université de Saint-Etienne (7,720 students)
  34, rue Francis Baulier, 42023 Saint-Etienne Cedex
  Major Programs: Law; Economics; Science; Arts & Letters; Foreign Languages; Medicine; History; Geography
  Diplomas: DEUG, L, M, MST, DESS, DEA

Université de Strasbourg I (Université Louis Pasteur) (14,321 students)
  4, rue Blaise Pascal, 67070 Strasbourg Cedex
  Major Programs: Medicine; Dentistry; Pharmacy; Science; Engineering; Social Sciences, Economics
  Diplomas: DEUG, L, M, MSG, *Magistère, Ing.*, DESS, DEA, *Doct.*
  Affiliated Institution: IREM

Université de Strasbourg II (Université des Sciences Humaines) (8,937 students)
  22, rue Descartes, 67084 Strasbourg Cedex
  Major Programs: Arts & Letters; Social Sciences; Theology; Physical Education
  Diplomas: DEUG, L, M, DESS, DEA, *Doct.*

Université de Strasbourg III (Université des Sciences Juridiques, Politiques, Sociales et de Technologie) (5,814 students)
  Place d'Athènes, 67084 Strasbourg Cedex
  Major Programs: Law, Economics; Journalism; Applied Research Technology
  Diplomas: DEUG, L, M, MST, DESS, DEA, *Doct.*
  Affiliated Institution: CPAG

Université de Tours (Université François Rabelais) (15,513 students)
  3, rue des Tanneurs, 37041 Tours Cedex
  Major Programs: Arts & Letters; Law, Economics; Medicine; Pharmacy, Science; Social Sciences
  Diplomas: DEUG, DEUST, L, M, MST, DESS, DEA, *Doct.*

Université de Toulon et du Var (3,063 students)
  Avenue de l'Université, 83130 Le Garde
  Major Programs: Law and Economics; Science
  Diplomas: DEUG, L, M, MST

Université de Toulouse I (Université des Sciences Sociales) (13,483 students)
  Place Anatole France, 31070 Toulouse Cedex
  Major Programs: Law; Economics, Business
  Diplomas: DEUG, DEUST, L, M, MIAG, *Magistère*, DESS, DEA, *Doct.*
  Affiliated Institution: CPAG

Université de Toulouse II (Université de Toulouse le Mirail) (15,000 students)
   109 bis, rue Vauquelin, 31081 Toulouse Cedex
Major Programs: Social Sciences; Arts & Letters; Mathematics for Social Sciences
Diplomas: DEUG, DEUST, L, M, MST, DESS, DEA, Doct.

Université de Toulouse III (Université Paul Sabatier) (22,755 students)
   118, route de Narbonne, 31077 Toulouse Cedex
Major Programs: Medicine; Dentistry; Pharmacy; Physical Education; Science, Mathematics, Engineering
Diplomas: DEUG, L, M, MST, MIAG, *Magistère*, DESS, DEA, Doct.
Affiliated Institution: IREM

Université de Valenciennes et du Hainaut-Cambrésis (4,400 students)
   Le Mont Houy, 59326 Valenciennes Cedex
Major Programs: Science; Social Sciences; Art; Law, Economics, Business; Engineering
Diplomas: DEUG, DEUST, L, M, MST, *Ing*.

Université de Bourges—established in 1986 as **Université de Technologie du Centre de la France** (University of Technology of Central France). (259–300 students)
Major Programs: MST in automatic production; quality control and international trade

Private Universities

Private universities award national degrees of higher education by authority of the Ministry of Education either independently or in association with public universities. Degrees and diplomas specific to each institution *(diplômes d'université)* are also awarded.

Faculté Libre, Autonome et Cogérée d'Economie et de Droit de Paris/FACO (300 students)
   115, rue de Notre-Dame-des-Champs, 75006 Paris
Major Programs: Economics; Law
Diplomas: Specific to the institution

Faculté Libre de Droit de Valence
   12, rue Louis-Gallet, 26000 Valence
Major Program: Law
Diploma (in affiliation with the University of Grenoble II): DEUG

Faculté Libre de Paris
   223, rue du Faubourg Saint Honoré, 75008 Paris
Major Programs: Arts & Letters; Foreign Languages; Social Sciences
Diplomas: DEUG, L, M in association with the Universities of Paris IV and Paris X

Faculté Libre de Philosophie Comparée (260 students)
   70, avenue Denfert-Rochereau, 75014 Paris Cedex
Major Programs: Law; Economics; Social Sciences
Diplomas (in affiliation with University of Paris IV): DEUG, L, M

Faculté Libre de Theologie Evangélique
   85, Avenue de Cherbourg, 78740 Vaux-sur-Seine Cedex
Major Program: Theology
Diplomas: Specific to the institution

Fédération Universitaire et Polytechnique de Lille (9,500 students)
   60, Boulevard Vauban, 59046 Lille Cedex

Major Programs: Law; Literature & Humanities; Medicine; Science; Economics; Theology
Diplomas: DEUG, L, M, DEA, *Doct.*

Institut Catholique de Paris (14,685 students)
21, rue d'Assas, 75270 Paris Cedex
Major Programs: Canonic Law; Foreign Languages; History; Literature; Philosophy
Diplomas (in affiliation with the University of Paris IV): DEUG, L, M

Institut Catholique de Toulouse (5,100 students)
31, rue de la Fonderie, 31068 Toulouse Cedex
Major Programs: Theology; Canonic Law; Philosophy, Literature
Diplomas: DEUG, L, M, DEA, *Doct.*

Institut Protestant de Théologie (approx. 350 students)
83, boulevard Arago, 75014 Paris. The institution has a branch in Montpellier.
Major Program: Theology
Diplomas: Specific to the institution

Université Catholique de Lyon (4,700 students)
25, rue du Plat, 69288 Lyon Cedex
Major Programs: Theology; Philosophy; Pedagogy; Law; Social Sciences; Languages & Literature; Science; Sacred Music
Diplomas: D, L, M, DEA, *Doct.*

Université Catholique de l'Ouest (4,300 students)
30, place André-Leroy, 49005 Angers Cedex
Major Programs: Theology; Literature; History; Languages, Psychology; Education; Physical Education; Mathematics
Diplomas: DEUG, L, M, DEA, *Doct.*

Appendix B

Institutions Which Award the *Diplôme d' Ingénieur*

Institutions are listed in alphabetical order. The name of each school is followed by its formal abbreviation, the city where it is located and the total enrollment in the 1985–86 academic year in parentheses. Student records will often bear the full name of the institution; however, it is not unusual for the abbreviation to appear following the title of *diplôme d'ingénieur*. **C.P.** = *classes préparatoires*.

Name of School and Location	Entrance Requirements	Length of Studies	Diploma Conferred
Centre d'Etudes Supérieures Industrielles/CESI, Paris (320)	BTS/DUT + 5 years work experience	22 months	*Dip. d'Ing. Diplômé du CESI*
Centre d'Etudes Supérieures des Techniques Industrielles/CESTI, Saint-Ouen (170)	*Bacc.* + 2 years C.P.	3 years	*Dip. d'Ing.*
Centre National d'Etudes Agronomiques des Régions Chaudes/CNEARC-ESAT, Montpellier (10)	*Dip. d'Ing.*	2 years	*Dip. d'Ing. d'Agronomie Tropicale*
Centre National Supérieur de Mécanique et de Microtechniques/ENSMM, Besançon (315)	*Bacc.* + 2 years C.P./DEUG/DUT/BTS	3 years	*Dip. d'Ing. ENSMM*
Centre Universitaire des Sciences et Techniques/CUST (Université de Clermont-Ferrand II) (483)	DEUG	3 years	*Dip. d'Ing. CUST de l'Université de Clermont I*
Conservatoire National des Arts et Métiers/CNAM, Paris	Open	variable	*Dip. d'Ing. CNAM*
Cours Supérieur d'Armement/CoSAr, Paris (12)	*Bacc.* + 2 years C.P./DEUG	2 years	*Dip. d'Ingénieur de l'Armée de Terre, Diplôme du CoSAr*
Cours Supérieur d'Engins Missiles/COSEM, Paris (6)	*Bacc.* + 2 years C.P./DEUG	18 months + 5 months practical training	*Dip. d'Ingénieur de l'Armée de Terre, Diplôme du COSEM*

APPENDIX B

School	Entry Requirement	Duration	Diploma
Ecole de l'Air/EA, Salon de Provence (183)	Bacc. + 2 years C.P.	3 years	*Dip. d'Ingénieur de l'Ecole de l'Air*
Ecole d'Application des Hauts Polymères/EAHP, Strasbourg (32)	*Dip. d'Ing./Maîtrise*	2 years	*Dip. d'Ing. de l'EAHP*
Ecole Catholique d'Arts et Métiers/ECAM, Lyon (246)	Bacc.	5 years	*Dip. d'Ing. ECAM*
Ecole Centrale de Lyon/ECL (640)	Bacc. + 2 years C.P.	3 years	*Dip. d'Ing. ECL*
Ecole Centrale des Arts et Manufactures/ECP, Paris (1071)	Bacc. + 2 years C.P.	3 years	*Dip. d'Ing. des Arts et Manufactures*
Ecole Française de Papeterie de Grenoble/EFPG (78)	Bacc. + 2 years C.P./DEUG	3 years	*Dip. d'Ing. EFPG*
Ecole Française de Radioélectricité, d'Electronique et d'Informatique/EFREI, Paris (257)	Bacc.	4 years	*Dip. d'Ing. EFREI*
Ecole des Ingénieurs de la Ville de Paris/IVP (50)	Bacc. + 2 years C.P.	3 years	*Dip. d'Ing. de l'Ecole des Ingénieurs de la Ville de Paris*
Ecole Nationale de l'Aviation Civile/ENAC, Toulouse (190)	Bacc. + 2 years C.P.	3 years	*Dip. d'Ing. ENAC*
Ecole Nationale du Génie Rural des Eaux et Forêts/ENGREF, Paris (150)	*Dip. d'Ing.* of the Ecole Polytechnique and *Dip. d'Ing.* of the Institut National Agronomique	27 months	*Dip. d'Ing. du Corps du Génie Rural, des Eaux et des Forêts/Dip. d'Ing. Civil du Génie Rural, des Eaux et des Forêts/Dip. d'Ing. Civil des Forêts*
Ecole Nationale d'Ingénieurs de Belfort/ENIBe (370)	Bacc.	4 years	*Dip. d'Ing. de l'ENIBe*
Ecole Nationale d'Ingénieurs de Brest/ENIBr (311)	Bacc.	4 years	*Dip. d'Ing. de l'ENIBr*
Ecole Nationale d'Ingénieurs de Metz/ENIM (453)	Bacc.	4 years	*Dip d'Ing. de l'ENIM*

200   APPENDIX B

Ecole Nationale d'Ingénieurs de Saint-Etienne/ENISE (398)	Bacc.	5 years	Dip. d'Ing. de l'ENISE
Ecole Nationale d'Ingénieurs de Tarbes/ENIT (352)	Bacc.	5 years	Dip. d'Ing. de l'ENIT
Ecole Nationale d'Ingénieurs des Techniques des Industries Agricoles et Alimentaires/ENITIAA, Nantes (124)	Bacc. + 1 year C.P.	3 years	Dip. d'Ing. des Techniques des Industries Agricoles et Alimentaires
Ecole Nationale d'Ingénieurs des Travaux Agricoles d'Angers/ENITAH (133)	Bacc. + 1 year C.P.	3 years	Dip. d'Ing. des Techniques Horticoles
Ecole Nationale d'Ingénieurs des Travaux Agricoles de Bordeaux/ENITAB (150)	Bacc. + 1 year C.P.	3 years	Dip. d'Ing. des Techniques Agricoles de l'ENITAB
Ecole Nationale d'Ingénieurs des Travaux Agricoles de Clermont-Ferrand/ENITAC (202)	Bacc. + 1 year C.P.	3 years	Dip. d'Ing. des Techniques Agricoles de l'ENITAC
Ecole Nationale d'Ingénieurs des Travaux Agricoles de Dijon/ENITAD (147)	Bacc. + 1 year C.P.	3 years	Dip. d'Ing. des Techniques Agricoles de l'ENITAD
Ecole Nationale d'Ingénieurs des Travaux des Eaux et Forêts/ENITEF, Nogent/Vernisson (98)	Bacc. + 2 years C.P.	3 years	Dip. d'Ing. des Techniques Forestières
Ecole Nationale d'Ingénieurs des Travaux Ruraux et des Techniques Sanitaires/ENITRTS, Strasbourg (168)	Bacc. + 2 years C.P.	3 years	Dip. d'Ing. des Techniques de l'Equipement
Ecole Nationale de la Météorologie/ENM Toulouse (162)	Graduates of Ecole Polytechnique/Maîtrise	2 years	Dip. d'Ing. Civil de la Météorologie
Ecole Nationale des Ponts et Chaussées/ENPC, Paris (411)	Bacc. + 2 years C.P./Graduates of the Ecole Polytechnique	3 years	Dip. d'Ing. de l'ENPC
Ecole Nationale de la Santé Publique/ENSP, Rennes (20–30)	Dip. d'Ing.	1 year	Dip. d'Ing. du Génie Sanitaire de l'ENSP

APPENDIX B

Ecole Nationale des Sciences Géographiques/ ENSG, Saint-Mande (149)	Bacc. + 2 years C.P.	3 years / 2 years	Dip. d'Ing. de l'ENSG/Dip. du Corps des Ingénieurs Géographes/ Dip. d'Ing. Civil Géographe
Ecole Nationale Supérieure de l'Aéronautique et de l'Espace/ENSAE/SUP' AERO, Toulouse (393)	Bacc. + 2 years C.P./ Graduates of the Ecole Polytechnique	3 years	Dip. d'Ing. de l'ENSAE
Ecole Nationale Supérieure d'Agronomie et des Industries Alimentaires de Nancy/ ENSAIA (302)	Bacc. + 2 years C.P./DEUG	3 years	Dip. d'Ing. Agronome de l'ENSAIA/Dip. d'Ing. des Industries Alimentaires de l'ENSAIA
Ecole Nationale Supérieure Agronomique de Montpellier/ENSAM (294)	Bacc. + 2 years C.P.	3 years	Dip. d'Ing. Agronome de l'ENSAM
Ecole Nationale Supérieure Agronomique de Rennes/ENSAR (380)	Bacc. + 2 years C.P.	3 years	Dip. d'Ing. Agronome de l'ENSAR
Ecole Nationale Supérieure Agronomique de Toulouse/ENSAT (186)	Bacc. + 2 years C.P.	3 years	Dip. d'Ing. Agronome de l'ENSAT
Ecole Nationale Supérieure des Arts et Industries de Strasbourg/ENSAIS (492)	Bacc. + 2 years C.P.	3 years	Dip. d'Ing. de l'ENSAIS
Ecole Nationale Supérieure des Arts et Industries Textiles/ENSAIT, Roubaix (147)	Bacc. + 2 years C.P./DEUG/ DUT	3 years	Dip. d'Ing. des Arts et Industries Textiles
Ecole Nationale Supérieure d'Arts et Métiers/ ENSAM, Paris (768)	Bacc. + 2 years C.P.	3 years	Dip. d'Ing. de l'ENSAM
Ecole Nationale Supérieure de Biologie Appliquée à la Nutrition et à l'Alimentation/ ENSBANA, Dijon (140)	Bacc. + 2 years C.P./DEUG	3 years	Dip. d'Ing.
Ecole Nationale Supérieure de Céramique Industrielle/ENSCI, Limoges (110)	Bacc. + 2 years C.P.	3 years	Dip. d'Ing. Céramiste de l'ENSCI

APPENDIX B

Ecole Nationale Supérieure de Chimie de Clermont-Ferrand/ENSCCF (134)	Bacc. + 2 years C.P./DEUG	3 years	Dip. d'Ing. Chimiste ENSCCF
Ecole Nationale Supérieure de Chimie de Lille/ENSCL (140)	Bacc. + 2 years C.P./DEUG	3 years	Dip. d'Ing. ENSCL
Ecole Nationale Supérieure de Chimie de Montpellier/ENSCM (156)	Bacc. + 2 years C.P./DEUG	3 years	Dip. d'Ing. Chimiste de l'ENSC de Montpellier
Ecole Nationale Supérieure de Chimie de Mulhouse/ENSCMU (94)	Bacc. + 2 years C.P./DEUG	3 years	Dip. d'Ing.-Chimiste ENSCMU
Ecole Nationale Supérieure de Chimie de Paris/ENSCP (185)	Bacc. + 2 years C.P./DEUG	3 years	Dip. d'Ing. ENSCP
Ecole Nationale Supérieure de Chimie et de Physique de Bordeaux/ENSCPB (150)	Bacc. + 2 years C.P./DEUG	3 years	Dip. d'Ing. de l'ENSCPB
Ecole Nationale Supérieure de Chimie de Rennes/ENSCR (120)	Bacc. + 2 years C.P./DEUG	3 years	Dip. d'Ing. ENSCR
Ecole Nationale Supérieure de Chimie de Strasbourg/ENSCS (102)	Bacc. + 2 years C.P./DEUG	3 years	Dip. d'Ing. ENSCS
Ecole Nationale Supérieure de Chimie de Toulouse/ENSCT (163)	Bacc. + 2 years C.P./DEUG	3 years	Dip. d'Ing.-Chimiste de l'ENSCT
Ecole Nationale Supérieure d'Electricité et de Mécanique/ENSEM, Nancy (276)	Bacc. + 2 years C.P./DEUG	3 years	Dip. d'Ing. ENSEM
Ecole Nationale Supérieure d'Electrochimie et d'Electrométallurgie de Grenoble/ENSEEG (275)	Bacc. + 2 years C.P./DEUG	3 years	Dip. d'Ing. de l'ENSEEG
Ecole Nationale Supérieure d'Electronique et de ses Applications/ENSEA, Cergy (320)	Bacc. + 2 years C.P./DEUG	3 years	Dip. d'Ing. Electronicien de l'ENSEA
Ecole Nationale Supérieure d'Electronique et de Radioélectricité de Bordeaux/ENSERB (187)	Bacc. + 2 years C.P./DEUG	3 years	Dip. d'Ing. ENSERB

APPENDIX B

Ecole Nationale Supérieure d'Electronique et de Radioélectricité de Grenoble/ENSERG (325)	Bacc. + 2 years C.P./DEUG	3 years	Dip. d'Ing. ENSERG
Ecole Nationale Supérieure d'Electrotechnique, d'Electronique, d'Informatique et d'Hydraulique de Toulouse/ENSEEIHT (704)	Bacc. + 2 years C.P./DEUG	3 years	Dip. d'Ing. de l'ENSEEIHT
Ecole Nationale Supérieure Féminine d'Agronomie/ENSFA, Rennes (150)	Bacc.	4 years	Dip. d'Ing. de l'ENSFA
Ecole Nationale Supérieure de Géologie Appliquée et de Prospection Minière/ENSG, Nancy (170)	Bacc. + 2 years/DEUG	3 years	Dip. d'Ing. de l'ENSG
Ecole Nationale Supérieure d'Horticulture/ENSH, Versailles (74)	Bacc. + 4 years (Diplôme d'Agronomie Générale/Maîtrise)	2 years	Dip. d'Ing. de l'ENSH
Ecole Nationale Supérieure d'Hydraulique de Grenoble/ENSHG (180)	Bacc. + 2 years C.P./DEUG	3 years	Dip. d'Ing. de l'ENSHG
Ecole Nationale Supérieure des Industries Agricoles et Alimentaires/ENSAIA, Massy (189)	Bacc. + 2 years C.P./DEUG	3 years	Dip. d'Ing. des Industries Agricoles et Alimentaires
Ecole Nationale Supérieure des Industries Chimiques/ENSIC, Nancy (210)	Bacc. + 2 years C.P./DEUG	3 years	Dip. d'Ing. des Industries Chimiques (ENSIC)
Ecole Nationale Supérieure des Industries Textiles de Mulhouse/ENSITM (54)	Bacc. + 2 years C.P./DEUG	3 years	Dip. d'Ing. de l'ENSITM
Ecole Nationale Supérieure d'Informatique et de Mathématiques Appliquées de Grenoble/ENSIMAG (340)	Bacc. + 2 years C.P./DEUG	3 years	Dip. d'Ing. de l'ENSIMAG
Ecole Nationale Supérieure d'Ingénieurs de Caen/ISMRA (280)	Bacc. + 2 years C.P./DEUG	3 years	Dip. d'Ing. de l'ISMRA

School	Entry Requirement	Duration	Diploma
Ecole Nationale Supérieure d'Ingénieurs de Constructions Aéronautiques/ENSICA, Toulouse (225)	Bacc. + 2 years C.P./DEUG	3 years	Dip. d'Ing. de Constructions Aéronautiques (ENSICA)
Ecole Nationale Supérieure d'Ingénieurs Electriciens de Grenoble/ENSIEG (682)	Bacc. + 2 years C.P./DEUG	3 years	Diplôme National de l'Ecole Nationale Supérieure d'Ingénieurs Electriciens de Grenoble
Ecole Nationale Supérieure d'Ingénieurs des Etudes et Techniques d'Armement/ENSIETA, Arcueil and Brest (343)	Bacc. + 2 years C.P.	4 years	Dip. d'Ing. de l'ENSIETA
Ecole Nationale Supérieure d'Ingénieurs de Mécanique et d'Energetique de Valenciennes/ENSIMEV (Université de Valenciennes) (131)	Bacc. + 2 years C.P./DEUG	3 years	Dip. d'Ing. de l'ENSIMEV
Ecole Nationale Supérieure de Mécanique/ENSM, Nantes (512)	Bacc. + 2 years C.P./DEUG	3 years	Dip. d'Ing. ENSM
Ecole Nationale Supérieure de Mécanique et d'Aérotechnique/ENSMA, Poitiers (256)	Bacc. + 2 years C.P./DEUG	3 years	Dip. d'Ing. ENSMA
Ecole Nationale Supérieure de la Métallurgie et de l'Industrie des Mines/ENSMIM, Nancy (235)	Bacc. + 2 years C.P.	3 years	Dip. d'Ing. Civil des Mines de l'Ecole Nationale Supérieure des Mines de Nancy/Dip. d'Ing. en Génie Industriel
Ecole Nationale Supérieure de Meunerie et des Industries Céréalières/ENSMIC, Paris	Dip. d'Ing.	1 year	Dip. d'Ing. Meunier
Ecole Nationale Supérieure des Mines de Paris/EMP (370)	Bacc. + 2 years C.P./Graduates of the Ecole Polytechnique	3 years	Dip. d'Ing. Civil des Mines (EMP)/Dip. d'Ing. au Corps National des Mines
Ecole Nationale Supérieure des Mines de Saint-Etienne/EMSE (223)	Bacc. + 2 years C.P.	3 years	Dip. d'Ing. Civil des Mines de l'Ecole Nationale Supérieure des Mines de Saint-Etienne

APPENDIX B

School	Entry Requirement	Duration	Diploma
Ecole Nationale Supérieure du Pétrole et des Moteurs/ENSPM, Rueil-Malmaison (170)	Dip. d'Ing./Maîtrise	11–18 months	Dip. d'Ing. de l'ENSPM
Ecole Nationale Supérieure de Physique de Marseille/ENSPM (186)	Bacc. + 2 years C.P.	3 years	Dip. d'Ing. ENSPM
Ecole Nationale Supérieure de Physique de Strasbourg/ENSPS (130)	Bacc. + 2 years C.P./DEUG/DUT	3 years	Dip. d'Ing. de l'ENSPS
Ecole Nationale Supérieure des Sciences Agronomiques Appliquées/ENSSAA, Dijon (70)	Dip. d'Ing. d'Agronome	2 years	Dip. d'Ing. Civil de l'ENSSAA/ Dip. d'Ing. du Corps d'Agronomie
Ecole Nationale Supérieure des Techniques Avancées/ENSTA, Paris (389)	Bacc. + 2 years C.P. Dip. d'Ing.	3 years 2 years	Dip. d'Ing. ENSTA
Ecole Nationale Supérieure des Techniques Industrielles et des Mines d'Alès/ENSTIMA (358)	Bacc. + 1 year C.P.	4 years	Dip. d'Ing. de l'ENSTIMA
Ecole Nationale Supérieure des Techniques Industrielles et des Mines de Douai/ENSTIMD (249)	Bacc. + 1 year C.P.	4 years	Dip. d'Ing. de l'ENSTIMD
Ecole Nationale Supérieure des Télécommunications/ENST/TELECOM, Paris (435)	Bacc. + 2 years C.P./ Graduates of the Ecole Polytechnique	3 years	Dip. d'Ing. de l'Ecole Nationale Supérieure des Télécommunications (ENST)
Ecole Nationale Supérieure des Télécommunications de Bretagne/ENST/BR, Brest (244)	Bacc. + 2 years C.P.	3 years	Dip. d'Ing. de l'Ecole Nationale Supérieure des Télécommunications de Bretagne (ENST/BR)
Ecole Nationale des Travaux Publics de l'Etat/ ENTPE, Vaulx-en-Velin (511)	Bacc. + 2 years C.P.	3 years	Dip. d'Ing. de l'ENTPE
Ecole Navale/EN, Lanveoc-Crozon (140)	Bacc. + 2 years C.P.	3 years	Dip. d'Ing. EN
Ecole Polytechnique/EP/X, Palaiseau (672)	Bacc. + 2 years C.P.	2 years	Dip. d'Ing. de l'Ecole Polytechnique

Ecole de Polytechnique Féminine/EPF, Sceaux (620)	*Bacc.*	5 years	*Dip. d'Ing. de l'Ecole Polytechnique Féminine*
Ecole Spéciale de Mécanique et d'Electricité/ESME/SUDRIA, Paris (620)	*Bacc.*	5 years	*Dip. d'Ing. Mécanicien-Electricien/Dip. d'Ing. Mécanicien-Electronicien*
Ecole Spéciale Militaire de Saint-Cyr/ESM, Coëtquidan (56)	*Bacc.* + 2 years C.P.	3 years	*Dip. d'Ing. de l'Ecole Spéciale Militaire de Saint-Cyr*
Ecole Spéciale des Travaux Publics, du Bâtiment et de l'Industrie/ETP, Paris (1114)	*Bacc.* + 2 years C.P.	3 years	*Dip. d'Ing. des Travaux du Bâtiment (ETP)/Dip. d'Ing. des Travaux Publics (ETP)/Dip. d'Ing. Mécanicien-Electricien (ETP)/Dip. d'Ing. Géomètre (ETP)*
Ecole Supérieure d'Agriculture d'Angers/ESA (360)	*Bacc.*	5 years	*Dip. d'Ing. en Agriculture de l'ESA d'Angers*
Ecole Supérieure d'Agriculture de Purpan/ESAP, Toulouse (414)	*Bacc.*	5 years	*Dip. d'Ing. en Agriculture de l'ESAP*
Ecole Supérieure d'Application des Corps Gras/ESACG, Pessac (10)	*Dip. d'Ing.*	1 year	*Dip. d'Ing. ESACG*
Ecole Supérieure du Bois/ESB, Paris (100–120)	*Bacc.* + 2 years C.P.	3 years	*Dip. d'Ing. de l'ESB*
Ecole Supérieure de Chimie Industrielle de Lyon/ESCIL, Villeurbanne (203)	*Bacc.* + 2 years C.P./DEUG/DUT	3 years	*Dip. d'Ing. Chimiste de l'ESCIL*
Ecole Supérieure de Chimie de Marseille/ESCM (173)	*Bacc.*	5 years	*Dip. d'Ing. Chimiste de l'Université d'Aix-Marseille (Ingénieur Chimiste U.AM)*
Ecole Supérieure de Chimie Organique et Minérale/ESCOM, Paris (113)	*Bacc.*	5 years	*Dip. d'Ing. ESCOM*
Ecole Supérieure du Cuir et des Peintures, Encres et Adhésifs/ESCEPEA, Lyon (80)	*Bacc.* + 2 years C.P./DEUG	3 years	*Dip. d'Ing. de l'ESCEPEA*

APPENDIX B

Ecole Supérieure d'Electricité/ESE/SUPELEC, Gif-sur-Yvette (1015)	Bacc. + 2 years C.P./DEUG Dip. d'Ing.	3 years 2 years	Dip. d'Ing. ESE Dip. d'Ing. en Informatique Avancée de l'ESE
Ecole Supérieure d'Electronique de l'Armée de Terre/ESEAT, Cesson-Sevigné (48)	Graduates of Saint-Cyr Military Academy/DEUG	2 years	Dip. d'Ing. de l'Armée de Terre
Ecole Supérieure d'Electronique de l'Ouest/ESEO, Angers (225)	Bacc.	5 years	Dip. d'Ing. Electronicien ESEO
Ecole Supérieure de l'Energie et des Matériaux/ESEM (Université d'Orléans) (94)	DEUG	3 years	Dip. d'Ing.
Ecole Supérieure de Fonderie/ESF, Bagneux (30)	BTS Dip. d'Ing.	2 years 1 year	Dip. d'Ing. or Diplôme de Technicien de l'Ecole Supérieure de Fonderie
Ecole Supérieure du Génie Militaire/ESGM, Versailles (30)	Dip. d'Ing.	20 months	Dip. d'Ing. de l'Armée de Terre/Diplôme de l'Ecole Supérieure du Génie Militaire
Ecole Supérieure des Géomètres et Topographes/ESGT, Evry (99)	Bacc. + 2 years C.P.	3 years	Dip. d'Ing. de l'ESGT
Ecole Supérieure des Industries du Caoutchouc/ESICA, Montrouge (8–12)	Dip. d'Ing.	14 months	Dip. d'Ing. du Caoutchouc
Ecole Supérieure des Industries Textiles d'Epinal/ESITE (52)	Bacc. + 2 years C.P./DEUG	3 years	Dip. d'Ing. de l'ESITE
Ecole Supérieure d'Ingénieurs en Electrotechnique et Electronique/ESIEE, Paris (410)	Bacc.	5 years	Dip. d'Ing. de l'ESIEE
Ecole Supérieure d'Ingénieurs en Génie Electrique/ESIG-ELEC, Rouen (450)	Bacc. + 2 years C.P./DEUG	3 years	Dip. d'Ing.
Ecole Supérieure d'Ingénieurs de Marseille/ESIM (250)	Bacc. + 2 years C.P.	3 years	Dip. d'Ing. de l'ESIM

APPENDIX B

Ecole Supérieure d'Ingénieurs et de Techniciens pour l'Agriculture/ESITPA, Le Vaudreuil (343)	Bacc.	4 years	Dip. d'Ing. en Agriculture de l'ESITPA
Ecole Supérieure de Métrologie/ESM, Douai (11)	Bacc. + 2 years C.P.	3 years	Dip. d'Ing. de l'Ecole Supérieure de Métrologie
Ecole Supérieure d'Optique/ESO, Orsay (140)	Bacc. + 2 years C.P./DEUG	3 years	Dip. d'Ing. de l'ESO (Institut d'Optique Théorique et Appliquée)
Ecole Supérieure de Physique et de Chimie Industrielles/ESPCI/PC, Paris (194)	Bacc. + 2 years C.P.	4 years	Dip. d'Ing. ESPCI Chimiste/Physicien
Ecole Supérieure des Sciences et Technologies des Industries du Bois/ESSTIB (Université de Nancy I) (25)	DEUG	3 years	Dip. d'Ing.
Ecole Supérieure de Soudure Autogène/ESSA, Paris (36)	Dip. d'Ing.	1 year	Dip. d'Ing. Soudeur ESSA
Ecole Supérieure des Techniques Aérospatiales/ESTA, Orsay (30–34)	Dip. d'Ing.	1 year	Dip. d'Ing. ESTA
Ecole Supérieure des Techniques Industrielles et des Textiles/ESTIT, Villeneuve d'Ascq (106)	Bacc.	5 years	Dip. d'Ing. de l'ESTIT
Ecole Technique Supérieure des Travaux Maritimes/ETSTM (20)	Bacc. + 2 years C.P.	3 years	Dip. d'Ing. de l'Ecole Supérieure des Travaux Maritimes
Ecole Universitaire d'Ingénieurs de l'Université de Lille I/EUDIL (530)	DEUG	3 years	Dip. d'Ing. de l'EUDIL
Formation d'Ingénieurs de l'Université Paris Sud/FIUPSO (130)	DEUG	3 years	Dip. d'Ing.
Formations Supérieures d'Ingénieurs de l'Université de Paris-Nord/FSIPN (200)	DEUG	3 years	Dip. d'Ing. du Centre Scientifique et Polytechnique de l'Université Paris-Nord

APPENDIX B

Institution	Entry	Duration	Diploma
Formations Supérieures d'Ingénieurs en Matériaux/FSIM (Université de Paris XIII) (80)	DEUG	3 years	Dip. d'Ing.
Hautes Etudes Industrielles/HEI, Lille (547)	Bacc.	5 years	Dip. d'Ing. HEI
Institut Agricole et Alimentaire/IAA (Université de Lille I) (45)	DEUG	3 years	Dip. d'Ing.
Institut Catholique d'Arts et Métiers/ICAM, Lille (245)	Bacc.	5 years	Dip. d'Ing. ICAM
Institut de Chimie et Physique Industrielles de Lyon/ICPI (222)	Bacc.	5 years	Dip. d'Ing. Physicien Electronicien/ Dip. d'Ing. Chimiste/Dip. d'Ing. en Microélectronique
Institut d'Etudes Supérieures d'Industrie et d'Economie Laitières/IESIEL, Paris (15–20)	Dip. d'Ing.	13 months	Dip. d'Ing. de l'IESIEL
Institut Français du Froid Industriel/IFFI, Paris (100)	Dip. d'Ing.	1 year	Dip. d'Ing. Frigoriste
Institut de Génie Chimique/IGC, Toulouse (150)	Bacc. + 2 years C.P./DEUG/ DUT	3 years	Dip. d'Ing. du Génie Chimique (IGC)
Institut Industriel du Nord/IDN, Villeneuve d'Ascq (537)	Bacc. + 2 years C.P.	3 years	Dip. d'Ing. de l'IDN
Institut d'Informatique d'Entreprise/IIE, Evry (204)	Bacc. + 2 years C.P./DEUG/ DUT	3 years	Dip. d'Ing. de l'Institut d'Informatique d'Entreprise
Institut National Agronomique Paris-Grignon/ INA (552)	Bacc. + 2 years C.P.	3 years	Dip. d'Ing. Agronome de l'INA
Institut National des Sciences Appliquées de Lyon/INSA (3,000)	Bacc.	5 years	Dip. d'Ing. INSA
Institut National des Sciences Appliquées de Rennes/INSA (796)	Bacc.	5 years	Dip. d'Ing. INSA

Institut National des Sciences Appliquées de Rouen/INSA (156) (formerly Institut National Supérieur de Chimie Industrielle de Rouen)	Bacc.	5 years	Dip. d'Ing. INSA
Institut National des Sciences Appliquées de Toulouse/INSA (1043)	Bacc.	5 years	Dip. d'Ing. INSA
Institut National des Sciences et Techniques Nucléaires/INSTN, Paris (120)	Dip. d'Ing./Maîtrise/DEA	2 years	Dip. d'Ing. en Génie Atomique
Institut National des Télécommunications/INT, Evry (247)	Bacc. + 2 years C.P.	3 years	Dip. d'Ing. de l'Institut National des Télécommunications
Institut de Pétroléochimie et de Synthèse Organique Industrielle/IPSOI, Marseille (30–36)	Maîtrise Dip. d'Ing.	2 years 1 year	Dip. d'Ing. de l'Institut de Pétroléochimie et de Synthèse Organique Industrielle
Institut de Physique du Globe de Strasbourg/IPGS (Université de Strasbourg) (48)	DEUG	3 years	Dip. d'Ing. Géophysicien (IPGS) de l'Université Louis Pasteur
Institut de Recherche et d'Enseignement Supérieur aux Techniques de l'Electronique/IRESTE (Université de Nantes) (24)	Bacc. + 2 years C.P./DEUG/DUT	3 years	Dip. d'Ing. IRESTE
Institut des Sciences de l'Ingénieur/ISIM (Université de Montpellier II) (490)	DEUG	3 years	Dip. d'Ing. de l'ISIM
Institut des Sciences de l'Ingénieur/ISIN, Nancy (300)	Bacc.	5 years	Dip. d'Ing. ISIN
Institut des Sciences et des Techniques/IST/USMG (Université de Grenoble I) (40)	DEUG	3 years	Dip. d'Ing. Géotechnicien de l'Université de Grenoble I
Institut des Sciences et des Techniques/IST/PARIS VI (Université de Paris VI) (195)	DEUG	3 years	Dip. d'Ing. en Sciences et Technologie de l'Université Pierre et Marie Curie

APPENDIX B 211

Institut des Sciences et des Techniques/IST/POITIERS (Université de Poitiers) (60)	DEUG	3 years	*Dip. d'Ing. de l'Université de Poitiers*
Institut Supérieur Agricole de Beauvais/ISAB (360)	Bacc.	5 years	*Dip. d'Ing. en Agriculture de l'Institut Supérieur Agricole de Beauvais (ISAB)*
Institut Supérieur d'Agriculture de Lille/ISA (300)	Bacc.	5 years (effective 1986)	*Dip. d'Ing. en Agriculture de l'Institut Supérieur d'Agriculture de Lille*
Institut Supérieur d'Agriculture Rhône-Alpes/ISARA, Lyon (240)	Bacc.	4 years	*Dip. d'Ing. en Agriculture de l'Institut Supérieur d'Agriculture Rhône-Alpes*
Institut Supérieur du Béton Armé/ISBA, Marseille (20)	*Dip. d'Ing.*	1 year	*Dip. d'Ing. ISBA*
Institut Supérieur d'Electronique du Nord/ISEN, Lille (341)	Bacc.	5 years	*Dip. d'Ing. ISEN*
Institut Supérieur d'Electronique de Paris/ISEP (356)	Bacc.	5 years	*Dip. d'Ing. ISEP*
Institut Supérieur des Matériaux et de la Construction Mécanique/ISMCM, Saint-Ouen (40–60)	*Dip. d'Ing. Maîtrise*	12 months 24 months	*Dip. d'Ing. ISMCM*
Institut Textile de France/ITF, Boulogne-Billancourt (6–8)	*Dip. d'Ing.*	1 year	*Dip. d'Ing. Textile ITF*
Institut Universitaire des Sciences de l'Ingénieur en Thermique-Enérgétique et Matériaux/IUSITEM (Université de Nantes) (48)	DEUG	3 years	*Dip. d'Ing.*

Institut Universitaire des Sciences pour l'Ingénieur-Génie Industriel des Systèmes Automatiques/GISAI (Université d'Aix-Marseille III) (48)	DEUG	3 years	*Dip. d'Ing.*
Institut Universitaire des Systèmes Thermiques Industrielles de l'Université de Provence/IUTSI-UP (Université d'Aix-Marseille I) (30)	DEUG	3 years	*Dip. d'Ing.*

Appendix C

Postsecondary Schools of Business and Commerce

The following is a list of major postsecondary private and public schools of business currently operating in France. The name of each institution is given with its acronym, location, and, where available, enrollment size.

The following initialisms have been used in listing two schools: ESCAE = Ecole Supérieure de Commerce et d'Administration des Entreprises and IAE = Institut Administration des Entreprises. Initialisms for their corresponding diplomas are DESCAF = *Diplôme d'Etudes Supérieures Commerciales, Administratives et Financières* and CAAE = *Certificat d'Aptitude à l'Administration des Entreprises*. An asterisk following the name of a diploma indicates that the institution awards the *mastère*.

The letters in the recognition column indicate the following: N = institution is not recognized by the government; R = institution is recognized; U = institution is part of (or affiliated with) a public university; V = institution is recognized and diploma is sealed and issued by the Ministry of Education. As the Ministry of Education is constantly reviewing institutions for recognition, the U.S. admissions officer is advised to verify the status of the institution that is indicated on degree and diploma certificates.

Name of School and Location	Entrance Requirements	Length of Studies	Diploma Conferred	Recognition
Académie Commerciale Internationale	*Bacc.*	2 years	*Diplôme Supérieur d'Etudes Commerciales*	V
Centre d'Enseignement et de Recherche Appliqués au Management/ CERAM-ESCAE, Sophia-Antipolis (250)	*Bacc.* + 1 year C.P.	3 years	DESCAF/*	V
Centre d'Etudes de Commerce Exterieur/CECE, Marseille (60)	*Bacc.* + 4 years postsecondary study	9 months	*Certificat d'Etudes Supérieures en Commerce International*	R
Centre d'Etudes Supérieures Européennes de Management/CESEM, Reims, UK and Germany (600)	*Bacc.* + 1 year C.P.	4 years	*Diplôme d'Etudes Supérieures Européennes de Management/* DESEM + BA from UK or *Diplom-Betriebswirt* from Germany	R

Centre d'Etudes Supérieures du Management/CESMA, Ecully (90)	Bacc. + 4 years postsecondary study	10 months	Certificat d'Etudes Supérieures du Management	R
Centre d'Etudes Supérieures en Systèmes d'Informatique Automatisés de Gestion/CESSIAG, Toulouse (18)	Bacc. + 4 years postsecondary study	1 year	Certificat d'Etudes Supérieures en Systèmes d'Information Automatisés de Gestion (CESSIAG)	R
Centre de Formation aux Affaires/CEFA, Reims (20)	Bacc. + 3–4 years postsecondary study	38 weeks	Attestation du Centre de Formation des Affaires	R
Centre Supérieur des Transports Maritimes et Internationaux/CSTM, Marseille (30)	Bacc. + 4 years postsecondary study	9 months	Certificat d'Etudes Supérieures en Transport International	R
Conservatoire National des Arts et Métiers/CNAM, Paris and regional centers throughout France (variable)	Open DPC DESE	3–4 years part-time 3 years part-time 2 years part-time	Diplôme du Premier Cycle (DPC) Diplôme d'Etudes Supérieures Economiques (DESE) Diplôme d'Economiste	R
Cycle d'Etudes et de Formation à l'Audit et au Contrôle de Gestion/CEFACG, Toulouse (17)	Bacc. + 4 years postsecondary study	1 year	Certificat de Formation à l'Audit et au Contrôle de Gestion	R
Cycle d'Etudes Supérieures en Développement de l'Innovation/CESDI, Toulouse (15)	Bacc. + 3–4 years postsecondary study	1 year	Diplôme d'Etudes Supérieures en Développement de l'Innovation	R
Cycle de Formation Supérieure de Logistique Internationale/ACI/CFSLI, Paris	Bacc. + 2 years postsecondary study	9 months	Certificat de Formation Supérieure de Logistique Internationale	R
Ecole d'Administration de l'Armement/EAA, Arcueil (17)	Bacc. + 2 years postsecondary study	3 years	Diplôme de l'Ecole d'Administration de l'Armement	R
Ecole d'Administration et Direction des Affaires/EAD, Paris (300)	Bacc. + 1 year C.P.	3 years	Diplôme d'Administration et Direction (DAD)/Probatoire en Administration et Gestion (PAG)	R

APPENDIX C

School	Entrance Requirement	Duration	Diploma	Type
Ecole Européennes des Affaires/EAP, Paris, Oxford, Berlin (240)	Bacc. + 1 year C.P.	3 years	*Diplôme de l'EAP/**	V
Ecoles des Cadres du Commerce et des Affaires Economiques/EDC, Neuilly (1100)	Bacc.	3 years	*Certificat de Fin d'Etudes Supérieures, Economiques et Commerciales*	R
Ecole de Commerce et d'Administration/ECA, Paris (70)	Bacc.	3 years	*Certificat de Fin d'Etudes*	N
Ecole de Commerce de Chambery/ECC (180)	Bacc.	3 years	*Titre de l'Ecole de Commerce de Chambery*	R
Ecole de Direction d'Entreprises de Paris/EDEP (220)	Bacc.	3 years	*Certificat de Fin d'Etudes Supérieures de l'EDEP*	R
Ecole des Hautes Etudes Commerciales/HEC, Jouy-en-Josas (900)	Bacc. + 1 year C.P.	3 years	*Diplôme HEC/**	V
Ecole des Hautes Etudes Commerciales du Nord/EDHEC, Lille (480)	Bacc. + 1 year C.P.	3 years	*Diplôme EDHEC/**	V
Ecole du Marketing et de la Publicité/EMP, Paris (160)	Bacc.	2 years	*Certificat de Fin d'Etudes de l'EMP*	R
Ecole Nationale de la Statistique et de l'Administration-Division des Statisticiens et des Administrateurs/ENSAE, Malakoff (150)	Bacc. + 2 years postsecondary study	2 years	*Diplôme de Cadre de Gestion Statistique*	R
Ecole des Praticiens de Commerce International/EPSCI, Cergy-Pontoise (270)	Bacc.	3 years	*Certificat de Fin d'Etudes*	R
Ecole Privée de Préparation à la Pratique des Affaires/EPPA, Paris (120)	Bacc.	2 years	*Certificat de Fin d'Etudes*	N

216   APPENDIX C

Ecole Supérieure d'Administration des Entreprises/ESAE, Paris (300)	*Bacc.*	3 years	*Diplôme de l'Ecole ESAE*	R
Ecole Supérieure des Affaires de Grenoble/ESAG (Université de Grenoble II)	*Bacc.*	Variable	University degrees	U
Ecole Supérieure de Commerce de Lyon/ESC (540)	*Bacc.* + 2 years C.P.	3 years	*Diplôme de l'Ecole Supérieure de Commerce de Lyon*/*	V
ESCAE, Bordeaux (100)	*Bacc.*	4 years	DESCAF	V
ESCAE, Brest (200)	*Bacc.*	4 years	DESCAF	V
ESCAE, Clermont-Ferrand (270)	*Bacc.*	4 years	DESCAF	V
ESCAE, Dijon (300)	*Bacc.*	4 years	DESCAF	V
ESCAE, Grenoble (85)	*Bacc.*	4 years	DESCAF	V
ESCAE, Le Havre (100)	*Bacc.*	4 years	DESCAF	V
ESCAE, Lille (620)	*Bacc.*	4 years	DESCAF	V
ESCAE, Marseille-Luminy (700)	*Bacc.*	4 years	DESCAF	V
ESCAE, Montpellier (250)	*Bacc.*	4 years	DESCAF	V
ESCAE, Nantes (300)	*Bacc.*	4 years	DESCAF/*	V
ESCAE, Nice	*Bacc.*	4 years	DESCAF	V
ESCAE, Pau (300)	*Bacc.*	4 years	DESCAF	V
ESCAE, Poitiers (180)	*Bacc.*	4 years	DESCAF	V
ESCAE, Reims (420)	*Bacc.*	4 years	DESCAF/*	V
ESCAE, Rouen (476)	*Bacc.*	4 years	DESCAF/*	V
ESCAE, Toulouse (530)	*Bacc.*	4 years	DESCAF/*	V
Ecole Supérieure de Commerce Exterieur/ESCE, Paris (430)	*Bacc.*	3 years	*Diplôme d'Etudes Supérieures de l'ESCE*	R

APPENDIX C

Ecole Supérieure de Commerce de Paris/ESCP (850)	Bacc. + 1 year C.P.	3 years	Diplôme de l'Ecole Supérieure de Commerce de Paris/*	V
Ecole Supérieure de Dirigeants d'Entreprises/ESDE, Paris (600)	Bacc.	4 years	Certificat de Fin d'Etudes de l'ESDE	R
Ecole Supérieure de Gestion/ESG, Paris (580)	Bacc. + 1 year C.P.	3 years	Ancien Elève de l'Ecole Supérieure de Gestion	R
Ecole Supérieure de Gestion et Informatique/ESGI, Paris (250)	Bacc.	3 years	Expert en Informatique de Gestion d'Ecole Supérieure de Gestion et d'Informatique	R
Ecole Supérieure de Gestion et Finances/ESGF, Paris (300)	Bacc.	4 years	Attaché de Direction Financière de l'Ecole Supérieure de Gestion et Finances	R
Ecole Supérieure Libre des Sciences Commerciales Appliquées/ESLSCA, Paris (750)	Bacc. + 1 year C.P.	3 years	Diplôme ESLSCA	V
Ecole Supérieure Privée d'Administration du Commerce et de l'Industrie/ESACI, Arcueil (140)	Bacc.	3 years	Diplôme de l'Ecole	R
Ecole Supérieure des Sciences Commerciales d'Angers/ESSCA (485)	Bacc.	4 years	Diplôme de l'ESSCA	V
Ecole Supérieure des Sciences Economiques et Commerciales/ESSEC, Cergy-Pontoise (840)	Bacc. + 1 year C.P.	3 years	Diplôme ESSEC/*	V
European Business School/EBS, Paris (620)	Bacc.	4 years	Diplôme de Fin d'Etudes de l'EBS	R
IAE, Aix-en-Provence (110)	Bacc. + 4 years postsecondary study	1 year	CAAE	U

218   APPENDIX C

IAE, Amiens (70)	Bacc. + 4 years postsecondary study	1 year	CAAE	U
IAE, Bordeaux (400)	Bacc. + 4 years postsecondary study	1 year	CAAE	U
IAE, Caen (40)	Bacc. + 4 years postsecondary study	1 year	CAAE	U
IAE, Clermont-Ferrand (40)	Bacc. + 4 years postsecondary study	1 year	CAAE	U
IAE, Grenoble (100)	Bacc. + 4 years postsecondary study	1 year	CAAE	U
IAE, Lille	Bacc. + 4 years postsecondary study	1 year	CAAE	U
IAE, Lyon	Bacc. + 4 years postsecondary study	1 year	CAAE	U
IAE, Montpellier (25)	Bacc. + 4 years postsecondary study	1 year	CAAE	U
IAE, Nice (80)	Bacc. + 4 years postsecondary study	1 year	CAAE	U
IAE, Paris (1800)	Bacc. + 4 years postsecondary study	1 year	CAAE	U
IAE, Pau (100)	Bacc. + 4 years postsecondary study	1 year	CAAE	U
IAE, Poitiers (120)	Bacc. + 4 years postsecondary study	1 year	CAAE	U
IAE/Institut de Gestion de Rennes/IGR	Bacc. + 4 years postsecondary study	1 year	CAAE	U

APPENDIX C

IAE, Rouen	Bacc. + 4 years postsecondary study	1 year	CAAE	U
IAE, Strasbourg (170)	Bacc. + 4 years postsecondary study	1 year	CAAE	U
IAE, Toulouse (375)	Bacc. + 4 years postsecondary study	1 year	CAAE	U
Institut Agro-Alimentaire International/IAAI, Brest (10)	Bacc. + 4 years postsecondary study	9 months	Diplôme de Fin d'Etudes du Cycle Agro-Alimentaire International	R
Institut Commercial de Nancy/ICN (280)	Bacc. + 1 year postsecondary study	3 years	Diplôme de l'Institut Commercial de Nancy	R
Institut Commercial Supérieur/ICS-BEGUE, Paris (700)	Bacc.	4 years	Diplôme de l'Institut BEGUE	R
Institut d'Economie d'Entreprise et de Formation Sociale pour Ingénieurs/IEFSI, Lille (40)	Diplôme d'Ingénieur	1 year	Diplôme de l'IEFSI	V
Institut d'Economie Scientifique et de Gestion/IESEG, Lille (280)	Bacc.	3 years	Certificat de Fin d'Etudes de l'IESEG	R
Institut d'Etudes des Relations Internationales/ILERI, Paris (350)	Bacc.	4 years	Diplôme Supérieur de Recherches	N
Institut d'Etudes Supérieures des Techniques de l'Organisation/IESTO, Paris (200)	Bacc. + 4 years postsecondary study	1 year	Diplôme d'Etudes Supérieures des Techniques de l'Organisation	R
Institut Européen d'Administration des Affaires/INSEAD, Fontainebleau (1500)	Bacc. + 4 years postsecondary study	10 months	MBA	R
Institut Européen des Affaires/IEA, Paris (450)	Bacc.	5 years	Ancien Elève de l'Institut Européen des Affaires	R
Institut Européen d'Etudes Commerciales/IECS, Strasbourg (260)	Bacc.	4 years	Diplôme de l'IECS	R

220   APPENDIX C

Institut de Formation d'Animateurs Conseillers d'Entreprises/IFACE, Paris (30)	*Bacc.* + 3 years work experience	22 months	*Attestation de Fin d'Etudes*	R
Institut de Formation Alternée à la Gestion/IFAG, Paris (540)	*Bacc.*	3 years	*Certificat de Fin d'Etudes de l'IFAG*	R
Institut de Formation au Commerce International/IFCI, Clermont-Ferrand (20)	*Bacc.* + 4 years postsecondary study	9 months	*Diplôme de l'IFCI*	R
Institut Franco-Américain du Management/IFAM, Paris (450)	*Bacc.*	3 years	*Diplôme de l'IFAM*	N
Institut George Chetechine/IGC, Rueil-Malmaison (40)	*Bacc.*	3 years	*Diplôme IGC*	N
Institut de Gestion International Agro-Alimentaire/IGIA, Cergy-Pontoise (50)	*Bacc.* + 4 years postsecondary study	1 year	*Certificat de Fin d'Etudes IGIA*	R
Institut de Gestion de Personnel/IGP, Paris (70)	*Bacc.* + 2 years postsecondary study	2 years	*Certificat de l'Institut de Gestion Sociale*	R
Institut de Gestion Sociale/IGS, Paris (90)	*Bacc.* + 4 years postsecondary study	16 months	*Certificat de l'Institut de Gestion Sociale*	R
Institut de Hautes Etudes de Droit Rural et d'Economie Agricole/IHEDREA, Paris (450)	*Bacc.*	4 years	*Diplôme de l'IHEDREA*	R
Institut des Etudes de l'Information et de la Communication-Université de Paris IV/CELSA (500)	DEUG Maîtrise	2 years 1 year	*Maîtrise d'Information et de Communication/Diplôme du CELSA DEA/DESS*	U
Institut Libre des Hautes Etudes Economiques et Commerciales/INSEEC, Bordeaux and Paris (680)	*Bacc.*	3 years	*Diplôme de l'INSEEC/Certificat d'Etudes Supérieures de Gestion Commerciale Administrative et Financière*	R

APPENDIX C

Institut du Management et de l'Achat Industriel/MAI (ESCAE-Bordeaux) (20)	Bacc. + 4 years postsecondary study	1 year	Certificat d'Etudes Supérieures de Management de l'Achat Industriel	R
Institut de Management Hôtelier International/IMHI, Cergy-Pontoise (80)	Bacc. + 3 years postsecondary study	2 years	Certificat de Fin d'Etudes	R
Institut National de la Formation des Cadres Supérieurs de la Vente/ICSV, Paris (80)	Bacc. + 2 years postsecondary study + 3 years work experience	2 years	Diplôme d'Enseignement Supérieur	V
Institut National d'Informatique de Gestion/INIG, Paris (60)	Bacc. + 4 years postsecondary study	1 year	Certificat de Scolarité	R
Institut National des Télécommunications-Section Gestion/INT, Evry (40)	Bacc. + 2 years postsecondary study	3 years	Diplôme de l'Institut National des Télécommunications	R
Institut pour la Diffusion de la Recherche Active Commerciale/IDRAC, Montpellier and Paris (630)	Bacc.	3 years	BTS after 2 years/Certificat de Fin d'Etudes de l'IDRAC after 1 additional year	R
Institut des Petites et Moyennes Entreprises/IPME, Paris (210)	Bacc.	3 years	Diplôme de l'Institut	R
Institut Portuaire d'Enseignement et de Recherche/IPER, Le Havre (18)	Bacc. + 4 years postsecondary study	9 months	Certificat de Fin d'Etudes	R
Institut de Préparation à l'Administration et à la Gestion/IPAG, Paris (200)	Bacc.	4 years	Certificat de Fin d'Etudes de l'IPAG	R
Institut Supérieur des Affaires/ISA, Jouy-en-Josas (100)	Bacc. + 4 years postsecondary study + 5 years managerial experience	18 months	Diplôme ISA	V

APPENDIX C

Institut Supérieur de Commerce International de Dunkerque/ISCID (60)	Bacc. + 1 year C.P.	3 years	*Diplôme*	R
Institut Supérieur de Commerce de Paris/ISC (480)	Bacc. + 1 year C.P.	3 years	*Diplôme de Fin d'Etudes*	V
Institut Supérieur de Gestion/ISG, Paris	Bacc.	3 years	*Diplôme ISG*	N
Institut Supérieur de Gestion de Personnel/Faculté Libre Internationale Pluridisciplinaire/ISGP-FACLIP, Paris (135)	Bacc.	3–4 years	*Diplôme d'Etudes Supérieures/Diplôme d'Etudes Supérieures Approfondies*	R
Institut Supérieur des Sciences, Techniques et Economie Commerciales/ ISTEC, Paris (150)	Bacc.	3 years	*Certificat d'Aptitude aux Fonctions d'Ingénieur en Marketing*	R
Institut Supérieur Technique d'Outre Mer/ISTOM, Le Havre (60)	Bacc.	4 years	*Diplôme d'Etudes Supérieures des Techniques d'Outre Mer (DESTOM)*	V
MBA Institute, Paris (90)	Bacc.	4 years	Bachelor's Degree	N
Management de la Distribution/MD (Université de Lille II) (50)	Bacc. + 2 years postsecondary study	1 year	*Diplôme d'Université*	U
Université de Lyon I-Formation Supérieure Technico-Commerciale/ FSTC (30)	Bacc. + 2 years postsecondary study	1 year	*Diplôme d'Université en Développement Commercial et Industriel*	U
Université des Sciences et Techniques du Languedoc-Montpellier II-Cycle de Formation Supérieure Technico-Commerciale (60)	Bacc. + 2 years postsecondary study	1 year	*Diplôme Universitaire d'Etudes Supérieures Technico-Commerciales (DUESTC)*	U
Université de Valenciennes-Formation Supérieure Technico-Commerciales (30)	Bacc. + 2 years postsecondary study	8 months	*Diplôme d'Université d'Etudes Supérieures Technico-Commerciales*	U

Appendix D

Special Institutions

Collège de France, 11, place Marcelin Berthelot, 75005 Paris.

A public institution in which major professors lecture on a variety of literary and scientific topics related to their research. The Collège de France does not award degrees. Lectures are free and open to the public.

Conservatoire National des Arts et Métiers/CNAM, 292, rue Saint-Martin, 75141 Paris Cedex 03. The CNAM has branches throughout France.

A public institution dedicated to continuing education and research in business, engineering, and science.

Bureau des Longitudes, Palais de l'Institut, 3, rue Mazarine, 75006 Paris.

A public research institution specializing in astronomy, celestial mechanics, and geophysics. The institution does not award degrees.

Ecole des Hautes Etudes en Sciences Sociales, 54, boulevard Raspail, 75006 Paris.

A public institution dedicated to doctoral studies and research in social sciences. Admission is highly selective and is based on research projects.
Diplomas: DEA, *Doct.*

Ecole Nationale d'Administration/ENA, 13, rue de l'Université, 75007 Paris.

A public institution administered by the office of the Prime Minister, the ENA is dedicated to training senior civil servants. Admission is by *concours* for applicants who have completed four years of university study or have graduated from a *grande école.* Civil servants who are less than 36 years old and who have completed five years of service, trade union leaders younger than 41 years and who have eight years of professional experience are also eligible to sit for a special entrance examination. The training at ENA lasts 29 months including 11 months' internship in government agencies and two months in business enterprises. No diploma is awarded for completion of the program, and graduates are posted in different government agencies or in the diplomatic corps in accordance with their exit rank.

Ecole Nationale des Chartes, 19, rue de la Sorbonne, 75005 Paris.

A public institution dedicated to teaching and research in art history; conservation; and paleography.
Diploma: Diplôme d'Archiviste Paléographe

Ecole Nationale de la Magistrature/ENM, 9, rue du Marechal Joffre, 33080 Bordeaux.

A public institution administered by the Ministry of Justice, the ENM trains judges and magistrates. Admission is by *concours* for candidates who have completed four years of university study *(maîtrise)* in law. Civil servants who have completed at least two years of higher education, are less than 40 years old and have served for at least four years are also eligible for the entrance examination. The 28-month program consists of classroom instruction and internships. No diploma is awarded for completing the program; graduates are assigned to various positions in accordance with their exit rank.

Ecole Pratique des Hautes Etudes, Palais de la Sorbonne, 46, rue Saint-Jacques, 75005 Paris.

A public institution dedicated to doctoral studies and to basic and applied research in chemistry; earth and life sciences; history; mathematics; philology; physics; religion.
Diplomas: DEA, *Doct.*

Institut Régional d'Administration/IRA (4 regional centers as follows):

quai des Martyrs de la Liberation, B.P. 208, 20200 Bastia (Corse).

103, rue Barthelemy Delespaul, 59046 Lille.

15, avenue de Lyon, 57070 Metz.

1, avenue Dutrievoz, 69100 Villeurbanne.

IRAs are public institutions dedicated to training middle-level civil servants. Admission is by *concours* and, since 1985, candidates must hold a *licence* and be younger than 30. The *concours* is also open to civil servants who have had four years of service and who are younger than 40. The training program is 12 months long and includes an internship. No diploma is awarded; graduates, who must serve the State for at least six years, are assigned to various agencies in accordance with their exit rank.

Museum d'Histoire Naturelle, Jardin des Plantes, 57, rue Cuvier, 75005 Paris.

A public research institution in natural history. Lectures are free and open to the public.

Observatoire de Paris, Avenue de l'Observatoire, 75014 Paris. (Branches in Meudon and at the Universities of Besançon; Clermont-Ferrand; Bordeaux; Nice; and Strasbourg)

A public institution dedicated to research in astronomy, radioastronomy, space science, statistics.

Palais de la Decouverte, Avenue Franklin Roosevelt, 75008 Paris.

A public research institution in astronautics; astronomy and space science; biology; chemistry; computer science; earth sciences; electricity; history of science; mathematics; medicine; nuclear physics; physics. The Palais de la Decouverte maintains a planetarium, a library and a photo-library and a cinema. It organizes exhibitions and lectures open to the public.

Acronyms

Bac./Bacc.	*Baccalauréat*	
BC	*Brevet des Collèges*	Certificate of Lower Secondary Education
BEP	*Brevet d'Enseignement Professionnel*	Certificate of Vocational Education
BT	*Brevet de Technicien*	Technician's Certificate
BTA	*Brevet de Technicien Agricole*	Agricultural Technician's Certificate
BTn	*Baccalauréat de Technicien*	Technical *Baccalauréat*
BTS	*Brevet de Technicien Supérieur*	Higher Technician's Certificate
BTSA	*Brevet de Technicien Supérieur Agricole*	Higher Technician's Certificate in Agriculture
CAAE	*Certificat d'Aptitude à l'Administration des Entreprises*	Certificate of Qualification in Business Administration
CAELP	*Certificat d'Aptitude à l'Education des Enfants et Adolescents Déficients ou Inadaptés*	Certificate of Qualification to Teach Deficient or Maladjusted Children and Adolescents
CAP	*Certificat d'Aptitude Pédagogique*	Certificate of Pedagogical Aptitude
CAP	*Certificat d'Aptitude Professionnelle*	Certificate of Vocational Qualification
CAPEPS	*Certificat d'Aptitude au Professorat d'Education Physique et Sportive*	Certificate of Qualification to Teach Sports and Physical Education
CAPES	*Certificat d'Aptitude au Professorat de l'Enseignement Secondaire*	Certificate of Qualification to Teach Secondary Education
CAPET	*Certificat d'Aptitude au Professorat de l'Enseignement Technique*	Certificate of Qualification to Teach Technical Education
CE	*Cycle Elémentaire*	Elementary Cycle
CFEN	*Certificat de Fin d'Etudes Normales*	Certificate of Completion of Normal School Studies
CFES	*Certificat de Fin d'Etudes Secondaires*	Certificate of Completion of Secondary Education
CHU	*Centre Hospitalo-Universitaire*	University Hospital Center
CM	*Cycle Moyen*	intermediate cycle
CNAM	*Conservatoire National des Arts et Métiers*	National Conservatory of Arts and Crafts
CNEC	*Centre National d'Enseignement par Correspondence*	National Center for Correspondence Education
CNOUS	*Centre National des Oeuvres Universitaires et Scolaires*	National Center for University and School Works (Student Affairs)
CNRS	*Centre National de la Recherche Scientifique*	National Center for Scientific Research
CP	*Cycle Préparatoire*	preparatory cycle
CPA	*Classes Préparatoires d'Apprentissage*	Apprenticeship Training Classes

CPECF	*Certificat Préparatoire aux Etudes Comptables et Financières*	Preparatory Certificate for Studies in Accounting and Finance
CPPN	*Classes Préprofessionnelles de Niveau*	Pre-vocational Remedial Classes
CPR	*Centre Pédagogique Régional*	Regional Pedagogical Center
DALF	*Diplôme Approfondi de Langue Française*	Advanced Diploma of French Language
DCEM	*Deuxième Cycle d'Etudes Médicales*	Second Cycle of Medical Studies
DEA	*Diplôme d'Etudes Approfondies*	Diploma of Advanced Studies
DECS	*Diplôme d'Etudes Comptables Supérieures*	Diploma of Higher Studies in Accounting
DEFA	*Diplôme d'Etudes Fondamentales en Architecture*	Diploma of Foundation Studies in Architecture
DELF	*Diplôme Elémentaire de Langue Française*	Elementary Diploma of French Language
DES	*Diplôme d'Etudes Spécialisées*	Diploma of Specialized Studies
DESCAF	*Diplôme d'Etudes Supérieures Commerciales, Administratives et Financières*	Diploma of Higher Studies in Commerce, Administration and Finance
DESS	*Diplôme d'Etudes Supérieures Spécialisées*	Diploma of Higher Specialized Studies
DEST	*Diplôme d'Etudes Supérieures Techniques*	Diploma of Higher Technical Studies
DEUG	*Diplôme d'Etudes Universitaires Générales*	Diploma of General University Studies
DEUST	*Diplôme d'Etudes Universitaires Scientifiques et Techniques*	Diploma of University Scientific and Technical Studies
DNAT	*Diplôme National d'Arts et Techniques*	National Diploma of Arts and Crafts
DNSEP	*Diplôme National Supérieur d'Expression Plastique*	Higher National Diploma of Artistic Expression
DPCT	*Diplôme de Premier Cycle Technique*	Diploma of First Technical Cycle
DPLG	*Diplôme d'Architecte Diplômé par le Gouvernement*	Government Diploma in Architecture
DU	*Diplôme Universitaire*	University Diploma
DUT	*Diplôme Universitaire de Technologie*	University Diploma of Technology
ENA	Ecole Nationale d'Administration	National School of Administration
ENI	*Ecole Nationale d'Ingénieurs*	National School for Engineers
ENITA	*Ecole Nationale d'Ingénieurs de Travaux Agricoles*	National School for Agricultural Works Engineers
ENNA	*Ecole Normale Nationale d'Apprentissage*	National Normal School of Apprenticeship
ENS	*Ecole Normale Supérieure*	Higher Normal School
ENSA	*Ecole Nationale Supérieure d'Agronomie*	Higher National School of Agriculture
EPCSCP	*Etablissement Public à Caractère Scientifique et Professionnel*	Public Scientific, Cultural and Professional Institution
ESCAE	*Ecole Supérieure de Commerce et d'Administration des Entreprises*	Higher School of Commerce and Business Administration
IAE	*Institut d'Administration d'Entreprises*	Institute of Business Administration

ACRONYMS

IEP	*Institut d'Etudes Politiques*	Institute of Political Studies
INSA	*Institut National de Sciences Appliquées*	National Institute of Applied Sciences
INSERM	Institut National de la Santé et de la Recherche Médicale	National Institute of Health and Medical Research
IUT	*Institut Universitaire de Technologie*	University Institute of Technology
LEGT	*Lycée d'Enseignement Général et Technique*	Comprehensive Upper-Secondary School
LP	*Lycée Professionnel*	Vocational Secondary School
MIAG	*Maîtrise d'Informatique Appliquée à la Gestion*	*Maîtrise* of Computer Science Applied to Business
MSG	*Maîtrise des Sciences de Gestion*	*Maîtrise* of Business Science
MST	*Maîtrise des Sciences et Techniques*	*Maîtrise* of Science and Technology
MSTCF	*Maîtrise des Sciences et Techniques Comptables et Financières*	*Maîtrise* of Science and Techniques in Accounting and Finance
PCEM	*Premier Cycle d' Etudes Médicales*	First Cycle of Medical Studies
STS	*Section de Techniciens Supérieurs*	Higher Technicians' Section
TD	*Travaux Dirigés*	Tutorials
TP	*Travaux Pratiques*	Practical/Laboratory Work
UER	*Unité d'Enseignement et de Recherche*	Teaching and Research Unit
UFR	*Unité de Formation et de Recherche*	Teaching and Research Unit
UPA	*Unité Pédagogique d'Architecture*	Architectural Pedagogical Unit
UV	*Unité de Valeur*	Unit of Value

Useful Addresses

General Information

Centre d'Information et de Documentation Jeunesse/CIDJ, 101 quai Branly, 75740 Paris Cedex 15, France.

Publishes pamphlets on education in all fields including addresses of institutions where programs are offered.

Centre International d'Etudes Pédagogiques, 1, avenue Léon Journault, 92310 Sèvres Cedex, France.

Organizes visits, seminars and other long- and short-term programs for foreign visitors interested in French education and in the teaching of French as a foreign language.

Centre National de Documentation sur l'Enseignement Privé, 107 rue de l'Université, 75007 Paris, France.

Publishes information on private educational institutions.

Centre National de Documentation Pédagogique/CNDP, 29, rue d'Ulm, 75230 Paris Cedex, France.

Publishes information on secondary and postsecondary academic programs and curricula.

Direction de la Cooperation et des Relations Internationales, 173, boulevard Saint Germain, Paris Cedex 07, France.

The international relations arm of the Ministry of Education, this office provides information on all aspects of education in France for foreign correspondents.

Franco-American Commission for Educational Exchange, 9, rue Chardin 75016 Paris, France.

Fulbright Commission and the USIS student advising center.

Institut National de la Recherche Pédagogique/INRP, 29, rue d'Ulm, 75230 Paris Cedex 05, France.

The research arm of the Ministry of Education.

Ministère de l'Education, 110, rue de Grenelle, 75357 Paris Cedex 07, France.

Higher Education

Direction de l'Enseignement Supérieur, 61–65, rue Dutot, 75732 Paris Cedex 15, France.

National headquarters for higher education administration. The information section publishes numerous guides to higher education.

L'Etudiant, 27, rue du Chemin Vert, 75011 Paris, France.

A private publisher of useful directories, magazines, and a series of books on higher and professional education.

USEFUL ADDRESSES

Office National d'Information sur les Enseignements et les Professions/ONISEP, 46–52, rue Albert, 75225 Paris Cedex 05, France.

A public information service which prepares and distributes information on educational opportunities and programs in all fields.

International Education/French for Foreigners/Exchange Programs

Bureau pour l'Enseignement de la Langue et de la Civilisation Françaises à l'Etranger/BELC, 9, rue Lhomond 75005 Paris, France.

Dedicated to promoting the teaching of French language and culture abroad.

Centre International d'Etudes Pédagogiques (see above).

Centre National des Oeuvres Universitaires et Scolaires, 69, quai d'Orsay, 75007 Paris, France.

Provides information and assistance for foreign students.

Franco-American Commission for Educational Exchange (see above).

Ministère des Affaires Etrangères (Relations Culturelles), 34–36, rue la Pérouse, 75016 Paris, France.

Art, Dance, Drama, Music

Ministère de la Culture, 3, rue Valois, 75042 Paris Cedex 01, France.

Administers all public schools and conservatories of art, dance, drama and music.

Business

Fondation Nationale pour l'Enseignement de la Gestion des Entreprises/FNEGE, 2, avenue Hoche, 75008 Paris, France.

Information and publications on business education.

Engineering and Business

Comité d'Etudes sur les Formations d'Ingénieurs/CEFI, 2, avenue Hoche, 75008 Paris, France.

Publishes studies on French engineering education.

Conférence des Grandes Ecoles, 60, boulevard St. Michel, 75272 Paris Cedex 06, France.

The association of *grandes écoles* publishes detailed information on member institutions and their academic programs.

Health Professions

Secretariat d'Etat à la Santé, 1, place de Fontenoy, 75050 Paris, France.

Information on paramedical education.

Social Professions

Ministère des Affaires Sociales, 124, rue Sadi-Carnot, 92170 Vanves, France.

Information on social work and social services education.

Glossary

Admis	Passed or admitted
Admis avec mention	Passed with honors
Admission sur titre	Admission by virtue of a title
Agrégation	Competitive examination for secondary teachers
Agrégé	Holder of an *agrégation*
Agronomie	Agricultural science/agronomy
Ajourné	Failed
Année Scolaire/Universitaire	Academic Year
Année	Year
Annuaire	Directory
Antérieur	Previous/Prior
Appliqué	Applied
Appréciation	Evaluation
Apprentissage	Apprenticeship
Arrêté	Governmental rule
Arts Plastiques	Studio/Plastic Arts
Arts Appliqués	Applied/Graphic Arts
Assez Bien	Good
Attestation	Authenticating Document
Auditeur Libre	Auditor
Baccalauréat Technique	Technical *baccalauréat*
Baccalauréat	Secondary school leaving examination
Bachelier	Holder of a *baccalauréat*
Bachelier de l'Enseignement du Second Degré	Holder of a *Baccalauréat* of Secondary Education
Beaux Arts	Fine Arts
Bien	Good
Bourse	Scholarship/Grant
Brevet	Certificate/Permit/Patent
Cadre	Executive
Cinquième	Fifth
Classe Préparatoire	Preparatory Class for *grandes écoles*
Classe Terminale	Final year of secondary school
Classe	Grade
Classe Primaire	Elementary school grade
Collège	Lower secondary school
Comptabilité	Accounting
Comptable	Accountant
Concours	Competition, competitive examination
Conformément	In accordance with
Connaissance	Knowledge

GLOSSARY

Conseil	Council
Contrôle Continu	Continuous assessment
Cours Magistral	Lecture
Cours	Class, private school
Crèche	Day care center
Dactylographie	Typing
Décret	Decree
Demande d'Inscription	Admission application
Dérogation	Special consideration
Dessin	Design, Drawing
Dessinateur	Draftsman
Deuxième	Second
Dispense	Exemption
Dixième	Tenth
Donné à	Issued at (place)
Doyen	Dean
Droit	Law
Durée	Duration, Length
Echec	Failure
Echoué	Failed
Ecole Maternelle	Nursery School
Ecole	School
Ecrit	Written
Elève	Student (elementary and secondary school)
Enseignant	Teacher, instructor
Enseignement	Education
Enseignement du Second Degré	Secondary education
Epreuve Orale de Contrôle	Validation oral examination
Epreuve	Examination
Etablissement	Institution
Etats Unis	United States
Etranger	Foreign, foreigner
Etudes	Studies
Etudiant	Student (postsecondary)
Examen Partiel	Mid-term examination
Exercer	To practice (a profession)
Exigé	Required
Exiger	To require
Facultatif	Optional
Faible	Weak
Formation	Education, training
Frais	Fees
Français	French
Génie	Engineering
Gestion	Business administration, management
Grand Etablissement	Special institution of research
Grande Ecole	Highly selective institution of higher education
Habileté	Qualified, entitled

Haut	High
Hebdomadaire	Weekly
Heure	Hour
Homologué	Indexed at a level
Homologue	Counterpart
Horaire	Timetable, schedule
Huitième	Eighth
Infirmier	Nurse
Ingénieur	Engineer
Ingénieur Diplômé	Engineer with a diploma
Inscription	Enrollment, registration
Inscrit	Enrolled, registered
Instituteur	Elementary school teacher
Jardin d'enfants	Nursery school
Kinésithérapie	Physical therapy
Laborantin	Laboratory analyst
Langue vivante	Modern language
Langue étrangère	Foreign language
Langue classique	Ancient language
Licencié	Holder of a *licence*
Livret scolaire	Report card
Loi	Law
Lycée	Upper secondary school
Maître de Conférence	Assistant Professor
Maître	Teacher, school master
Maitière	Subject
Médaille	Medal
Médaillé	Holder of a *médal*
Médecin	Physician
Mémoire	Research paper
Mention	Mention, distinction (grade)
Métier	Profession, trade, craft
Mi-temps	Half-time
Mois	Month
Moyenne du goupe	Class average
Moyenne générale	Overall average
Moyenne	Average
Naissance	Birth
Né/e le	Born on
Neuvième	Ninth
Niveau	Level
Nom de famille	Family name
Nom	Last name
Note	Grade
Obtenu	Obtained
Oenologue	Winemaker
Orthophoniste	Speech therapist

GLOSSARY

Passable — Satisfactory for passing
Plein temps — Fulltime
Prénom — First name
Primaire (Classe) — Elementary school grade
Privé — Private
Prix — Prize
Professeur — Secondary or postsecondary faculty
Promotion — Class (class of 19—)

Réadaptation — Rehabilitation
Recalé — Failed
Recherche — Research
Reconnu — Recognized
Recteur — Rector
Reçu — Passed an examination
Redoubler — To repeat a class
Réglements — Regulations
Relevé de notes — Statement of grades
Relevé — Statement
Rentrée — The reopening of school
Ressortissant — Native, citizen of (country)
Réussi — Passed

Sage-femme — Midwife
Santé — Health
Santé publique — Public health
Sciences physiques — Physical sciences
Sciences naturelles — Natural sciences
Secondaire — Secondary
Secrétariat — Registrar's office
Septième — Seventh
Sixième — Sixth
Stage — Internship, practical training

Thérapeute — Therapist
Titre — Title
Titulaire — Holder of a title
Travail — Work
Travaux pratiques — Practical, laboratory work
Travaux manuels — Handicrafts
Travaux dirigés — Tutorials
Très bien — Very good
Troisième — Third

Unité de valeur — Unit of value
Unité de formation et de recherche — Teaching and research unit
Unité d'enseignement et de recherche — Teaching and research unit
Unité capitalisable — Unit of continuing education

Visa — Seal
Visé — Sealed

Useful References

General Information

Elvin, Lionel, ed. "France." In *The Educational Systems in the European Community, A Guide*, pp. 111–134. Windsor: The NFER-Nelson Publishing Company Ltd., 1981.

Contains a detailed description of the administrative structure of French higher education. Available in the U.S. from Humanities Press, Inc., Atlantic Highlands, NJ 07716.

Le Monde de l'Education (A monthly educational magazine published by *Le Monde*).

Available by subscription in the United States from SPEEDIMPEX, 45-45 39th Street, Long Island City, NY 11104.

Lewis, H.D. *The French Education System.* New York: St. Martin's Press, 1985.

Useful for background information on French education stressing the political aspects of educational planning and administration. Available from St. Martin's Press, 175 Fifth Avenue, New York, NY 10010.

Minot, Jacques, ed. *Les Universités après la loi sur l'Enseignement Supérieur du 26 janvier 1984.* Paris: Berger-Levrault, 1984.

A detailed account of the status of French universities under the 1984 reform. Contains entries on university history, reforms, organization and administration, academic programs, research, student life, international exchange, faculty and staff. Available from Berger-Levrault, 229, bd. Saint-Germain, 75007 Paris, France.

Neave, Guy. "France." In *The School and the University: An International Perspective*, pp. 10–45. Edited by Burton R. Clark. Berkeley: University of California Press, 1985.

Wanner, Raymond E. *France: A Study of the Educational System of France and A Guide to the Placement of Students in Educational Institutions in the United States.* Washington, D.C.: American Association of Collegiate Registrars and Admissions Officers, 1975.

Available from University Microfilms International, Ann Arbor, MI 48016.

Secondary Education

Aperçu du Système Educatif Français. Sèvres: Centre International d'Etudes Pédagogiques, 1985.

Available from the Centre International d'Etudes Pédagogiques, 1, avenue Léon Journault, 92310 Sèvres, France.

Croissandeau, Jean-Michel. *Le Guide du Lycée.* Paris: Editions du Seuil, 1986.

A most comprehensive description of secondary education designed for students and parents and written by the Editor of *Le Monde de l'Education*. Available from Editions du Seuil, 27, rue Jacob, 75006 Paris, France.

Organization of the French Educational System Leading to the Baccalauréat. Washington, D.C.: Cultural Services of the French Embassy, 1987.

USEFUL REFERENCES

A very good description of secondary education and especially the *baccalauréat* curriculum. Available from The Cultural Service, French Embassy, 4101 Reservoir Road, Washington, D.C. 20007-2178.

Primary and Secondary Education in France. Washington, D.C.: Cultural Services of the French Embassy, 1985.

See above for source address.

Postsecondary Education

Annuaire National de l'Enseignement Supérieur. Paris: L'Etudiant. (annual)

A comprehensive listing of all institutions of higher education in France. Available from l'Etudiant, 27, rue du Chemin Vert, 75011 Paris, France.

Bac ou Pas Bac, Que Faire Après. Paris: ONISEP. (annual)

A guide to postsecondary education by profession. Available from ONISEP, 46-52, rue Albert, 75013 Paris Cedex 13, France.

Connaître les Filières de l'Enseignement Supérieur. Paris: Ministère de l'Education Nationale.

An authoritative guide to higher education in France by discipline. Available from Information et Orientation, Direction des Enseignements Supérieurs, 61-65, rue Dutot, 75732 Paris Cedex 15, France.

Higher Education in France: University Studies—1985. Washington, D.C.: Cultural Services of the French Embassy.

See above for source address.

Précis de l'Enseignement—Tome I—Enseignement Supérieur, Ecoles d'Ingénieurs. Paris: La Documentation Pratique, 1985.

A comprehensive listing of engineering schools with an entry on each institution, including admission requirements, program structure, courses and hours. Available from La Documentation Pratique, 62, Galerie Vivienne, 75002 Paris, France.

Précis de l'Enseignement—Tome II—Enseignement Supérieur, Gestion et Techniques de Gestion. Paris: La Documentation Pratique, 1986.

A comprehensive listing of business schools with an entry on each institution including admission requirements, program structure, courses and hours. Available from La Documentation Pratique, 62, Galerie Vivienne, 75002 Paris, France.

International Education/Study Abroad

Cours de Français pour Etudiants Etrangers. Paris: Association pour la Diffusion de la Pensée Française. (annual)

A guide to French language and civilization programs offered by French universities, organizations and institutions affiliated with universities, as well as independent programs. Available from the Association pour la Diffusion de la Pensée Française, 9, rue Anatole-de-la-Forge, 75017 Paris, France.

Je Vais en France. Paris: Centre National des Oeuvres Universitaires et Scolaires, 1987.

Designed for foreign students who wish to study in France, this publication gives an excellent overview of French education with special emphasis on the practical aspects of study and student life in France. May be consulted at French Cultural Offices in the United States.

Index

académie, xiii, 14, 16, 26, 31, 35
accounting, 48, 49, 50, 54, 55, 66, 68, 82, 125, 127–129, 137
admission. *See specific fields; institutions; and levels of education*
agrégation, 60, 135, 137–138, 176
agricultural education, 82, 83, 88–89, 109–117, 172–173
Ancien Elève de l'Ecole du Louvre, 157, 184
architecture, 151–154, 180–181
art education, 51, 58, 83, 154–158, 181–184
attestation, 43, 45, 76, 153
audioprosthesis, 142

baccalauréat, xiv, 3, 4, 5–28, 40; types of, 5, 14–18, 81, 121, 165
Baccalauréat de l'Enseignement du Second Degré, 5, 14
Baccalauréat de Technicien, 5, 14
Baccalauréat Professionnel, 9, 14, 29, 165
Brevet d'Enseignement Professionnel/BEP, xiv, 29, 165
Brevet de Technicien/BT, xiv, 29, 30, 83, 165
Brevet de Technicien Agricole, 109
Brevet de Technicien Supérieur/BTS, xiv, 30, 81, 83–85, 109, 118, 125, 156, 157, 161, 162, 170, 182; *d'Analyses Biologiques*, 144
Brevet de Technicien Supérieur Agricole/ BTSA, 109, 171
Brevet des Collèges, 3, 15, 165
Bureau des Longitudes, 223
Bureau pour l'Enseignement de la Langue et de la Civilisation Françaises/ BELC, 80
business education, 31, 32, 35, 65–66, 67, 88, 118–130, 135; admission, 119, 121, 123–124, 125, 126, 128, 129; *classes préparatoires*, 119, 121, 123, 128, 173; credentials, 63, 118, 119, 120–121, 122, 125, 126, 127, 128, 129, 162, 173–175; curriculum, 123, 124–125, 128–129; examinations, 119, 121, 123, 124–125, 128–129; programs, 68, 72, 81, 82, 83, 118, 121, 124–129; schools, 118-120, 121–125, 213–222. *See also grande école;* technical education; university education

Centre International d'Etudes Pédagogiques/CIEP, 80
Centre National de la Recherche Scientifique/CNRS, 71, 74
Centre National des Oeuvres Universitaires et Scolaires/CNOUS, 34
Centre Pédagogique Régional/CPR, 131, 137
Centres de Formation de Professeurs Techniques, 135
Certificat d'Aptitude à l'Administration des Entreprises/CAAE, 127, 174
Certificat d'Aptitude à l'Education des Enfants et Adolescents Déficients ou Inadaptés, 132, 175
Certificat d'Aptitude à l'Enseignement dans les Lycées Professionnels/CAELP, 133, 175
Certificat d'Aptitude à la Pratique Psychomusicale, 160, 185
Certificat d'Aptitude au Professorat d'Education Physique et Sportive/ CAPEPS, 135, 176
Certificat d'Aptitude au Professorat de l'Enseignement Général des Collèges/ CAPEGC, 134
Certificat d'Aptitude au Professorat de l'Enseignement Secondaire/CAPES, 60, 134–135, 137, 138, 176
Certificat d'Aptitude au Professorat de l'Enseignement Technique/CAPET, 135, 137, 176
Certificat d'Aptitude au Professorat Technique/CAPT, 135, 176
Certificat d'Aptitude Pédagogiques/CAP, 131
Certificat d'Aptitude Professionnelle/CAP, xiv, 29, 165
Certificat d'Etudes Approfondies d'Architecture, 154, 181
Certificat d'Etudes Spéciales, Mention Orthodontie, 141, 177
Certificat d'Initiation Plastique, 155, 156, 181
Certificat d'Université de Musicothérapie, 160, 185

INDEX

Certificat de Capacité d'Orthophoniste, 143, 178
Certificat de Capacité en Droit, 39–40, 166
Certificat de Fin d'Etudes, 120, 122, 173–174
Certificat de Fin d'Etudes Normales/CFEN, 131, 175
Certificat de Fin d'Etudes Secondaires/CFES, 26, 166
Certificat de Synthèse Clinique et Thérapeutique, 140, 176
Certificat Pratique de Langue Française, 79, 169
Certificat Préparatoire aux Etudes Comptables et Financières/CPECF, 128, 174
chiropody, 143, 147
classes préparatoires. See Classes Préparatoires aux Grandes Ecoles; grande école
Classes Préparatoires aux Grandes Ecoles, xiv, 136, 151, 154; agriculture, 110–111, 117; business, 119, 121, 123, 173; Ecoles Normales Supérieures, 136–137, 176; engineering, 88–91, 170
collège, xii, 2, 3, 29, 133, 134, 135, 165
Collège de France, 31, 223
Commission des Titres d'Ingénieur/CTI, 86–87, 111, 112, 115
compulsory education, xii, xiv, 1
concours, 87, 88, 163; d'internat de spécialité, 140. See also specific programs; fields; institutions; and levels of education
Conferénce des Grandes Ecoles, 104, 126
Conservatoire National des Arts et Métiers/CNAM, 35, 86, 101, 103, 223
Conservatoire National Supérieur d'Art Dramatique, 161
Conservatoire National Supérieur de Musique de Lyon, 160, 185
Conservatoire National Supérieur de Musique de Paris, 160, 185
continuing education, 86, 87, 96, 101, 149
Corps d'Ingénieurs de l'Etat, 92
credentials. See Placement Recommendations; specific credentials; institutions; programs; and levels of education
curriculum. See specific institutions; programs; and levels of education
cycles, 1, 2–3, 28–29. See also architecture; continuing education; medicine; university education

dance, 161
dentistry, xiv, 139, 141
diploma: national, 14, 39–40, 41, 162; state, 83, 139, 142, 162; university, 40, 41, 68, 139, 162
diplôme accrédité, 68
Diplôme Approfondi de Langue Française/DALF, 79, 169
Diplôme d'Agronomie Générale, 110–111, 113, 116, 172
Diplôme d'Architecte de l'Ecole Nationale Supérieure des Arts et Industries de Strasbourg, 154, 181
Diplôme d'Architecte Diplômé par le Gouvernement/DPLG, 152, 180
Diplôme d'Archiviste Paléographe, 158, 184
Diplôme d'Art Dramatique du Conservatoire National Supérieur, 161, 186
Diplôme d'Enseignement Spécialisé Complémentaire, 140
Diplôme d'Etat: medical studies, 139–140, 141, 142, 176; music, 161; paramedical studies, 142, 144, 145, 146, 147, 148, 177–179; Placement Recommendations, 173, 176, 177–179, 180, 186; social education, 149, 150, 180; technical education, 83, 170, 182; veterinary medicine, 117, 173
Diplôme d'Etudes Approfondies/DEA, 40, 71, 72–73, 76, 77, 79–80, 103, 140, 154, 168, 171
Diplôme d'Etudes Comptables Supérieures/DECS, 128–129, 130, 174
Diplôme d'Etudes Fondamentales en Architecture/DEFA, 151, 180
Diplôme d'Etudes Françaises, 79, 169
Diplôme d'Etudes Politiques, 69–71, 167
Diplôme d'Etudes Supérieures Commerciales, Administratives et Financières/DESCAF, 119, 120, 173
Diplôme d'Etudes Supérieures d'Instituteur, 131, 175
Diplôme d'Etudes Supérieures Spécialisées/DESS, 40, 71–72, 75, 77, 80, 127, 154, 167

Diplôme d'Etudes Supérieures Techniques/ DEST, 101, 172
Diplôme d'Etudes Universitaires Générales/ DEUG, xiv, 39, 40, 43–44, 47–61, 101, 135, 166
*Diplôme d'Etudes Universitaires Scientifiques et Techniques/*DEUST, 40, 43, 46, 60, 166
Diplôme d'Expert Comptable, 128, 129, 175
Diplôme d'Ingénieur, 71, 77, 86, 88, 92, 95, 101, 103, 104, 111, 116, 119, 170–171, 173, 198–211
Diplôme d'Ingénieur Agronome, 110–116, 172
Diplôme d'Ingénieur de l'Institut Textile de France, 104
Diplôme d'Ingénieur des Techniques Agricoles, 115, 173
*Diplôme d'Université/*DU, 40, 41, 139
Diplôme d'Université de Musicothérapie, 160, 185
Diplôme de Baccalauréat de Technicien, 14, 165
Diplôme de Bachelier de l'Enseignement du Second Degré, 14, 15, 165
Diplôme de Docteur-Ingénieur, 74, 77, 78, 171
Diplôme de Fin d'Etudes, 120, 173–174
Diplôme de l'Ecole Nationale Supérieure de Création Industrielle, 155, 182
Diplôme de l'Ecole Nationale Supérieure des Arts Decoratifs, 155, 182
Diplôme de l'Ecole Nationale Supérieure des Arts et Techniques du Théâtre, 161, 186
Diplôme de l'Ecole Spéciale d'Architecture, 154, 181
Diplôme de l'Ecole Supérieure d'Art Dramatique du Théâtre National de Strasbourg, 161, 186
Diplôme de l'Institut Français de Restauration des Oeuvres d'Art, 157, 184
Diplôme de l'Institut Supérieur de Cinéma et de l'Audiovisuél, 157, 183
Diplôme de Muséologie de l'Ecole du Louvre, 157, 184
Diplôme de Premier Cycle de l'Ecole du Louvre, 157, 158, 184
*Diplôme de Premier Cycle Technique/*DPCT, 101, 171
Diplôme de Psychologue Scolaire, 133, 175
Diplôme Elémentaire de Langue Française/ DELF, 79, 169

Diplôme National d'Arts et Techniques/ DNAT, 155, 156, 181
Diplôme National d'Etudes Photographiques, 157, 183
Diplôme National d'Etudes Supérieures de la Musique, 160, 184
Diplôme National d'Oenologie, 110, 172
*Diplôme National Supérieur d'Expression Plastique/*DNSEP, 154–155, 156, 182
Diplôme Supérieur d'Arts Appliqués, 156, 182
Diplôme Supérieur d'Arts Plastiques, 154, 183
Diplôme Supérieur d'Etudes Françaises, 79, 169
Diplôme Supérieur en Travail Social, 149, 179
*Diplôme Universitaire/*DU, 46, 154, 168
*Diplôme Universitaire de Technologie/*DUT, xiv, 40, 81–83, 84, 95, 118, 170; *de Biologie Appliquée,* 144; *Option Animation Culturelle,* 150
diplôme visé, 119, 120, 126, 173
*Diplômes d'Etudes Spécialisées/*DES, 140, 142
diplômes revêtus du visa officiel, 119
Doctorat, xiv, 37, 40, 71, 72, 73–78, 80, 103, 111, 137, 168, 171; *d'Etat,* 74, 77–78, 168; *de l'Université,* 78; *de Spécialité,* 75; *de Troisième Cycle,* 74, 75, 77, 78, 168
drama, 51, 161, 186

école d'application, 103, 116
école d'architecture, 151–153
école d'ingénieur, 72, 88
Ecole de Danse de l'Opéra de Paris, 161
Ecole des Chartes, 157–158
Ecole des Hautes Etudes Cinématographiques, 157
Ecole des Hautes Etudes Commerciales/ HEC, 121, 123, 124–125
Ecole des Hautes Etudes en Sciences Sociales, 223
Ecole des Langues Orientales, 35
Ecole du Louvre, 157
Ecole Nationale d'Administration/ENA, 69, 92, 223
Ecole Nationale de la Magistrature/ENM, 224

INDEX 239

Ecole Nationale de la Photographie, 157
Ecole Nationale des Chartes, 223
Ecole Nationale Louis Lumière, 157
Ecole Nationale Supérieure de Création Industrielle/ENSCI, 155
Ecole Nationale Supérieure des Arts Décoratifs/ENSAD, 155
Ecole Nationale Supérieure des Arts et Industries de Strasbourg/ENSAIS, 151, 154
Ecole Nationale Supérieure des Arts et Techniques du Théâtre, 161
Ecole Nationale Supérieure des Beaux Arts/ENSBA, 154, 183
Ecole Normale Nationale d'Apprentissage/ ENNA, 133
Ecole Polytechnique, 31, 35, 91, 92, 93, 103, 116
Ecole Pratique des Hautes Etudes, 224
Ecole Spéciale d'Architecture/ESA, 151, 153–154
Ecole Supérieure d'Art Dramatique du Théâtre National de Strasbourg, 161
Ecole Supérieure de Commerce de Lyon/ Sup de Co-Lyon, 121
Ecole Supérieure de Commerce de Paris/ ESCP, 119, 121, 123
Ecole Supérieure des Sciences Economiques et Commerciales/ESSEC, 121, 123
Ecoles Nationales d'Ingénieurs/ENI, 101, 198–212
Ecoles Nationales d'Ingénieurs des Travaux Agricoles/ENITA, 112, 114, 198–212
Ecoles Nationales Supérieures d'Agronomie/ ENSA, 110, 115
Ecoles Normales Supérieures/ENS, 31, 68, 135–137, 138
Ecoles Supérieures de Commerce et d'Administration des Entreprises/ESCAE, 119, 121, 213–222
educational laws, xii, xiv, 14, 31, 32, 35, 36–37, 43, 47
Elève Diplômé de l'Ecole du Louvre, 157, 184
engineering, 31, 32, 35, 72, 86–108, 121, 136, 137; admission, 81, 88, 89–91, 95, 101, 104; credentials, 74, 77, 78, 86, 92, 93, 95, 96, 101, 103, 104, 105, 119, 162, 170–172; curriculum, 90, 93–94, 96–100, 102, 104–105; examinations, 88, 89–91, 101; programs, 81, 82, 83, 84, 91–108; schools, 86, 87, 105–108, 198–213. *See also grande école*
enrollment, 3, 9, 33, 34, 35–36, 78, 86, 87, 93, 96, 102, 111
Etablissement Public à Caractère Scientifique, Culturel et Professionnel/EPCSCP, 32, 33
établissements reconnu par l'Etat, 120, 121, 125, 174
Examen Spécial d'Entrée à l'Université, 39, 166
examinations, xiii, 162. *See also concours; specific fields; institutions; programs; and levels of education*
expert comptable, 127

Français langue étrangère, 79

grading, 18–28, 42–43, 47, 83, 162–163
grande école, xiv, 31, 33, 35, 68, 71, 86, 87–92, 109, 121–125, 128; admission, 81, 88, 89–91, 110, 116–117, 123–124, 126; credentials, 67, 92, 93, 103–105, 110–111, 119, 125–126, 162, 171, 173, 174; curriculum, 90, 93–94, 104–105, 111–112; programs, 91–92, 93–94, 103–108, 110–112, 116–117, 124–125, 135–136; schools, 91, 103, 105–108, 118. *See also Classes Préparatoires aux Grandes Ecoles; concours*

Habilitation à Diriger des Recherches, 38, 40, 74–75, 168
Harvard University, 126
higher education, xii, xiv, 31–161, 166–186

ingénieur diplômé, 101, 104
Institut Européen d'Administration des Affaires/INSEAD, 126
Institut Français de Restauration des Oeuvres d'Art, 157
Institut National de la Santé et de la Recherche Médicale/INSERM, 71
Institut Régional d'Administration/IRA, 224
Institut Supérieur du Cinéma et de l'Audiovisuel, 157

Instituts d'Administration des Entreprises/
    IAE, 127
*Instituts d'Etudes Politiques/*IEP, 69, 72,
    123
*Instituts Universitaires de Technologie/*IUT,
    xiv, 31, 33, 36, 38, 46, 81–83, 84, 95,
    118, 142, 149
international education, 78–80, 126

Jardin des Plantes, 31

law, xiv, 31, 35, 47, 48–49, 60, 68, 69, 77,
    128, 129
licence, xiv, 39–40, 44, 59, 60–61, 62, 63,
    79, 134, 135, 137, 166
lycée, xii, 2, 3–28, 29, 31, 83, 88, 109, 118,
    121, 134, 135, 137, 157–158, 161

magistère, 67–69, 167
maîtrise, xiv, 39–40, 45, 59, 60, 62–67, 79,
    127, 135, 137, 167
*Maîtrise d'Informatique Appliquée à la
    Gestion/*MIAG, 63, 127, 167
*Maîtrise de Sciences Sociales Appliquées au
    Travail*, 149, 179
*Maîtrise des Sciences de Gestion/*MSG, 63,
    65–66, 67, 127, 167
*Maîtrise des Sciences et Techniques/*MST,
    62–63, 64–65, 127, 128, 167
*Maîtrise des Sciences et Techniques
    Comptables et Financières/*MSTCF, 128
Master of Business Administration, 126
*Mastère/*MS, 101, 103–108, 125–126, 171,
    174
mathematics, 48, 55, 60, 63, 67, 68, 69,
    88, 89, 90, 91, 131, 135, 138
Médailles, 158–159, 160, 161, 184
medical laboratory technology, 143, 144,
    162
medicine, xiv, 31, 35, 38, 139–142, 176–
    177
midwifery, 142
ministries: Agriculture, 33, 109; Culture,
    33, 154, 155, 158; Defense, 33; Finance,
    38; Health, 33, 139, 142, 144, 147, 150;
    Housing and Urban Affairs, 33, 151,
    152; Industry, 33, 86, 155; Labor, 86;
    Social Affairs, 33, 149, 150;
Telecommunications, 33; Youth and
    Sports, 150; Universities, 32. *See also*
    Ministry of Education
Ministry of Education, xii, xiv; higher
    education, 31, 32, 33, 34, 36, 37, 38, 39,
    46, 67, 68, 72, 75, 77, 78, 79, 83, 86,
    118, 119, 120, 121, 125, 126, 128, 138,
    151, 162; secondary education, 14, 18
moyenne générale, 42
Museum d'Histoire Naturelle, 224
music education, 48, 51–52, 58, 60, 158–
    161, 184–186

Napoleonic University, 31, 35
nursing, 143, 144–145

Observatoire de Paris, 31, 224
occupational therapy, 145, 146
option internationale du baccalauréat, 18
Ordre des Architectes, 151
Ordre des Comptables, 129

Palais de la Decouverte, 224
paramedical education, 142–148, 177–179
pharmacy, xiv, 31, 35, 139, 141–142
physical therapy, 143, 146–147, 148
Placement Recommendations, 78, 125,
    165–186
première d'adaptation, 29
preschool education, xiv, 1
primary education, xii, xiii, xiv, 1–2, 35
private education, xii, xiii, 31, 34, 35, 37,
    69, 83, 86, 118, 120, 121, 126, 134, 142,
    144, 146, 147, 151, 153, 156, 160, 161,
    183, 213–222
Prix, 160, 185
*Professeurs d'Enseignement Général des
    Collèges/*PEGC, 133–134
public education, xiii, 34, 69, 86, 127,
    144, 146, 151, 152–153, 157, 158, 160,
    213–222

radiology, 143, 147
rehabilitation counselors, 147, 160
relevé de notes, 16, 43, 162

INDEX

secondary education, xiii, xiv, 2–30, 35, 88; admission, 2, 3, 4; credentials, 3, 4, 5–28, 165–166; curricula, 2–3, 4, 5–9, 10–14, 30; examinations, 3, 14, 17–26; grading, 18–28. See also *baccalauréat; collège; lycée*
seconde de détermination, 4, 30
sections d'études spécialisées, 2
Sections de Technicien Supérieur/STS, 83, 109, 118
social professions, 81, 83, 149–150, 179–180
speech therapy, 143

teacher training, xiii, 33, 131–138; admission, 131, 132, 133, 134, 135, 136, 137; credentials, 60, 131, 132, 133, 134, 135, 137, 175–176; curriculum, 132, 136–137; examinations, 131, 132, 134–135, 136, 137–138; programs, 48, 58, 79–80, 131–138, 150; schools, 136
technical education: academic calendar, 81; admission, 81, 83; credentials, 5, 14, 17, 30, 81–85, 121, 165, 170; curriculum, 7–8, 12–13, 82, 84, 85, 121, 123; examinations, 83; grading, 83; programs, 4, 5, 9, 10, 14, 20–26, 37, 81–85, 118; secondary, 4, 89; short

higher, 32, 33, 81–85, 120. See also *baccalauréat; Instituts Universitaires de Technologie*/IUT; vocational education
transcripts, 43, 88

Unité d'Enseignement et de Recherche/UER, 36, 37
Unité de Formation et de Recherche/UFR, 37, 38, 69; *à Derogation*, 38, 81
unité de valeur/UV, 43, 59, 60, 65
unités pédagogiques d'architecture/UPA, 151
university education, xiv, 31–32, 35–80; academic calendar, 39; admission, 14, 29, 39–40, 43, 60, 62, 63, 64, 68, 69, 71, 72, 73, 74, 77, 78, 79; credentials, 39–40, 41, 43–46, 47–78, 79–80, 166–169; examinations, 39, 42, 46, 47, 60, 68, 69, 73, 78–79; faculty, 37–38, 40, 42; grading, 42–43, 47; institutions, 68–69, 163, 187–197; programs, 37, 40, 43–80. See also agricultural education; business education; engineering; medicine; teacher training

veterinary medicine, 116–117, 173
vocational education, xii, xiv, 3, 9, 14, 28–30, 34, 165. See also *baccalauréat*

NATIONAL COUNCIL ON THE EVALUATION OF FOREIGN EDUCATIONAL CREDENTIALS

The Council is an interassociational group that serves as a forum for developing consensus on the evaluation and recognition of certificates, diplomas, and degrees awarded throughout the world. It also assists in establishing priorities for research and publication of country, regional, or topical studies. One of its main purposes is to review and modify admissions and placement recommendations drafted by World Education Series authors or others who might ask for such review. (The practices followed in fulfilling this purpose are explained on page 164).

Chairperson—Stan Berry, Director of Admissions, Washington State University, Pullman, WA 99163.

Vice-Chairperson/Secretary—Andrew J. Hein, Assistant Dean, The Graduate School, University of Minnesota, Minneapolis, MN 55455.

MEMBER ORGANIZATIONS AND THEIR REPRESENTATIVES

American Association of Collegiate Registrars and Admissions Officers—Chairperson of the World Education Series Committee, Kitty M. Villa, Assistant Director, International Office, University of Texas, Austin, TX 78716; Virginia Gross, Assistant Director, Admissions, University of Iowa, Iowa City, IA 52242; June Hirano, Award Services Officer, East-West Center, Honolulu, HI 96848.

American Association of Community and Junior Colleges—Philip J. Gannon, President, Lansing Community College, Lansing, MI 48901.

American Council on Education—Joan Schwartz, Director, Registries, Center for Adult Learning & Educational Credentials, ACE, Washington, DC 20036.

College Entrance Examination Board—Sanford C. Jameson, Director, Office of International Education, CEEB, Washington, DC 20036.

Council of Graduate Schools—Ann Fletcher, Assistant Dean, Graduate Studies, Stanford University, Stanford, CA 94305.

Institute of International Education—Martha Renaud, Director, Placement & Special Services Division, IIE, New York, NY 10017.

National Association for Foreign Student Affairs—Robert Brashear, Associate Director of Admissions, University of Houston-University Park, Houston, TX 77004; William H. Smart, Associate Director, International Education, Oregon State University, Corvallis, OR 97331-2122; Valerie Woolston, Director, International Education Services, University of Maryland-College Park, College Park, MD 20742.

OBSERVER ORGANIZATIONS AND THEIR REPRESENTATIVES

USIA—Anne C. Bellows, Education and Cultural Exchange Specialist, Student Support Services Division, Office of Academic Programs, USIA, Washington, DC 20547.

AID—Hattie Jarmon, Education Specialist, Office of International Training, U.S. Department of State/AID, Washington, DC 20523.

New York Education Department—Mary Jane Ewart, Associate in Comparative Education, State Education Department, The University of the State of New York, Albany, NY 12230.